The
HEARTBEAT
of Old Testament Theology

T0338811

Acadia Studies in Bible and Theology

Craig A. Evans, General Editor

The last two decades have witnessed dramatic developments in biblical and theological study. Full-time academics can scarcely keep up with fresh discoveries, recently published primary texts, ongoing archaeological work, new exegetical proposals, experiments in methods and hermeneutics, and innovative theological syntheses. For students and nonspecialists, these developments are confusing and daunting. What has been needed is a series of succinct studies that assess these issues and present their findings in a way that students, pastors, laity, and nonspecialists will find accessible and rewarding. Acadia Studies in Bible and Theology, sponsored by Acadia Divinity College in Wolfville, Nova Scotia, and in conjunction with the college's Hayward Lectureship, constitutes such a series.

The Hayward Lectureship has brought to Acadia many distinguished scholars of Bible and theology, such as Sir Robin Barbour, John Bright, Leander Keck, Helmut Koester, Richard Longenecker, Martin Marty, Jaroslav Pelikan, Ian Rennie, James Sanders, and Eduard Schweizer. The Acadia Studies in Bible and Theology series reflects this rich heritage.

These studies are designed to guide readers through the ever more complicated maze of critical, interpretative, and theological discussion taking place today. But these studies are not introductory in nature; nor are they mere surveys. Authored by leading authorities in the field, the Acadia Studies in Bible and Theology series offers critical assessments of the major issues that the church faces in the twenty-first century. Readers will gain the requisite orientation and fresh understanding of the important issues that will enable them to take part meaningfully in discussion and debate.

The
HEARTBEAT
of Old Testament Theology

THREE CREEDAL EXPRESSIONS

MARK J. BODA

Baker Academic
a division of Baker Publishing Group
Grand Rapids, Michigan

© 2017 by Mark J. Boda

Published by Baker Academic
a division of Baker Publishing Group
P.O. Box 6287, Grand Rapids, MI 49516-6287
www.bakeracademic.com

Printed in the United States of America

Library of Congress Cataloging-in-Publication Data
Names: Boda, Mark J., author.
Title: The heartbeat of Old Testament theology : three creedal expressions / Mark J. Boda.
Description: Grand Rapids : Baker Academic, 2017. | Includes bibliographical references and index.
Identifiers: LCCN 2016046727 | ISBN 9780801030895 (pbk.)
Subjects: LCSH: Bible. Old Testament—Theology. | Bible—Theology.
Classification: LCC BS1192.5 .B63 2017 | DDC 230/.0411—dc23
LC record available at https://lccn.loc.gov/2016046727

In keeping with biblical principles of creation stewardship, Baker Publishing Group advocates the responsible use of our natural resources. As a member of the Green Press Initiative, our company uses recycled paper when possible. The text paper of this book is composed in part of post-consumer waste.

17 18 19 20 21 22 23   7 6 5 4 3 2 1

For Stephen

Ad majorem Dei gloriam

Contents

Abbreviations

General and Bibliographic

AIL	Ancient Israel and Its Literature
alt.	altered translation
AnBib	Analecta Biblica
AOAT	Alter Orient und Altes Testament
AT	author's translation
BBR	*Bulletin for Biblical Research*
Bib	*Biblica*
BSac	*Bibliotheca Sacra*
BZAW	Beihefte zur Zeitschrift für die alttestamentliche Wissenschaft
CBQ	*Catholic Biblical Quarterly*
chap.	chapter
CurBR	*Currents in Biblical Research*
DCH	*Dictionary of Classical Hebrew*, ed. David J. A. Clines, 9 vols. (Sheffield: Sheffield Phoenix, 1993–2014)
Eng.	English Bible numbering
esp.	especially
FAT	Forschungen zum Alten Testament
HALOT	*Hebrew and Aramaic Lexicon of the Old Testament*, by L. Koehler, W. Baumgartner, and J. J. Stamm, trans. and ed. M. E. J. Richardson, 4 vols. (Leiden: Brill, 1994–99)
HBM	Hebrew Bible Monographs
HBT	*Horizons in Biblical Theology*
HSM	Harvard Semitic Monographs
HSS	Harvard Semitic Studies

IBHS	*An Introduction to Biblical Hebrew Syntax*, by B. K. Waltke and M. O'Connor (Winona Lake, IN: Eisenbrauns, 1990)
Int	Interpretation
JAOS	*Journal of the American Oriental Society*
JBL	*Journal of Biblical Literature*
JETS	*Journal of the Evangelical Theological Society*
JSOTSup	Journal for the Study of the Old Testament Supplement Series
JTISup	Journal of Theological Interpretation, Supplements
KJV	King James Version
LHBOTS	Library of Hebrew Bible/Old Testament Studies
MSJ	*Master's Seminary Journal*
NASB	New American Standard Bible
NETS	*A New English Translation of the Septuagint*, ed. A. Pietersma and B. G. Wright (New York: Oxford University Press, 2007)
NIV	New International Version
NIVAC	NIV Application Commentary
NLT	New Living Translation
NRSV	New Revised Standard Version
NSBT	New Studies in Biblical Theology
NT	New Testament
OBT	Overtures to Biblical Theology
OG	Old Greek
OT	Old Testament
OTL	Old Testament Library
SBJT	*Southern Baptist Journal of Theology*
SBL	Society of Biblical Literature
SBLSP	Society of Biblical Literature Seminar Papers
SBT	Studies in Biblical Theology
SJT	*Scottish Journal of Theology*
TB	Theologische Bücherei
VT	*Vetus Testamentum*
VTSup	Supplements to Vetus Testamentum
WMANT	Wissenschaftliche Monographien zum Alten und Neuen Testament
WTJ	*Westminster Theological Journal*
WUNT	Wissenschaftliche Untersuchungen zum Neuen Testament
ZAW	*Zeitschrift für die alttestamentliche Wissenschaft*

Old Testament

Gen.	Genesis	Num.	Numbers
Exod.	Exodus	Deut.	Deuteronomy
Lev.	Leviticus	Josh.	Joshua

Judg.	Judges	Lam.	Lamentations
Ruth	Ruth	Ezek.	Ezekiel
1–2 Sam.	1–2 Samuel	Dan.	Daniel
1–2 Kings	1–2 Kings	Hosea	Hosea
1–2 Chron.	1–2 Chronicles	Joel	Joel
Ezra	Ezra	Amos	Amos
Neh.	Nehemiah	Obad.	Obadiah
Esther	Esther	Jon.	Jonah
Job	Job	Mic.	Micah
Ps(s).	Psalm(s)	Nah.	Nahum
Prov.	Proverbs	Hab.	Habakkuk
Eccles.	Ecclesiastes	Zeph.	Zephaniah
Song	Song of Songs	Hag.	Haggai
Isa.	Isaiah	Zech.	Zechariah
Jer.	Jeremiah	Mal.	Malachi

New Testament

Matt.	Matthew	1–2 Thess.	1–2 Thessalonians
Mark	Mark	1–2 Tim.	1–2 Timothy
Luke	Luke	Titus	Titus
John	John	Philem.	Philemon
Acts	Acts	Heb.	Hebrews
Rom.	Romans	James	James
1–2 Cor.	1–2 Corinthians	1–2 Pet.	1–2 Peter
Gal.	Galatians	1–3 John	1–3 John
Eph.	Ephesians	Jude	Jude
Phil.	Philippians	Rev.	Revelation
Col.	Colossians		

Preface

Reflection on the topics within this volume began many years ago as I was embarking on my doctoral studies at the University of Cambridge. I was told that British doctorates produced great researchers because of the singular focus on a dissertation on a limited topic or portion of text, while American doctorates were more conducive to teaching because of the demand of coursework, comprehensive exams, and dissertation. Knowing that I would most likely teach introductory courses in OT in North America, I carefully chose my dissertation topic: Neh. 9. It was a special passage, one that recited the entire history of Israel from creation to exile. And my method was primarily traditio-historical, that is, investigating the relationship of this prayerful recitation of the story of Israel to the rest of the OT. My hope was to gain comprehensive exposure to the content and critical study of the OT while remaining limited to a single passage. I was first exposed to Neh. 9 through Gerhard von Rad and his careful work on the short historical creeds. I was drawn to von Rad because he provided a critical approach to the redemptive-historical approach that I had learned from followers of the Old Princeton theologian Geerhardus Vos. Thus, as I began my journey into the academic study of the OT through Neh. 9, I was motivated by my interest in OT and Biblical Theology, and it is a relief to finally have an opportunity to express more fully my thoughts on the inner structure of OT theology. The influence of Neh. 9 and von Rad will be evident from the beginning,

but it will soon become clear that I've discovered much, much more
as I have explored the OT over the past twenty years.

My students were the first to hear lectures on the topics that I investigate in this book. I used early expressions of my thoughts found
in this book as my lecture for students when I was candidating at
Canadian Theological Seminary and McMaster Divinity College. I
chose these lectures because they expressed my passion and identity
as an OT scholar, that is, that I was interested in its theological message. But it was the Hayward Lectureship at Acadia Divinity College,
Acadia University on October 21–23, 2013, that afforded me the opportunity to take my thoughts to a new level and expand them into
the present book. I am grateful to Craig Evans for his kind invitation
and to the warm hospitality that I enjoyed while in Wolfville, Nova
Scotia, especially as I was hosted by Craig and Virginia Evans and
Glen and Darlene Wooden. The opportunities to preach at the Manning Memorial Chapel and to spend focused time with students and
faculty discussing the content of the lectures were stimulating, and
I hope helpful for those who participated. Many thanks to President
Harry Gardner for his warm welcome while on campus. Also I am
thankful to Jim Kinney at Baker Academic for guiding the process of
turning the lecture notes into the present book and patiently waiting
for the arrival of the manuscript.

The research and writing of this book have taken place over many
years within the academy, and my hope is that this book will be a helpful resource for those mentoring an emerging generation of students
of the Bible. The book showcases an approach to the core theology
of the OT that not only engages the OT text but also shows the connection between this core OT theology and the NT and the life of
the community that embraces both Old and New Testaments. In a
postscript, I present the sermon I preached at Acadia that served as
an invitation to intimacy with the God who is revealed and confessed
throughout the Scriptures. In an appendix, I provide a slightly revised
edition of an earlier article that presents my theological hermeneutic
for Biblical Theology and then what I hope is a basic procedure with
an example to guide students of the Bible in reading the OT in a biblical theologically responsible way. I have included this long appendix
to provide theological orientation and practical advice for others to

continue the tradition of biblical-theological reflection, whether for assignments in the academy, for sermons and Bible studies in the church, or for personal enrichment in the home.

I hope that this book will draw the uninitiated into the theological riches of the OT and motivate those who have already found these riches to explore new ways to communicate these riches to a church and world in need of the God to whom they witness. The ultimate goal, however, is that all that has been written will prompt greater glory to the God who is revealed and confessed throughout the Old and New Testaments.

I dedicate this book to my son Stephen, whose organ weekly sings praises to this God who is the focus of this book. My greatest hope as a father is that you will experience all the goodness of the God of the Scriptures in the abundant life available to you through Jesus Christ and the indwelling Holy Spirit.

Ego ex eorum numero me esse profiteor qui scribunt proficiendo, et scribendo proficient.

(Augustine, *Epistle* 143.2, via John Calvin)

Mark J. Boda
Hamilton, Ontario

1

Taking the Pulse
of Old Testament Theology

Past and Present

I am a person who likes to track progress, and in no place is that more important to me than at my local gym, where two or three times a week I mount an elliptical trainer for a thirty-minute workout. This machine is a high-tech wonder, tracking my steps, distance, and most important of all, my heartbeat. By my grasping two handles this elliptical trainer reads the speed of my heartbeat. At the end of my workout a summary report shows how long I trained within the optimum pulse rate for my size and age. In the normal pace of life I don't even notice my heartbeat, but through the miracle of technology I am able to take my pulse. My elliptical trainer identifies my heartbeat as a single rhythm, but more sophisticated instruments, such as a stethoscope or an EKG monitor, reveal that multiple rhythms compose my heartbeat.

I invite you to don your theological stethoscope and listen for the heartbeat that represents the very core of the theology of the

OT. We are not the first to practice biblical cardiology. The OT and NT themselves provide evidence that the writers of the Scriptures were interested in taking the heartbeat of the biblical witness, whether that was Zechariah identifying the heartbeat of the prophets (Zech. 1:3–4) or Jesus the heartbeat of the law and the prophets (Matt. 7:12). Even the history of scholarship in the twentieth century provides a helpful case study as we begin to take the pulse of OT theology.

The past century of biblical scholarship bears witness to the rising and falling, revising and fracturing of the discipline of OT theology, sometimes foreshadowing, oftentimes paralleling, the dominant hermeneutical agenda of the times. With the supremacy of diachronic presuppositions and methodologies at the beginning of the twentieth century, it is not surprising that OT theology had in large part been silenced across the OT guild in favor of the study of the history of religion. Taking their lead from Wellhausen's work in the late nineteenth century, OT scholars used the biblical text mainly as a source for accessing the religious ideology of the ancient Hebrew people as it evolved from nature religion to its heights in prophetic monotheism before its demise in priestly legalism.[1]

A loosening of the diachronic stranglehold on the study of the OT in the period between the World Wars prompted the revival of OT theology. Although the historical study of the Hebrew people, religion, and literature had laid bare the historical context of the OT, it was time to allow the ancient texts once again to speak theologically. In a way, this shift from the history of religion to OT theology foreshadowed the mid-twentieth-century shift from diachronic to synchronic hermeneutical paradigms, represented in New Criticism and Structuralism.[2]

There are examples in the second half of the twentieth century of an approach to OT theology more akin to classic Christian systematic theology, focusing on categories such as theology (God), anthropology (humanity), soteriology (salvation), and eschatology

---

1. See Spieckermann, "God's Steadfast Love," for superb examples of the differences between the disciplines of OT theology and history of religion.

2. For the categories (which I have revised and updated) employed below, see Hasel, *Basic Issues*.

(future state).[3] At the same time there are others who continued to approach OT theology through the lens of history of religions.[4] However, these approaches have been overshadowed by four key figures who dominated the discipline in the second half of the twentieth century: Walther Eichrodt, Gerhard von Rad, Brevard Childs, and Phyllis Trible.[5] Eichrodt focused on covenant as the central theme of OT theology. Von Rad leveraged the development of traditions in the OT to trace key streams in OT theology. Childs attended to the canon of the OT to identify the shape of OT theology. Trible sought to shift focus from text to reader and the hermeneutical framework for reflection on OT theology.

Eichrodt is representative of a series of thematic approaches that emerged in the second half of the twentieth century and beyond. His approach is best described as a cross-section thematic approach, one that structures OT theology around a theme or topic that lays bare "the inner structure of religion."[6] This entails selectivity, as the OT theologian is searching for (a) prominent idea(s). Others have adopted a thematic approach without limiting themselves to a single theme. Terrien's presence versus absence, Hanson's teleological versus cosmic, and Westermann's deliverance versus blessing are representative of many who have used two contrastive themes to structure OT theology.[7] At the core of Brueggemann's courtroom approach to OT theology lies the dialectic of core testimony versus countertestimony, which produces a "tension" that "belongs to the very character and substance of OT faith" and that "precludes and resists resolution."[8] Many, however, have adopted a multiplex thematic approach along

3. Baab, *Theology of the Old Testament*; Köhler, *Old Testament Theology*.

4. Schmidt, *Faith of the Old Testament*; Gunneweg, *Biblische Theologie des Alten Testaments*; Gerstenberger, *Theologies in the Old Testament*; cf. Perdue, *Reconstructing Old Testament Theology*, 25–75.

5. Eichrodt, *Theologie des Alten Testaments*; Eichrodt, *Theology of the Old Testament*; von Rad, *Theologie*; von Rad, *Old Testament Theology*; Childs, *Introduction*; Childs, *Old Testament Theology*; Childs, *Biblical Theology of the Old and New Testaments*; Trible, *God and the Rhetoric of Sexuality*; Trible, "Feminist Hermeneutics and Biblical Theology."

6. Hasel, *Basic Issues*, 49.

7. Terrien, *Elusive Presence*; Hanson, *Dynamic Transcendence*; Westermann, *Elements*.

8. Brueggemann, *Theology of the Old Testament*, 400.

the lines advocated by Gerhard Hasel.[9] This approach eschews any limitations on themes traced through the OT, encouraging reflection on any and all themes that arise from OT exegesis.[10]

Von Rad's approach is representative of a series of approaches that have been called diachronic. Von Rad focused on the development of the historical traditions (including the premonarchial traditions of Genesis–Joshua and the monarchial traditions that follow) and the prophetic traditions of Israel.[11] In tracing the historical traditions, von Rad showcases not only his diachronic approach to interpreting the text (sensitive to the development of the text over time) but also the diachronic dimension of the content of the text (sensitive to the presentation of a salvation history).[12] This attention to diachronic development for writing OT theology can also be discerned in the work of Christoph Barth, although he focuses on the presentation of a salvation history with little interest in the development of the text over time.[13] Geerhardus Vos also fits within this approach even though he focuses more on the presentation of revelatory history, which he identifies as inseparable from redemptive history.[14] His revelatory history is twofold: the Mosaic epoch and the prophetic epoch, with the first focused on revelation and events associated with the era of Moses and the second on events associated with the era of the prophets, understood particularly as guardians of the theocratic kingdom ruled by the monarch.

Brevard Childs structures his OT theology according to the canonical identity of the text.[15] Those who have followed Childs's lead have

9. Hasel, *Basic Issues*, 111–14; cf. Youngblood, *Heart of the Old Testament*; Dyrness, *Themes*; Alexander and Rosner, eds., *New Dictionary of Biblical Theology*.

10. One might place within this stream Gerstenberger, *Theologies in the Old Testament*, who does not adopt the typical canonical sensibility of Hasel, for instance, but seeks sensitivity to the complexity of religious voices within the OT text.

11. Von Rad, *Old Testament Theology*, whose first volume is subtitled: "The Theology of Israel's Historical Traditions," and second volume: "The Theology of Israel's Prophetic Traditions."

12. On this approach, see chap. 2 below.

13. Barth, *God with Us*. John Kessler's work takes seriously the diverse perspectives based on key theological tradition streams in the OT in a way that is akin to von Rad's approach; cf. Kessler, *Old Testament Theology*.

14. Vos, *Biblical Theology*.

15. Childs, *Introduction*; Childs, *Old Testament Theology*; Childs, *Biblical Theology of the Old and New Testaments*.

adopted one of the thematic approaches articulated above, usually a multiplex approach. Childs focused on the final form of the text with attention to the unique witness of the OT before bringing it into conversation with NT theology to produce a Biblical Theology. Elmer Martens has suggested an intertextual approach that focuses on the many intertextual links (allusions to characters, episodes, vocabulary) between canonical texts in the OT.[16] Paul House and Waltke and Yu also focus on the final form of the text, but they focus attention particularly on the theological witness of the individual books within the OT.[17] Others have given attention to the theological witness within specific sections of the OT canon and/or according to the overall shape of the OT canon.[18]

In recent years, however, one can discern a significant shift toward ideological approaches to OT theology. Phyllis Trible signaled this shift long ago when she called biblical theologians to take biblical hermeneutics more seriously.[19] Ideological approaches abandon the façade of objective description of OT theology and embrace contemporary identities that provide a lens through which to view the text. The scholarship traced by Leo Perdue in his helpful volume highlights the diversity of approaches that have emerged from this hermeneutical shift, including liberation, ethnic, feminist, mujerista, womanist, Jewish, postmodern, and postcolonial biblical interpretation and theology.[20]

Whereas the diachronic focus of biblical studies at the beginning of the century, with its emphasis on the evolution of religion in Israel, left little room for expressing a unified theology in the OT, the synchronic methods of the middle part of the century that began with great intentions of a synthetic unity increasingly contributed to the disunity of the OT as a corpus, first through tracing multiple tradition streams, later through investigating multiple themes, and

16. Martens, "Reaching."

17. House, *Old Testament Theology*; Waltke and Yu, *Old Testament Theology*.

18. Morgan, *Between Text and Community*; Zuck et al., *Biblical Theology of the Old Testament*; Hubbard et al., *Studies in Old Testament Theology*; Chapman, *Law and the Prophets*; Dempster, *Dominion and Dynasty*; Boda, *Severe Mercy*.

19. Trible, "Feminist Hermeneutics and Biblical Theology," 448–66.

20. See the superb review of various approaches in Perdue, *Reconstructing Old Testament Theology*, 76–339.

ultimately through consideration of the unique perspectives of the various books. The geometric expansion of themes and claims resulted in the hermeneutical fatigue of postfoundational OT theology and the conclusion that OT theology was merely a perspectival exercise. The constant in each era is the claim of diversity, whether that diversity is located within the evolving community that lay behind the text, in the varied canon that lay within the text, or in the fractured communities that interpreted the text.[21]

Is there any way ahead? Can we speak any longer of a theology that lies at the core of the OT? Are our claims of theology merely perspectival projections, or can we identify something in these ancient texts that witnesses to some form of unity in the biblical corpus?

The present book focuses on what I think lies at the core of OT theology. Of course, my own perspective ("I think") is key to this statement. I am fully aware that I am limited by my own hermeneutical journey, one that has involved reflection on the OT from my childhood within the Christian tradition until the present day. My journey has involved, however, consistent and deep engagement with the OT itself as I have read and taught these texts over the past four decades, nearly three of which have been spent in graduate education. I have also had the privilege of dialoguing with the best in scholarship on the OT, both confessional and secular, and from this have drawn insights that have endured for generations. I have honestly articulated my own hermeneutic and my approach to OT theology in the appendix below: "Biblical Theology and the Old Testament."[22] But let me begin with a short definition of my purpose in this book, a short articulation of my methodology, and then the dominant image I have adopted for the presentation of my topic.

The core purpose of the study of theology is, of course, reflection on God, and for the study of OT theology and Biblical Theology, reflection on the presentation of God in the OT and the NT. The enterprise of theology entails also reflection on the meaning of creation both human and nonhuman in relation to God, which explains why topics such as anthropology, soteriology, eschatology, and ecclesiology

---

21. On the future of OT theology, see the reflective comments of Brueggemann, "Futures in Old Testament Theology."

22. See also the introduction to Boda, *"Return to Me,"* 19–34.

are also included in studies of "theology." But it is important to remember that the main purpose of theology is deep and disciplined reflection on God. This present project seeks to describe what is foundational to the revelation and confession of God within the OT with sensitivity to how this revelation and confession is reflected as well in the NT. While the focus is on God, we will soon see that one can never abstract God from creation, especially humanity, among whom the canon was formed.

The methodology I have adopted is a selective intertextual-canonical approach that identifies core expressions of God that appear throughout the OT canon. It is "selective" in the sense that Eichrodt noted long ago: certain topics in the biblical witness seem to constitute its "inner structure," and it is important to highlight these topics that provide cohesion to the OT and the NT. It is "canonical" in that its focus is on the texts that are found within the canon in a form that has been accepted within a particular community of faith. As a Protestant I am part of a community that has adopted a certain set of texts as canonical. While I am aware that there are other communities of faith, both Christian and Jewish, that have adopted a different set of texts, it is also evident to me that the theological elements I have selected in this present study of OT theology are not exclusive to the Protestant canon (whether the particular books or the manuscript traditions employed) but can be discerned in all the major canonical traditions in Christian and Jewish faith. I have focused on the OT because it is my area of expertise and I do think it is important to give the OT a voice within biblical-theological reflection, even though I do show how the emphases of the OT find echoes in the NT. Finally, my method is "intertextual" in that it focuses on repeated use of particular phrases, expressions, and structures throughout the breadth of the OT and the NT. These topics are identified by close attention to what is ubiquitous throughout the biblical texts.

With this I have identified my particular approach to biblical cardiology. My selective intertextual-canonical method is the medical tool I have honed to discern the heartbeat and the patterns that are evidence of the core life principle that animates the biblical witness. I am going to argue for three basic rhythms that compose the heartbeat of the OT, identified with three basic creeds that can be discerned throughout the OT: the narrative, character, and relational creeds. In OT theology we will see that the three basic creedal rhythms reflect, on the one side, God's plan to form a redemptive community (Israel) and, on the other side, God's plan to transform all creation.

So join me as we take our theological stethoscopes and place them on the Scriptures to listen carefully for the heartbeat that shows that the Scriptures are indeed "living and active" (Heb. 4:12; cf. John 6:63, 68; Acts 7:38) and words by which we may truly live (Lev. 18:5; cf. Deut. 32:47; Ezek. 20:11, 13; Neh. 9:29).[23]

23. Throughout the book, I will generally draw citations of Scripture from the NASB translation, modified at times to reflect my own translation choices.

2

The Narrative Rhythm

God's Historical Action

The scholars who discerned the first basic rhythm of the heartbeat of the OT produced their greatest work at the midpoint of the twentieth century. In the previous chapter I identified these scholars with what I called the "diachronic" approach. This approach takes its lead from the narrative shape of the OT corpus, taking seriously the fact that the Bible is not ordered like the classic works of systematic theologies nor according to the thematic schemata of many OT theologies. Three scholars, in particular, were key contributors to the development of this approach.

Geerhardus Vos, professor of biblical theology at Princeton Theological Seminary, was a key conservative voice. His book *Biblical Theology: Old and New Testaments* appeared in 1948, the year before his death. In it he outlined the importance of historical progression for biblical-theological reflection: "Biblical Theology deals with the material from the historical standpoint, seeking to exhibit the organic growth or development of the truths of Special Revelation from the primitive preredemptive Special Revelation given in Eden to the close of the New Testament canon."[1] This view emerged from his reflection on the nature of the Bible itself, what he described as "The historic progressiveness of the revelation-process," with revelation focusing on "the interpretation of redemption."[2] Vos's emphasis on the history of revelation that was focused on interpreting redemption led to the division of his reflection into OT and NT and then a subdivision of the OT section into the Mosaic epoch of revelation (subdivided into pre-Noachian, Noachian, patriarchal, and Moses periods) and the prophetic epoch of revelation.

George Ernest Wright, OT professor and archaeologist, wrote his book *God Who Acts* (1952) during his tenure at McCormick Seminary prior to joining the faculty at Harvard Divinity School. As the title suggests, Wright approached OT theology as "a recital or proclamation of the redemptive acts of God, together with the inferences drawn therefrom."[3] At the core of OT theological expression is a narrative of God's actions. For him revelation is accomplished through action, not through disclosure. "Biblical theology is *the confessional recital of the redemptive acts of God*."[4] This emphasis on the redemptive act rather than the revelation thus distinguishes him from Vos, but they share sensitivity to the historical progression as key to theological content in and theological reflection on the OT.

Six years after Wright's work, the German Gerhard von Rad, professor of Old Testament at Heidelberg, lent his support to the diachronic emphasis of both Vos and Wright. His work traced the development of traditions throughout the OT.[5] While seeing progression in the emergence of the theology of the OT as did Vos, he shifted the focus from divine revelation to the religious experience of the Israelite community. At the same time he provided important insights into what constituted the core redemptive acts of God that had been the focus of Wright's earlier work. For von Rad, OT theology "unfolds as a dynamic story instead of a static system of religious ideas."[6]

1. Vos, *Biblical Theology*, 5.
2. Ibid., 14.
3. G. Wright, *God Who Acts*, 11.
4. Ibid., 13.
5. Von Rad, *Theologie*; von Rad, *Old Testament Theology*.
6. Here described by Barth, *God with Us*, 5.

The most important insight from von Rad is his highlighting of three recitations of early traditions of Israel as the key to unlocking the secret of the preliterary history of the "Hexateuch" (Genesis–Joshua). These recitations in Deut. 6, 26, and Josh. 24 provided evidence for him of an underlying theological expression in ancient Israel: *das kleine geschichtliche Credo*, or "the short historical creed."

Vos's emphasis on the revelation of God, Wright's focus on the actions of God, and von Rad's isolation of a creedal set of actions were not sufficiently heeded in the OT guild, where topical approaches continued to dominate.

The goal of this chapter is to take a closer look at this creedal core that von Rad has championed before introducing in subsequent chapters two other different yet complementary creedal traditions that are also essential to OT theology. The consistent use of these creedal traditions throughout the OT corpus points to the important role they must play in any construal of the theology of the OT.[7] These three creeds constitute the triple rhythms of the heartbeat of OT theology.

Narrative as Creed

Taking his lead from both George Ernest Wright and Gerhard von Rad, Christoph Barth, son of Karl Barth, identified the fact that "God Acts" as "The Heart of the Matter." He based this claim on three pieces of evidence from the OT: the thematic structure of the Pentateuch as "the story of Israel's origins in the mighty acts of God," the presence of commemorations of "God's redemptive acts" throughout the hymns and prayers of the Psalter, and the regular occurrence of "confessional summaries of history in the Old Testament."[8] As Barth,

7. Despite the importance of Deut. 6:4–5 within Judaism, it is not ubiquitously cited throughout the OT (see Zech. 14:9). While some may point to the fact that Deut. 6:6–9 commands these words to be kept in the heart and taught to children, displayed on body and home, the fact is that a similar command appears in Deut. 11:18 and yet it is not given the priority that Deut. 6:4–5 is given. Contra Moberly, *Old Testament Theology*, 7–40, who speaks of Deut. 6:4–9 as a passage "whose foundational and focal nature can readily be demonstrated." Jesus did point to the importance of Deut. 6:4–5 for ethics, as it encapsulates human response to Yahweh.

8. Barth, *God with Us*, 5; for other scholars who follow a redemptive-historical approach, see VanGemeren, *Progress*; Goldsworthy, *According to Plan*. Klink and

so we take our point of departure from von Rad's *kleine geschichtliche Credo*, or short historical creed.[9]

Deuteronomy 6:21–23 is a superb example of such a creed.

> We were slaves to Pharaoh in Egypt, and Yahweh brought us from Egypt with a mighty hand. Moreover, Yahweh showed great and distressing signs and wonders before our eyes against Egypt, Pharaoh and all his household; He brought us out from there in order to bring us in, to give us the land which He had sworn to our fathers.

This short recitation of God's redemptive act on Israel's behalf is here provided as the theological foundation for a parent's answer to a child's question concerning the purpose of the laws in the life of the Israelites.

The example in Deut. 26:5–9 depicts the declaration of a similar summary in the context of the presentation of firstfruits at the temple facilitated by a priest:[10]

> My father was a wandering Aramean, and he went down to Egypt and sojourned there, few in number; but there he became a great, mighty and populous nation. And the Egyptians treated us harshly and afflicted us, and imposed hard labor on us. Then we cried to Yahweh, the God of our fathers, and Yahweh heard our voice and saw our affliction and our toil and our oppression; and Yahweh brought us out of Egypt with a mighty hand and an outstretched arm and with great terror and with signs and wonders; and He has brought us to this place and has given us this land, a land flowing with milk and honey.

The final example, from Josh. 24:2–13, is presented not as a human confession about God's redemptive acts but rather as divine revelation

---

Lockett, *Understanding Biblical Theology*, 57–122, distinguish between those who approach Biblical Theology as "History of Redemption" and those who approach it as "Worldview-Story."

9. See von Rad, *Old Testament Theology*, 1:121, who notes: "Re-telling remains the most legitimate form of theological discourse in the Old Testament," with thanks to Goldingay, *Israel's Gospel*, 32. Von Rad has been criticized over the years. See, e.g., Carmichael, "New View"; Cody, "'Little Historical Creed' or 'Little Historical Anamnesis'?"

10. Von Rad (*Old Testament Theology*, 1:121–22) called Deut. 26:5–9 "the most important" among the narrative creeds.

("thus says Yahweh, the God of Israel") that forms the theological foundation for Joshua's call for covenant response from the people at the end of the conquest.

> From ancient times your fathers lived beyond the River, *namely*, Terah, the father of Abraham and the father of Nahor, and they served other gods. Then I took your father Abraham from beyond the River, and led him through all the land of Canaan, and multiplied his descendants and gave him Isaac. To Isaac I gave Jacob and Esau, and to Esau I gave Mount Seir to possess it; but Jacob and his sons went down to Egypt. Then I sent Moses and Aaron, and I plagued Egypt by what I did in its midst; and afterward I brought you out. I brought your fathers out of Egypt, and you came to the sea; and Egypt pursued your fathers with chariots and horsemen to the Re[e]d Sea. But when they cried out to Yahweh, He put darkness between you and the Egyptians, and brought the sea upon them and covered them; and your own eyes saw what I did in Egypt. And you lived in the wilderness for a long time. Then I brought you into the land of the Amorites who lived beyond the Jordan, and they fought with you; and I gave them into your hand, and you took possession of their land when I destroyed them before you. Then Balak the son of Zippor, king of Moab, arose and fought against Israel, and he sent and summoned Balaam the son of Beor to curse you. But I was not willing to listen to Balaam. So he had to bless you, and I delivered you from his hand. You crossed the Jordan and came to Jericho; and the citizens of Jericho fought against you, *and* the Amorite and the Perizzite and the Canaanite and the Hittite and the Girgashite, the Hivite and the Jebusite. Thus I gave them into your hand. Then I sent the hornet before you and it drove out the two kings of the Amorites from before you, *but* not by your sword or your bow. I gave you a land on which you had not labored, and cities which you had not built, and you have lived in them; you are eating of vineyards and olive groves which you did not plant.

Von Rad linked these foundational creedal expressions to the worshiping community of Israel: "This creed presupposes the existence of an already canonical form of Salvation-History, which for its part therefore must be still older."[11] He identified the examples in Deut.

---

11. "Setzt . . . das Vorhandensein einer schon kanonisch gewordenen Form der Heilsgeschichte voraus, die ihrerseits also noch älter sein muss"; von Rad, *Gesammelte Studien*, 16; cf. von Rad, *Problem of the Hexateuch*, 8.

6, 26, and Josh. 24 as "liturgical forms" (*agendarische Formulare*) that betray their intimate connection to the cult, that is, the regular worship activities of the Israelite community. One can see, however, that these three examples are linked to three different settings in the life of Israel: the repeated opportunity for theological teaching by parents within a family unit, the repeated opportunity for worship by Israelites at the temple, and the one-time covenant expression of the nation as a whole.

These three examples also highlight another important observation by von Rad: the expansion of the events included, which developed from the simple reference to the exodus and conquest of the land in Deut. 6, to the expanded reference to the patriarch Jacob tradition along with the exodus and conquest in Deut. 26, to the greatly expanded references to all patriarchs, plagues, exodus, wilderness, and conquest in Josh. 24. Von Rad thus noticed what he called "free modifications of the creed in cultic lyric,"[12] seen not only in developments from Deut. 6 to Josh. 24 but also in many other passages in the OT, from three verses in Deut. 6 to sixty-seven verses in Ps. 78 (cf. Exod. 15; 1 Sam. 12:8; Pss. 78; 105; 106; 135; 136; Neh. 9).[13]

Von Rad used this evidence on the short historical creed as a way to explain the prehistory of the biblical canon and text, that is, to look at the tradition history of text within the community, and in particular the development of what he called the Hexateuch (Genesis–Joshua).[14] And while there may be questions about the usefulness of this evidence for tracing the development of the Bible, key to von Rad's legacy is his identification of this important aspect of the theology of the OT: first, that theology is expressed in summary form and, second, that this summary is expressed in a historical or narrative form.[15] This latter characteristic is not surprising in light of the dominance of history and narrative throughout the OT.

---

12. "Freie Abwandlungen des Credo in der Kultlyrik"; von Rad, *Gesammelte Studien*, 16; von Rad, *Problem of the Hexateuch*, 8.

13. Von Rad, *Gesammelte Studien*, 16; von Rad, *Problem of the Hexateuch*, 8.

14. See further Schmid, "Emergence and Disappearance."

15. Von Rad's insights have encouraged others since his time, and his legacy is best expressed in the following works: VanGemeren, *Progress*; Barth, *God with Us*; Bartholomew and Goheen, *Drama*; also note Westermann, *Elements*, 45–50. Cf. Bauckham, "Reading Scripture"; Brown, "Future of Biblical Theology."

The narrative creed represents the first rhythm in the heartbeat of the OT. In this rhythm we feel the declaration of the redemptive action of God toward Israel. This declaration comes either in the form of divine revelation, as already seen in Josh. 24, or in the form of human confession, as seen in Deut. 6 and 26. But there are many other examples throughout the OT, as this rhythm can be felt in nearly every book.

Through the narrative creed we discover the history of God's redemption through finite action, that is, particular acts within specific times of history. While the emphasis is on God and his acts, these acts are directed toward a community and involve key leaders who play an important role. Thus, the human participants are part of this narrative theology that traces God's actions and human responses within the grand story of redemption.[16]

Elements

In this creedal tradition in ancient Israel, theology is expressed as God's redemptive story described through finite verbs expressing past action.[17] The basic elements of this story include accounts of the following:

ancestors: election of Abraham, Isaac, Jacob, and/or Joseph
exodus: plagues, Reed Sea, rescue from Egypt
wilderness: care and discipline on the journey to Canaan
conquest: entrance into Canaan and/or conquest of land
land: life in a land of plenty
exile: expulsion from land

Texts that reflect this summarizing tradition include Exod. 15:1–19; Deut. 6:21–23; 26:5–9; 29:2–9; 32; Josh. 24:2–13; Judg. 2:1–3; 6:8–10;

16. As noted by Ooi (*Scripture and Its Readers*, 200), who identifies a common motif between Neh. 9, Ezek. 20, and Acts 7: "the interplay of divine initiative and human responsibility," pointing to the scriptural story as "a drama of human (non-) participation in God's initiative."

17. As Brueggemann, *Theology of the Old Testament*, 145, notes: "Israel is characteristically concerned with the action of God—the concrete, specific action of God." See the list of elements in Ooi, *Scripture and Its Readers*, 187.

11:16–24; 1 Sam. 12:8; Pss. 78; 105; 106; 135; 136; Neh. 9:6–31; Jer. 2:6–7; 32:17–23; Ezek. 20:5–29.

That God's redemption as story is a theological construction is clear from the opening line of the Decalogue: "I am Yahweh your God who brought you out of the land of Egypt" (Exod. 20:2). Here is a clear statement of self-revelation: "I am Yahweh your God," and this is linked to the redemptive-historical event of God's salvation of Israel from Egypt. This statement not only highlights the theological character of the redemptive narrative but also suggests its essential core.

Core Historical Actions: Exodus and Conquest

Even a cursory glance at the chart below reveals two consistent elements throughout these liturgical expressions. Common to nearly every passage is that which is expressed in concise form in Deut. 6:21–23 (cf. 1 Sam. 12:8).

> We were slaves to Pharaoh in Egypt, and Yahweh brought us from Egypt with a mighty hand. Moreover, Yahweh showed great and distressing signs and wonders before our eyes against Egypt, Pharaoh and all his household; He brought us out from there in order to bring us in, to give us the land which He had sworn to our fathers.

The two foundational actions of God are his "bringing out" (יצא Hiphil) for the exodus and his "bringing in" (בוא Hiphil) for the conquest.[18] This is a common word pair that denotes the completion

---

18. For יצא (Hiphil) in relation to the rescue from Egypt, see Exod. 6:13, 26; 7:4; 12:17, 42, 51; 16:6, 32; 20:2; 29:46; 32:23; Lev. 19:36; 22:33; 23:43; 25:38, 42, 55; 26:13; Num. 15:41; Deut. 1:27; 5:6, 15; 6:12; 8:14; 13:5, 10; 29:25; Judg. 2:12; 1 Kings 8:21; 9:9; 2 Chron. 6:5; 7:22; Jer. 7:22; 11:4; 32:21; 34:13; Ezek. 20:9, 10; Dan. 9:15. A secondary expression utilizes the verb עלה (Hiphil) for the rescue from Egypt, e.g., Exod. 32:4, 8, 11; 33:1; Lev. 11:45; Deut. 20:1; Josh. 24:17; 1 Sam. 12:6; 1 Kings 12:28; 2 Kings 17:7, 36; Ps. 81:10; Jer. 2:6; 11:7; 16:14; 23:7; Amos 2:10; 3:1; 9:7; Mic. 6:4. Notice Judg. 6:8, which uses both עלה (Hiphil) and יצא (Hiphil), and Judg. 6:13, in which Gideon quotes the words of the "ancestors" who told them: "Did not Yahweh bring us up [עלה Hiphil] from Egypt?" Cf. Brueggemann, *Theology of the Old Testament*, 174–76, who also refers to נצל, גאל, and פדה. For the verb בוא (Hiphil) for God giving entrance into the promised land, see, e.g., Exod. 6:8; 13:5, 11; 23:23; Lev. 18:3; 20:22; Num. 14:3, 8, 16, 24, 31; Deut. 6:10, 23; 7:1; 8:7; 9:28; 11:29; 30:5; 31:20, 23; Ezek. 20:15. At times the entrance into the promised land follows directly

Narrative	Exod.	Deut.				Josh.	Judg.			1 Sam.	Pss.					Neh.	Isa.	Jer.		Ezek.
Creed	15	6	26	29	32	24	2	6	11	12	78	105	106	135	136	9	63	2	32	20
ancestors			•			•				•		•				•			•	
exodus	•	•	•	•	•	•	•	•	•	•	•	•	•	•	•	•	•	•	•	•
wilderness				•	•	•	•		•		•	•	•	•	•	•	•	•		•
conquest	•	•	•	•	•	•	•	•	•	•	•	•	•	•	•	•	•	•	•	•
land		•			•					•			•			•		•		•
exile													•	•		•				

of an activity. Similar to the English saying "what goes up must come
down," in Hebrew what goes out must come in (e.g., Josh. 6:1, 22;
14:11; Pss. 41:7 [41:6 Eng.]; 121:8). This close association of the two
redemptive actions is suggested by the twin acts of parting water at
the Reed Sea (exodus) and the Jordan River (conquest). When one
compresses the creedal narrative into its smallest form, the wilderness
experience drops out, and the exodus and conquest are left. At the
core of Israel's story of salvation is release from a place of oppres-
sion and provision of a place of freedom. It is not just release from
a negative situation but also the provision of a positive situation.

The action of "bringing out" (יצא Hiphil) is regularly accompanied
by the phrase "with a mighty hand and an outstretched arm, with great
terror and with miraculous signs and wonders," a phrase that emphasizes the personal and miraculous character of this redemption. God's
redemption is accomplished by his personal involvement: his "hand"
and "arm" accomplish this salvation. His hand and arm are powerful
(mighty) and active (outstretched); he is a God who is able to save the
Israelites from their predicament. Furthermore, this act is a miracle
of God, beyond natural experience since it is realized through "signs
and wonders." God's omnipotence is able to accomplish salvation.
While this vocabulary provides insight into the foundational actions
of God related to the exodus, more detail is provided at times in this
narrative summary tradition, for instance, descriptions of the defeat
of the Egyptians through the plagues (e.g., Josh. 24:5; Neh. 9:10; Pss.
78:43–51; 105:27–36; 135:9; 136:10) as well as the great victory at the
Reed Sea (e.g., Josh. 24:6–7; Neh. 9:9, 11; Pss. 78:12–13; 106:9–11;
135:13–15; Isa. 63:12–14). But in all this the focus remains on Yahweh's
ability to rescue Israel from the oppressive circumstances of Egypt.

The action of "bringing in" (בוא Hiphil) is often linked with the
verb "to give" (נתן).[19] The land is carefully defined as a gift from
Yahweh, emphasizing the gracious action of a benevolent God. The

---

from the verb used for the rescue from Egypt, whether עלה (Hiphil; e.g., Exod. 3:8,
17) or יצא (Hiphil; e.g., Ezek. 20:6).

19. For the verb נתן for the gift of the land see Gen. 12:7; 13:15, 17; 15:7; 17:8; 24:7;
26:3, 4; 28:13; 35:12; 48:4; Exod. 6:4, 8; 12:25; 13:5, 11; 20:12; 32:13; 33:1; Lev. 14:34;
20:24; 23:10; 25:2, 38; Num. 13:2; 14:8; 15:2; 34:13; Deut. 1:8, 25, 35, 36; 2:29; 3:20,
28; 4:1, 21, 38, 40; 5:16, 31; 6:10, 18, 23; 7:13; 8:1; 9:6; 10:11; 11:9, 17, 21, 31; 12:10;
15:4, 7; 16:20; 17:14; 18:9; 19:1, 2, 3, 8, 10, 14; 21:1, 23; 24:4; 25:15, 19; 26:1, 2, 3; 27:2,

verbal forms used for both of these redemptive acts (bringing out and bringing in) place God as subject and Israel as object, further attestation of God's grace to a needy people. Linked to the verb "to give" (נתן) in relation to the land is the verb "to swear" (שבע Niphal),[20] pointing out that the gift of this land is based on a promise God made long before its fulfillment in the conquest. The recipients of this promise are usually identified as the ancestors depicted in the book of Genesis, reminding the people that this gift of land was not received in a moment and involved faithful trust by many generations. More detail is also provided at times for the conquest tradition, with some texts focusing on the provision of a land flowing with milk and honey (e.g., Deut. 26:9; Jer. 32:22; Ezek. 20:6, 15) and others on particular conflicts or battles (Balak, Sihon, Og, Jericho, e.g., Deut. 29:7–8; Josh. 24:8–12; Neh. 9:22; Pss. 135:10–12; 136:17–22).

Extending the Historical Actions

Reference to God swearing in relation to his core activity in the conquest is a reminder that while the exodus and conquest are the two most important events in Israel's redemptive history, other events also play a key role.

ANCESTORS

As already noted, the conquest tradition depicts the accounts of the ancestors as the period when Yahweh's promises to Israel were inaugurated. The narrative creed in Deut. 26 limits the review of the period of the ancestors to the figure of Jacob as a wanderer, that is, as one who was landless, first in his sojourn in Paddan-Aram and then in settlement in Egypt at the end of his life. The miracle is that the one whose family was but "few in number . . . became a great, mighty

---

3; 28:8, 11; 30:20; 31:7; 32:49, 52; 34:4; Josh. 1:2, 6, 11, 13, 15; 2:14; 5:6; 9:24; 21:43; 1 Chron. 16:18; 2 Chron. 20:7; Neh. 9:8, 15; Ps. 105:11; Jer. 11:5; 32:22; Ezek. 20:28, 42.

20. Gen. 24:7; 26:3; 50:24; Exod. 6:8; 13:5, 11; 32:13; 33:1; Num. 11:12; 14:23, 30; 32:11; Deut. 1:8, 35; 6:3, 10, 18, 23; 7:13; 8:1; 9:5; 10:11; 11:9, 21; 19:8; 26:3, 15; 28:11; 30:20; 31:7, 20, 21, 23; 34:4; Josh. 1:6; 5:6; 21:43; Judg. 2:1; Neh. 9:15; Jer. 11:5; 32:22; Ezek. 20:6, 15, 28, 42; 47:14; at times the verb דבר (Piel, "promised") is used instead: e.g., Gen. 28:15; Deut. 9:28; 19:8; 27:3.

and populous nation" (Deut. 26:5). Joshua 24 reaches back to Abraham's father, Terah, and emphasizes God not only taking Abraham out of the region and the idolatry of his father's household but also leading him to the promised land and multiplying his descendants. Reference is made to Isaac and Jacob, with a passing mention of Esau. Esau's possession of Mount Seir contrasts Jacob and his sons entering Egypt, a reminder that the ancestors are subsidiary to the climax of redemption at the exodus. First Samuel 12 devotes only four words to the ancestors, focusing on Jacob and his entrance into Egypt as foundational to the exodus tradition. In Ps. 105 the ancestors play a far greater role, filling fifteen verses (vv. 9–23). Attention is given to Abraham, Isaac, and Jacob and to Yahweh's consistent covenantal pursuit of them. Core to the relationship between Yahweh and the ancestors is the promise of land: "To you I will give the land of Canaan as the portion of your inheritance" (v. 11). The emphasis, however, is on the lack of fulfillment of this promise, as seen in their identity as "strangers" (גֵּרִים) in the land and their activity of wandering from nation to nation and kingdom to people (vv. 12–13). In the midst of this tenuous existence we are reminded of God's protection of this small family (vv. 14–15). Extensive room is given to the story of Joseph and how God used him to preserve the family through a great famine (vv. 16–22). Jacob's entrance into Egypt brings the ancestors' focus to a close (v. 23), setting up the exodus. Finally, Neh. 9 devotes only two verses to the ancestors (vv. 7–8) and focuses attention on the single figure of Abraham. Attention is given to God's choice of Abram in Ur of the Chaldees, the changing of Abram's name to Abraham, and the covenant established between Yahweh and Abraham, with its promise to give the land to Abraham's descendants. Interestingly, the only covenant mentioned in Neh. 9 is the one established with Abraham, and this covenant is prompted by the faithfulness that Yahweh found in Abraham's heart. In the prayer of Neh. 9 this Abrahamic phase is foundational for Israel's enduring claim to the land.

Wilderness

The wilderness tradition focuses on the forty-year experience of the community following the great deliverance from Egypt in the exodus (Deut. 29:5–6; 32:10–12; Pss. 78:14–42; 105:39–41; 106:13–33; 136:16; Neh. 9:12–21; Jer. 2:6; Ezek. 20:10–26). Within the narrative theological summaries, the wilderness is a place of God's gracious provision for his people through divine leadership in the pillar of cloud and fire as well as the gift of God's spirit, preservation of their clothing and footwear, and provision of food (manna and meat) and water. During the wilderness period the people are protected from enemy nations and even begin to gather territory in the Transjordan region, that is, the boundary of the promised land. In the wilderness the nation grows in numbers, further fulfillment of the Abrahamic promise of seed. The wilderness is also the place where the people receive the law, their guide for life in the land.

In these theological summaries, however, the wilderness is also consistently a place of rebellion, as the people complain over their conditions, attack their divinely appointed leaders (Ps. 106:16–18), engage in idolatry and pagan practices, break commandments including the Sabbath, refuse to enter the land, and intermingle with foreign nations (Pss. 78:18–19, 22, 32, 36–37, 40–42; 106:13–33; Neh. 9:16–18; Ezek. 20:13, 21). Some of the theological summaries depict God responding with discipline and judgment, others focus on God's gracious responses, and still others combine the two divine responses.

Life in the Land

As the exodus, so the conquest is at times followed by a depiction of an elongated period of Israel's life as a nation, in this case the long period of Israel's life in the promised land (Deut. 32:13–43; 1 Sam. 12:9–11; Neh. 9:24–30; Pss. 78:56–72; 106:34–40; Jer. 2:7; 32:23; Ezek. 20:28–29). Key components of this life-in-the-land tradition are God's gracious provision of leadership (1 Sam. 12:11; Ps. 78:68–72) and a fully functioning land with its fortified cities, fertile land, and developed agricultural infrastructure to support Israel's needs as well as desires. The depiction in Neh. 9:25 is: "they ate, were filled and grew fat, and reveled in Your great goodness."

This provision, however, leads to another key feature of the life-in-the-land tradition: the rebellion of the people against God. This rebellion often involves lack of adherence to God's voice and law, especially showcased in their worship of other gods and the use of idols (1 Sam. 12:10) as well as their profaning of the Sabbath and intermingling with the nations. As with the wilderness tradition, this rebellion provides theological insight into the life-in-the-land tradition. Yahweh is depicted as disciplining his people, a strategy designed to bring them to repentance. At times God is depicted as patient with his people, holding off punishment as well as sending prophetic messengers to warn the people. But often this grace is met with further rebellion and even the murder of these prophetic messengers.

Destruction and Exile

The rebellion of the people and divine disciplinary response in the life-in-the-land tradition lays the foundation for the final phase of the narrative theological summaries, which can be discerned only in a few late texts (Ps. 106; Neh. 9; Jer. 32; Ezek. 20). This phase is often referred to as exile (Ps. 106:41, 46; Jer. 32:37; Ezek. 20:23), but at times it includes the destruction of the city/land (Jer. 32:24) and loss of control over the land (Neh. 9:30, 36; Jer. 32:36). This final phase of the narrative creed highlights the climax of the people's rebellion against God.

John Goldingay highlights the importance of narrative to Israel's faith and identity: "It is of the essence of Israel to be a people with a story."[21] We have seen this in the first creedal expression in the OT, which teaches us that the core events in Israel's salvation history are fundamental to the theological expression of Israel and the OT. While many Christian approaches to theology and religion, especially in the West, collapse theology into abstractions about God, the OT shows us that one key way to summarize the faith of Israel is through telling the story of God's particular redemptive actions throughout the history of his people. These rehearsals of redemptive history highlight humanity's need for salvation by Yahweh and consistently focus attention on human fallenness. In this we see that God has acted with mercy as well as justice, rescuing his people time after time but also disciplining them in order to restore them to relationship with him.

---

21. Goldingay, *Israel's Gospel*, 30, who continues: "The Old Testament tells us who God is and who we are through the ongoing story of God's relationship with Israel."

Integrating the Historical Actions

While we have considered each of the key acts in the narrative creed separately, it is important to remember that they form a single story. Certainly the exodus and conquest are foundational, but the other events provide essential insights. The story in its fullest form is open ended, as one can discern also from the shape of the OT narrative collections. For instance, the Primary History (Genesis–2 Kings) ends with Jerusalem destroyed and the king and elite in exile, with some hope in the final verses with the release of Jehoiachin from captivity to eat at the king's table.[22] The Secondary History (1–2 Chronicles) ends with the invitation of Cyrus for the community to go up to Jerusalem from exile.[23] The fullest form of the narrative creed thus binds together the historical experience of the present, understood as a community looking in faith for restoration, with the historical experiences of the past. These past experiences are powerful theological portraits of Yahweh as their merciful and disciplinary God. They also are designed to shape the communities' response to their God as they cling to his grace, seek him by faith, and turn to him in penitential response.

Function

The narrative creed is presented not only as a theological encapsulation of Hebrew faith but also as a summary of God's self-revelation. While the people or their leaders confess it in Exod. 15; Deut. 6; 26; 29; 1 Sam. 12; Pss. 78; 105; 106; 135; 136; Isa. 63:7–14; Jer. 2:6; 32; and Neh. 9, God either directly or through his mouthpieces declares this summary of narrative theology in Josh. 24; Judg. 2; 6; Jer. 2:7; and Ezek. 20.

This theological rhythm can be discerned throughout the OT, sensed in contexts ranging from those focusing on obedience to the

22. For the open-ended nature of OT and NT stories, see the section titled "Power of Story" in chap. 8 below.

23. If Ezra–Nehemiah is included for literary or canonical reasons, then the Secondary History ends with Nehemiah seeking to resolve enduring problems among the community, hardly the restoration hoped for.

law and covenant (Deut. 6; 29; Josh. 24; 1 Sam. 12:6–12) to those expressing praise and thanksgiving (Exod. 15; Deut. 26; Pss. 105; 135; 136), repentance and request (Isa. 63:7–14; Neh. 9; Ps. 106), and even prophetic judgment and salvation (Judg. 2:1–3; 6:8–10; Jer. 2:6–7; 32:16–25; Ezek. 20).[24]

John Goldingay has reminded us of the importance of humanity within the narrative theology of the OT:

> The Old Testament story is not merely God's story. From the beginning it is the story of God and humanity, a story in which humanity has a key role to play in the achievement of God's purpose in the world. It is a story that could not exist without God's initiatives and responses (positive and negative) but also could not exist without Israel's responses and initiatives (positive and negative).[25]

The importance of humanity to OT theology is showcased in the narrative creed tradition. Sometimes the focus of the narrative creedal summary is solely on God's redemptive acts and the people's positive response (Deut. 6; 26; Josh. 24; Pss. 105; 135; 136). But in many cases this creedal summary speaks of God's redemptive and disciplinary acts and the people's positive and negative responses to these divine actions (Judg. 2:1–3; 6:8–10; 1 Sam. 12:8–11; Isa. 63:7–14; Jer. 2:6–7; 32:16–25; Pss. 78; 106; Neh. 9; Ezek. 20).

The narrative creeds employ different models to relate this history of God's response to human rebellion.[26] In some cases the story focuses on God's extraordinary patience and mercy in the face of rebellion (e.g., Deut. 32; Ezek. 20), while at other times the story relates God's discipline, designed to turn the people toward God in covenant relationship (Judg. 2:1–3; 6:8–10; 1 Sam. 12:8–11; Isa. 63; Jer. 32; Ezek. 16). At times both models are used within these narrative

---

24. See McCarthy, "What Was Israel's Historical Creed?," 52: "What is the 'little historical creed'?" It is "often a plea of faith . . . and one can multiply the ends for which it serves: hymns to praise God, words of thanksgiving, the basis of pleas for help, motivation for obedience to the law of God and so forth." See further Ooi (*Scripture and Its Readers*) on the differing functions of Neh. 9 and Ezek. 20 (as well as Acts 7 in the NT).

25. Goldingay, *Israel's Gospel*, 36.

26. See further Boda, *Praying the Tradition*, 81–87.

summaries (Pss. 78; 106; Neh. 9). The variety of models tracking the divine action in response to human action is a reminder that God's patience and discipline are both expressions of God's grace toward his people as he passionately pursues relationship with his people. It is also a reminder that one cannot place God in a predictable theological box, as we will soon see in Exod. 32–34.

Truly this narrative creed is a key rhythm of the heartbeat of OT theology. But is this the only rhythm we can sense? I would say not. Rather, another beat that can be felt throughout OT revelation and faith cannot be ignored. This beat does not compete with the narrative beat but rather provides a theological complement in a vastly different form: the character creed.

3

The Character Rhythm

God's Active Character

In our quest to take the pulse of OT theology we have so far sensed one key rhythm in the heartbeat of the OT: the narrative creed that describes Yahweh as a redemptive God through finite past action, that is, particular acts within specific times of history. But careful attention to the OT pulse reveals another discernible rhythm that OT scholarship has at times overlooked.

Character as Creed

Although George Ernest Wright focused the attention of OT scholarship on God's actions, he did acknowledge another way of describing God in the OT, what I will call the character creed. Commenting on Exod. 34:6–7, he admits that the "nearest the Bible comes to an abstract presentation of the nature of God by means of his 'attributes' is an old liturgical confession embedded in Exod. 34.6–7 and quoted in part in many other passages."[1]

> Yahweh, Yahweh God, compassionate and gracious, slow to anger, abundant in steadfast love and truth, keeping steadfast love for thousands, forgiving iniquity, rebellion, and sin; yet He will by no means leave [iniquity] unpunished, visiting the punishment for iniquity of parents on the children and on the children of children to the third and fourth generations. (AT)

In a footnote Wright states: "This confession is one of the very few in the Bible which is not a recital of events."[2] Wright observes correctly that this confession is found on many other occasions throughout the OT but somehow misses the significance of this fact. Its regular appearance reveals the important role it played in theological expression in ancient Israel (Exod. 34:6–7; Num. 14:18; Pss. 86:5, 15; 103:8; 111:4; 112:4; 116:5; 145:8; Joel 2:13; Jon. 4:2; Nah. 1:3; Neh. 9:17, 31; 2 Chron. 30:9; cf. Deut. 4:31; Ps. 78:38).[3] Brevard Childs treats this creed more judiciously when he writes:

> The frequent use through the rest of the Old Testament of the formula in [Exod. 34:6] by which the nature of God is portrayed . . . is an eloquent testimony to the centrality of this understanding of God's person . . . the biblical tradition itself understood the formulation as a reflection of a considerable history of Israel's relation with her God.[4]

Like its narrative counterpart, the character creed is an encapsulation of theology, only utilizing a different form.[5]

1. G. Wright, *God Who Acts*, 85; Sakenfeld, *Faithfulness*, 49, called this "the Exodus 34 Liturgical formula"; Spieckermann, "God's Steadfast Love," 305–27. Goldingay, *Israel's Faith*, 16, refers to Exod. 34:6–7 as "the classic formulation of Israelite systematic theology"; cf. Goldingay, *Israel's Gospel*, 32.
2. G. Wright, *God Who Acts*, 85n2.
3. Cf. Hamilton, *Exodus*, 576.
4. Childs, *Book of Exodus*, 612.
5. See Janzen, *Exodus*, 401, who refers to Exod. 34:6–7 as "a poetic summary of qualities," which along with the verbal distinction noted below may be another distinction from the narrative creed with its prosaic mode.

Elements

In this creedal tradition in ancient Israel, theology is expressed as God's redemptive character, described through consistent activity utilizing nonperfective/nonpreterite verbal forms (participles, nonperfective finite verbs) as well as personal attributes utilizing adjectives and nouns.[6] Instead of speaking of God as One who did this or that at a particular time (e.g., in the beginning God created the heavens and the earth; at the Reed Sea God delivered Israel), this tradition speaks of God as One who does this or that (e.g., participles: God is the one who creates, God is the one who delivers; or nonperfective finite verbs: God will deliver) and by extension as One who possesses these characteristics (e.g., nouns: God is the Creator, God is the Deliverer).

The foundational example in Exod. 34:6–7 shows clearly that the character creed is a theological construction. This example begins with the introduction "Yahweh, Yahweh," a declaration that finds its roots in the previous chapters in Moses's daring requests of God in the wake of the golden calf incident (Exod. 32–33). Concerned for God's potential rejection of the people, Moses initially pleads for God not to destroy the nation, a request to which God accedes (32:9–14). However, while Yahweh does call Moses to lead the people into the promised land, he refuses to accompany them personally, providing an angelic substitute (32:34–33:6), a reversal of God's original promise in Exod. 25:8 (29:45–46) that he would dwell in their midst.[7] The promise of a substitute only increases the desperation of Moses's intercession, which is played out in 33:12–23.

> Then Moses said to Yahweh, "See, You say to me, 'Bring up this people!' But You Yourself have not let me know whom You will send with me. Moreover, You have said, 'I have known you by name, and you have also found favor in My sight.'
>
> "Now therefore, I pray You, if I have found favor in Your sight, let me know Your ways that I may know You, so that I may find favor in Your sight. Consider too, that this nation is Your people."

6. Similarly, Brueggemann, *Theology of the Old Testament*, 213–28.
7. Fretheim, *Exodus*, 293–94.

And He said, "My presence shall go *with you*, and I will give you rest."

Then he said to Him, "If Your presence does not go *with us*, do not lead us up from here. For how then can it be known that I have found favor in Your sight, I and Your people? Is it not by Your going with us, so that we, I and Your people, may be distinguished from all the *other* people who are upon the face of the earth?"

Yahweh said to Moses, "I will also do this thing of which you have spoken; for you have found favor in My sight and I have known you by name."

Then Moses said, "I pray You, show me Your glory!"

And He said, "I Myself will make all My goodness pass before you, and will proclaim the name of Yahweh before you; and I will be gracious to whom I will be gracious, and will show compassion on whom I will show compassion."

But He said, "You cannot see My face, for no human can see Me and live!"

Then Yahweh said, "Behold, there is a place by Me, and you shall stand *there* on the rock; and it will come about, while My glory is passing by, that I will put you in the cleft of the rock and cover you with My hand until I have passed by. Then I will take My hand away and you shall see My back, but My face shall not be seen."

Moses begins this second phase of intercession by asking for specific details as to the identity of the angelic being whom Yahweh had promised to send with the people (33:12). Moses's request to "know Your ways" in the very next verse (33:13) may be directly related to his desire to know the specific details of the identity of the angelic being, that is, asking God how he will act in regard to the provision of the angelic being.[8] However, God's answer in 33:14 (promising his face) suggests that Moses is asking for something more, that is, to experience God's personal activity in regard to the conquest of the land. While God has promised the activity of his heavenly agent, Moses desires Yahweh to be directly involved. Yahweh agrees to this request by promising his "face" in 33:14. This view is strengthened by Moses's declaration in 33:16 that "Your going with us" is a sign

8. On "know your ways" as a seeking after "how God will act," see Janzen, *Exodus*, 396.

of God's favor. The phrase "Your going with us" echoes the earlier phrase "Your ways" in 33:13, and both of these phrases are linked to finding God's favor in their respective verses.

The function of Moses's request in 33:15 ("if Your face does not go *with us*, do not lead us up from here") is not entirely clear since Yahweh has just promised his face in 33:14. On the one hand, it may be merely a rhetorical stage in the dialogue by which Moses is just confirming what God has just agreed to in 33:14. On the other hand, it may be taking the request to another level, asking Yahweh to provide his face not only to Moses ("you" in 33:14 is singular) but also to the entire nation ("us" in 33:15; "I and Your people . . . us . . . we, I and Your people" in 33:16).[9] God's answer in 33:17 suggests the latter option is correct: "I will also do this thing of which you have spoken."

Thus, to this point God has promised that his "face" would accompany both leader and people into the promised land. This provides insight into the narrative aside found in Exod. 33:7–11, which is foundational for understanding the second phase of Moses's intercession (33:12–23; see further chap. 9, "Postscript: Calling for Response").[10]

Now Moses used to take the tent and pitch it outside the camp, a good distance from the camp, and he called it the tent of meeting. And everyone who sought Yahweh would go out to the tent of meeting which was outside the camp. And it came about, whenever Moses went out to the tent, that all the people would arise and stand, each at the entrance of their tent, and gaze after Moses until he entered the tent. Whenever Moses entered the tent, the pillar of cloud would descend and stand at the entrance of the tent; and Yahweh would speak with Moses. When all the people saw the pillar of cloud standing at the entrance of the tent, all the people would arise and worship, each at the entrance of their tent. Thus Yahweh used to speak to Moses face

9. For the view favored here, see Childs, *Book of Exodus*, 595; Moberly, *At the Mountain of God*, 75; Enns, *Exodus*, 582; Hamilton, *Exodus*, 566. Stuart, *Exodus*, 702n117, rejects this view because in 33:3 Yahweh refers to the nation as second-person singular. However, that does not mean the distinction is not in play later in the passage, especially because of the clear shift from Yahweh referring to the singular "you" to Moses referring to the plural "us."

10. That 33:7–11 is a narrative aside (off-line comment) is clear from the shift away from the narrative backbone preterites that dominate 33:1–6 and 33:12–23; cf. Heller, *Narrative Structure*, 430–56; Boda and Conway, *Judges*.

to face, just as one speaks to their friend. When Moses returned to
the camp, his servant Joshua, the son of Nun, a young man, would
not depart from the tent.

In 33:7–11 the narrator reveals the past regularly occurring encounters between Yahweh and Moses in the tent of meeting. This
description ends with the climactic and summarizing statement in
33:11 that "Yahweh used to speak to Moses face to face, just as one
speaks to their friend." The preceding verses highlight the contrast
of Moses with the experience of the people, who would remain at
a distance at the entrance to their tents as Moses experienced this
face-to-face encounter with Yahweh (33:8, 10). Thus, in 33:12–23
Moses secures the "face" of Yahweh, that face he had experienced
in the tent of meeting, for the entire community. The narrative has
progressed significantly from the beginning of chapter 32. Rather
than Yahweh destroying the community for their idolatry, Yahweh
has now not only promised their survival, but rather than sending
them on their way with a heavenly intermediary, he has also promised his "face," which before was only experienced by Moses in the
tent of meeting.

But Moses is not finished with his negotiation with God. Embold-
ened by God's promise of "My face," Moses asks Yahweh: "show me
Your glory" (33:18). What Moses calls "Your glory," God calls "My
goodness" (33:19) and "My glory" (33:22), both of which God says
will pass by (עבר) Moses.[11] Glory (כָּבוֹד) is used in Ps. 16:9 when
speaking of rejoicing with all one's being: heart and body, that is,
glory. In Ps. 108:2 (108:1 Eng.) "glory" parallels the word "heart,"
again suggesting a semantic association. This is why "glory" can be
so easily identified with God himself in the prophetic warnings of
exchanging the "glory" for idols (Jer. 2:11; cf. Ps. 106:20). But glory
is particularly something that one "sees" (Exod. 16:7; Isa. 35:2; 66:18;
Ezek. 44:4).[12] As "glory," "goodness" (טוּב) is used to speak of the
beauty of a person (Zech. 9:17), in particular the positive qualities

11. See Fretheim, *Exodus*, 300, for the paralleling of goodness and glory. Oswalt
("Exodus," 532) distinguishes between glory and goodness, with goodness referring
to his characteristics and glory to his presence.
12. Hamilton, *Exodus*, 568.

of God (cf. Pss. 25:7; 145:7).[13] Of course, Moses had already seen
God's glory (Exod. 16:7, 10; 19:9, 16; 24:15–18; 33:9; cf. 40:34), so this
request in Exod. 33–34 is probably intended to confirm the agreement
reached in 33:17.[14] In the negotiation Moses had been dialoguing
with Yahweh verbally but now wanted to experience God's manifest
presence as a confirmation. This is precisely what happens when
God's glory/goodness passes by in Exod. 34. God's revelation of his
glory/goodness (34:1–8) leads to Moses's formal request for Yahweh's
personal presence (34:9), to which God responds by renewing covenant (34:10–26).

Back in 33:19 Yahweh promised that his glory/goodness would pass
by Moses's "face," and this is precisely what happens in 34:6 ("then
Yahweh passed by his face"). Once again we encounter the word "face"
and this time related to the human partner. Thus, God has promised
his "face" for the leader and people in 33:12–17, and when asked to
then show his "glory," he promises that this "glory/goodness" would
pass by Moses's "face." This is all reminiscent of the "face-to-face"
relationship between Yahweh and Moses described in 33:11. But there
is a qualification in 33:20–23 as Yahweh declares "you cannot see My
face, for no human can see me and live" (33:20) and "My face shall
not be seen" (33:23).[15] This does sound odd in light of the explicit
reference to the "face-to-face" relationship Moses enjoyed with Yahweh according to 33:11 (see above) and the promise of Yahweh's accompanying "face" for the leader and people in 33:14. This tension
may be resolved by distinguishing between proximity: it is one thing
for the "face" of Yahweh to accompany the people and leader from a
distance, but another for them to have close access to this "face."[16] But

13. Childs, *Book of Exodus*, 596, "his benefits which are experienced by Israel,"
cf. Hosea 3:5; Jer. 31:12.

14. Enns, *Exodus*, 582, sees 33:18–23 as designed to get confirmation of God's
promise in v. 17; cf. Stuart, *Exodus*, 704.

15. Of course, there are references elsewhere to humans seeing the face of God
and yet surviving, a scenario that demands the gracious intervention of God; cf.
Gen. 32:31 [32:30 Eng.].

16. Sarna, *Exodus*, 214, notes that earlier instances of glory were always corporate,
at a distance, and at God's initiative, thus distinguished from Moses's request. See
Fretheim, *Exodus*, 299, who speaks of "the face/presence of God no longer enveloped
by the cloud (cf. 16:10; 40:34) or the fire (see 24:17)." Dozeman, *Commentary on
Exodus*, 729–30, explains this diachronically, distinguishing between glory as "the

this does not explain how Moses experienced "face-to-face" encounter in the tent of meeting on a regular basis (33:11). It may be that in 33:11 the emphasis was on "speaking" ("Yahweh used to speak to Moses face to face"), while here in 33:20–23 the emphasis is on "seeing."[17] Nevertheless, Yahweh makes clear that there are limits for human access to the divine character. Here we see how God discloses, and yet there remains part of God's character that lies beyond mere mortal comprehension. As Oswalt notes: "No matter how close a human . . . can come to God in personal experience, there is still an uncrossable barrier between the essence of the Transcendent One and that of his creatures, a barrier not even a Moses could cross."[18]

Key to the present work is God's promise in 33:19 that accompanying the revelation of his glory/goodness will be the self-proclamation of his "name." It is not surprising that the word "name" is used to speak of a person (Num. 1:2, 18, 20; 3:40, 43; 26:55) and even to indicate the destruction of a person (to cut off the name, Deut. 7:24; 9:14; 1 Sam. 24:21). Childs has expressed it succinctly: "The name of God, which like his glory and his face are vehicles of his essential nature."[19] And Janzen supports this by writing, "This means nothing less than God will now reveal a new core understanding of his identity or character."[20] It is important to note that this encounter between Yahweh and Moses involves both a personal experience of God's glorious presence and God's declaration of his name. Both are key to the encounter depicted in Exod. 34: Moses experiences God's presence but also hears God articulate his name.[21]

---

inner character of God, revealed in the divine name Yahweh (3:13–15)" in non-P History and the "Glory of Yahweh" in P (24:15–18). There are also cases where Yahweh speaks face to face with the community and yet they survive (cf. Deut. 5:4). In this case there must be a difference related to proximity.

17. See Num. 12:8, where we learn that Moses spoke with Yahweh "mouth to mouth" (פֶּה אֶל־פֶּה) but also that he beholds (נבט Hiphil) the "form of Yahweh" (תְּמוּנָה), a term that suggests a distinction between Yahweh and what Moses beheld; cf. Ps. 17:15, where "face" and "form" are paralleled.

18. Oswalt, "Exodus," 532.

19. Childs, *Book of Exodus*, 596.

20. Janzen, *Exodus*, 447–48.

21. Thus there is no reason to downplay subjective experience of God (seeing) with objective cognition of God (knowing), as do Fretheim, *Exodus*, 299; Stuart, *Exodus*, 701; Kinlaw and Oswalt, *Lectures*, 175; cf. Hamilton, *Exodus*, 570.

The revelation of Yahweh is one of the key goals of the book of Exodus, as can be seen in two early encounters between Yahweh and Moses. In Exod. 3 Moses tells God that the people will want to know the name of the God of their fathers who is commissioning him for this task (v. 13). And God says: "I AM WHO I AM. . . . Thus you shall say to the children of Israel, 'I AM has sent me to you'" (v. 14) and then qualifies this as: "Thus you shall say to the children of Israel, 'Yahweh, the God of your ancestors, the God of Abraham, the God of Isaac, and the God of Jacob, has sent me to you.' This is my name forever, and this is my memorial-name to all generations" (v. 15). This agenda of the revelation of Yahweh as the name of the God of the ancestors is evident also in Exod. 6. God declares to Moses, "I am Yahweh," and then reminds him that while he appeared to the ancestors Abraham, Isaac, and Jacob as God Almighty (*El Shaddai*), he did not reveal to them the name Yahweh. The revelation of this name is linked to his act of salvation in the exodus (v. 6) as well as the covenant ceremony at Sinai (v. 7), and his provision of the promised land (v. 8). While these redemptive acts and this relational intimacy are integral to the revelation of Yahweh, one should not miss the key moment of self-revelation that occurs near the end of the book of Exodus, at one of the times of greatest crisis in the life of Israel. By beginning with "Yahweh, Yahweh," Exod. 34:6–7 is clearly a moment of divine self-disclosure on a level that transcends any revelation that the ancestors Abraham, Isaac, and Jacob experienced.

Core Active Characteristics: Steadfast Love and Justice

As with the narrative creed, so with the character creed there are elements that consistently appear throughout the creedal tradition. In the case of the character creed, most have focused attention on the ubiquity of the initial nouns and adjectives throughout the Hebrew Bible:[22]

> compassionate and gracious,
> slow to anger, abundant in steadfast love and truth

22. See esp. Knowles, *Unfolding Mystery*; cf. Laney, "God's Self-Revelation."

This list occurs in Exod. 34:6; Pss. 86:15; 103:8; 145:8; Joel 2:13; Jon. 4:2; and Neh. 9:17. Among these passages, Exod. 34:6 and Ps. 86:15 include "and truth" at the end of this list. Additional passages contain variations of this creed: Pss. 25:6; 111:4; 2 Chron. 30:9; and Neh. 9:31 have only "compassionate and gracious"; Pss. 112:4; 116:5 have only "compassionate and gracious" but add "righteous"; Deut. 4:31 and Ps. 78:38 have only "compassionate"; Num. 14:18 has only "slow to anger and abundant in steadfast love"; and Nah. 1:3 has only "slow to anger" and adds "great in power." The various nouns and adjectives found in Exod. 34:6 have been identified as "ontological" statements that are distinguished from the "functional" statements expressed through nonperfective verbal phrases (participles, imperfect verb) that follow in Exod. 34:7 (cf. Num. 14:18):[23]

> keeping steadfast love for thousands,
> forgiving iniquity, rebellion, and sin;
> yet He will by no means leave [iniquity] unpunished,
> visiting the punishment for iniquity of parents on the chil-
> dren and on the children of children to the third and
> fourth generations. (AT)

While this distinction is true, shifting our focus at the outset from the ontological statements of Exod. 34:6 to the functional statements of 34:7 opens the way for us to consider another key dimension to the character creed tradition in the OT, as will soon become apparent.[24]

23. For this see Gentry and Wellum, *Kingdom through Covenant*, 142–44, who, drawing on unpublished material from John Meade and Stephen Dempster, note the distinction between "ontology" and positive and negative "function" in Exod. 34:6–7. See Dozeman (*Commentary on Exodus*, 736) for scholarly debate over whether 34:6 and 7 reflect "two distinct cultic formula" that were later combined. He concludes that they are "a unified confession."

24. Brueggemann, *Theology of the Old Testament*, 145, writes: "Israel is characteristically concerned with the action of God—the concrete, specific action of God—and not God's character, nature, being, attributes, except as those are evidenced in concrete actions." With the common link as the participial expressions we then see how attributes are typically founded on concrete actions of Yahweh. Thus, Knowles, *Unfolding Mystery*, 39: "At least for Israel, the divine identity is not a matter of metaphysical abstracts; rather, it is expressed in terms that describe God's gracious manner of acting within the divine-human relationship. And that divine identity is expressed in concrete action."

The nonperfective clauses (participles, imperfect) found in Exod. 34:7 stand in contrast to the narrative creed with its use of perfective and preterite verbal forms that focus on God's specific actions within redemptive history. Back in Exod. 33 Moses asked God to "let me know Your ways that I may know You" (33:13) and also "show me Your glory" (33:18). Yahweh qualifies this second request, promising his "goodness," which is closely related to proclaiming his "name" (33:19). It may be that we find here the foundation for the distinction between the two parts of Exod. 34:6–7, with God's revelation of his "ways" related to the nonperfective clauses found in Exod. 34:7 and God's revelation of his "goodness" related to the adjectives/nouns in Exod. 34:6. While God's ways in Exod. 33–34 refer to Moses's experience of God's personal activity (see above), such personal activity is seen as the kind of personal activity that he has come to expect of Yahweh. God's "goodness" refers to those more abstract qualities that are grasped from having experienced his personal activity consistently.

Human experience in general confirms the relationship between these two ways of describing a person.[25] We do not first encounter a person's attributes, but rather their actions. We watch how they act and function in life and relationships and from this begin to discern certain patterns. They crack great jokes; they criticize their colleagues; they express their love through thoughtful notes; they arrive at work late. This activity begins as finite and particular actions

---

25. See the superb work of Goldingay (*Israel's Faith*, 15) for the distinction between describing people through telling a story about them versus through analyzing their traits, portraying their qualities, and identifying their priorities. His first two volumes on OT theology reflect these two strategies: *Israel's Gospel* and *Israel's Faith*. He argues that these two strategies explain the shape of the OT and the NT canon, with the narrative books (Genesis–Esther, Matthew–Acts) focusing on the first strategy and the books that follow (Job–Malachi, Romans–Revelation) focusing on the second. I am trying to show in the present book that these two strategies can be discerned in two of the foundational creeds in the OT. Goldingay helpfully cites Hauerwas and Jones, *Why Narrative?*, 9: "Christian theology is poised between the poles of narrative and metaphysics, and both are required for an adequate theological method." The priority of the storyteller is made clear by Lash, *Theology on the Way to Emmaus*, 117. Also note Goldingay, *Israel's Gospel*, 37, where he cites Nussbaum, *Love's Knowledge*, 165: "the particular is in some sense prior to general rules and principles." The particular would include the events of the narrative creed that precede the general rules of the character creed. Here I am suggesting that there is even a distinction in the general rules and principles between recurring acts and characteristics.

(she wrote a great research paper today), but soon we see patterns (she wrote great research papers in every class this semester), which leads us to conclude that this is part of her regular activity (she is someone who writes great research papers). Over time we begin to think of this person not in terms of her typical activity (someone who writes great research papers) but rather in terms of an attribute of the person (she is a great researcher). God's ways could be understood as typical activity expressed through nonperfective verbs (especially participles).[26] God's goodness could be understood as his attributes. Exodus 34:7, with its focus on regular patterns of behavior, provides us with Yahweh's typical activities (function), while Exod. 34:6, with its focus on abstract characteristics, provides us with God's attributes (ontology). From one perspective we understand that these inner characteristics explain the typical activity. But from another perspective, especially that of humans who experience God's presence and person, the typical activity leads them to understand the inner characteristics. Thus I will start with the typical activity found in Exod. 34:7. Furthermore, I will start here because elsewhere in the OT we discover that the typical activity found in Exod. 34:7 points to a set of inner characteristics distinct from, yet no less important than, those found in Exod. 34:6 (see below).

One characteristic is repeated in both the ontological and functional descriptions of Yahweh in Exod. 34:6–7, and it appears at the intersection between the two lists. That characteristic is steadfast love (חֶסֶד):

> ... abundant in steadfast love (חֶסֶד) and truth,
> keeping steadfast love (חֶסֶד) for thousands ...

The placement and repetition of this term (חֶסֶד) points to its importance in the theological presentation of the OT, an importance confirmed by its ubiquity in the OT as well as its consistent mention in OT exegesis and theological works.

---

26. On this see the classic work of Crüsemann, *Studien zur Formgeschichte*, who speaks similarly of the participial praise tradition found throughout the Psalms and Prophetic Books.

Recent study of this Hebrew word חֶסֶד (steadfast love) has em-phasized the loyal or faithful dimension of this term, whether arising from legal obligation or voluntary choice.[27] This contrasts with ear-lier approaches to the word that focused on the merciful or gracious dimension of the term.[28] While not losing the faithful dimension of חֶסֶד, a translation such as "steadfast love" is best because this word is used regularly for loving and merciful character and actions in the OT. This debate among English scholars may be reflected in the way חֶסֶד is translated in the OG tradition in general and in Exod. 34:7 in particular.

keeping steadfast love	נֹצֵר חֶסֶד	καὶ δικαιοσύνην διατηρῶν καὶ ποιῶν ἔλεος	and preserving righteousness and doing mercy

A key difference between the Hebrew text of Exod. 34:7 and its Greek translation is seen in how a single Hebrew participle followed by a noun (נֹצֵר חֶסֶד; keeping steadfast love) is translated by two Greek participle-noun phrases (δικαιοσύνην διατηρῶν καὶ ποιῶν ἔλεος, pre-serving righteousness and doing mercy). The expected translation of the Hebrew words is διατηρῶν ἔλεος (preserving mercy), that is, the participle from the first phrase in the OG and the noun from the second phrase. Wevers suggests that the OG construction has arisen due to harmonization with Exod. 20:6, which translates עֹשֶׂה חֶסֶד לַאֲלָפִים (doing steadfast love toward thousands) as ποιῶν ἔλεος εἰς χιλιάδας (doing mercy unto thousands).[29] This would explain the use of ποιέω (doing) in Exod. 34:7 but not the use of δικαιοσύνη (righ-teousness). In the OG tradition δικαιοσύνη (righteousness) usually translates words cognate with the verb צדק (to be righteous; צְדָקָה

27. Snaith, *Distinctive Ideas*, 94–130; Glueck, *Hesed*; Sakenfeld, *Meaning of Hesed*; Sakenfeld, *Faithfulness*; Clark, *Hesed*. Snaith emphasizes faithfulness even though at times he admits mercy is in view.

28. See Fürst, *Hebrew and Chaldee Lexicon*, 468: "kindness, benevolence, com-plaisance, favour, love"; note translations like KJV (mercy, goodness), NASB (loving-kindness), NIV (love). *HALOT* glosses as "joint obligation . . . closeness, solidar-ity, loyalty" for human relationships and "faithfulness, goodness, graciousness" for divine-human relationships; *DCH* as "loyalty, faithfulness, kindness, love, mercy," thus intertwining both nuances; note translations like NRSV ("steadfast love"); NLT ("unfailing love"). Note the superb review of this issue by Harris, "חסד (Ḥsd)," 305–7.

29. See Wevers, *Notes*, 557.

righteousness 126×; צֶדֶק righteousness 81×; צַדִּיק righteous 7×),
but nine times it is used to translate חֶסֶד (steadfast love: Gen. 19:19;
20:13; 21:23; 24:27; 32:10; Exod. 15:13; 34:7; Prov. 20:22; Isa. 63:7)
and six times to translate אֱמֶת (truth: Gen. 24:49; Josh. 24:14; Isa.
38:19; 39:8; Dan. 8:12; 9:13).[30] This evidence suggests that in Exod.
34:7 the OG is bringing out two aspects of the meaning of חֶסֶד
(steadfast love), that associated with righteousness (δικαιοσύνην)
and that associated with mercy (ἔλεος).[31]

These two dimensions—the righteous consistency of Yahweh's
character and his merciful grace—of חֶסֶד (steadfast love) are evident
in what follows in Exod. 34:7. God's steadfast love means that he
holds firm to his covenant commitments, which involve both mercy
and discipline. He both forgives and punishes sin, and these are not
contradictory acts.

Thus, in Exod. 34:7 we see the fulfillment of Moses's request for
God to reveal his "ways," that is, his patterns of behavior, and this is
unpacked through the nonperfective clauses in Exod. 34:7.[32]

> keeping steadfast love for thousands,
> forgiving iniquity, rebellion, and sin;
> yet He will by no means leave [iniquity] unpunished,
> visiting the punishment for iniquity of parents on the chil-
>   dren and on the children of children to the third and
>   fourth generations. (AT)

The first line focuses on Yahweh's key characteristic of חֶסֶד (steadfast love). The second and fourth lines highlight two key outcomes
related to human sin: forgiveness and punishment, with the third line
representing the shift between the two outcomes. Reference is made to
forgiveness of all kinds of sin, utilizing the three main words for sin

30. Data from *Lexham Analytical Lexicon to the Septuagint*.
31. It may be that the OG has a text that repeats the doublet at the end of v. 6
(חֶסֶד וֶאֱמֶת) and translates it slightly differently when it is repeated as נֹצֵר אֱמֶת
וְעֹשֵׂה חֶסֶד. We have no manuscript for this suggestion.
32. Spieckermann, "God's Steadfast Love," notes the importance of the character
creed in Exod. 34:6–7 but focuses his attention on the quality of steadfast love (חֶסֶד).
This term's appearance in both the ontological and functional sections of this character
creed suggests its importance. It interlinks the two types of character statements.

in the OT (עָוֹן וָפֶשַׁע וְחַטָּאָה, iniquity, rebellion, sin),[33] but the text immediately reminds us that Yahweh does not leave such sin unpunished. This seems odd to many who have a view of forgiveness that does not involve punishment, but the OT regularly employs the word "forgiveness" in contexts where punishment is also carried out.[34] This understanding of forgiveness involves mitigated punishment. The sin demands a severe consequence, but this consequence is mitigated as an act of mercy by a holy God. The present narrative context of Exod. 32–34 is a superb example of this, as we see in Exod. 32:30–35, where Moses's search for atonement and forgiveness involves punishment of the offending parties. The nation deserved to be eliminated for this offense, but there is "forgiveness" that involves mitigated punishment. So also Num. 14, where the character creed is employed in its expanded form, showcases this principle in action. Following the recitation of the character creed, Moses requests God's forgiveness (14:19) and God declares pardon (14:20), but then God proceeds to announce punishment on the present generation (14:21–23), even if there remains hope for Caleb, Joshua, and the next generation (14:24–35).

By focusing on Exod. 34:7 we gain a perspective on the kinds of activity (ways) that are typical of Yahweh, and we see that his activity is based on חֶסֶד (steadfast love), which entails both positive and negative actions directed toward sin—forgiving yet disciplining—even though his positive activity (thousands) outlasts his negative activity (third/fourth generations).

Extending the Active Characteristics

The functional statements about Yahweh in Exod. 34:7 fulfill Moses's request for Yahweh to teach him his "ways" in Exod. 33:13, while the ontological statements about Yahweh in Exod. 34:6 fulfill Moses's request for Yahweh to show him his "glory" or at least his "goodness" in Exod. 33:18.

---

33. As Hamilton, *Exodus*, 576, notes, "34:7, when speaking of God's forgiveness, seems to search the Hebrew lexicon exhaustively to make sure to miss no 'sin' family word."

34. See Sklar, *Sin, Impurity, Sacrifice, Atonement*; Sklar, "Sin and Atonement"; Boda, *Severe Mercy*.

Yahweh, Yahweh,
the compassionate and gracious God,
slow to anger, abundant in steadfast love and truth

This initial set of attributes, expressed through adjectives and nouns in 34:6 and ubiquitous throughout the OT, begins with two adjectives, compassionate and gracious (רַחוּם וְחַנּוּן) followed by two attributive phrases that employ quantitative language: "long" of anger and abundant in steadfast love and truth (אֶרֶךְ אַפַּיִם וְרַב־חֶסֶד וֶאֱמֶת). The mercy of God (compassionate), expressed through the Hebrew term רַחוּם, is a regular feature of the character creed. The use of the closely related term רַחֲמִים (compassion) to refer to the pity of a mother for her threatened child in the bizarre legal scene in 1 Kings 3:26 and to Joseph's response upon recognizing his brothers in Gen. 43:30 (cf. Amos 1:11) highlights the emotionally charged quality of these terms.[35] This is confirmed by the fact that these words are often contrasted with the anger of God (Deut. 13:17; Zech. 1:13–16; Ps. 77:10 [77:9 Eng.]). The second term here, חַנּוּן (gracious), occurs thirteen times in the OT and in eleven of these occurrences in combination with רַחוּם (compassionate).[36] In all thirteen cases it refers to God's gracious character.[37]

The initial characteristic of God's passionate mercy toward his people is followed by two characteristics that emphasize the great quantity of two other characteristics.[38] Yahweh is "long of anger," which means that he has an immense capacity to withhold his anger.[39]

35. Notice the use of רַחֲמִים (compassionate) to refer to the surprising tender response of captors for their prisoners (e.g., 1 Kings 8:50; Ps. 106:46; Dan. 1:9; Neh. 1:11; 2 Chron. 30:9). That רַחוּם (compassionate) and רַחֲמִים (compassionate) are closely related can be seen in the easy replacement of the one for the other when paired with חֶסֶד (steadfast love); e.g., Pss. 25:6; 40:12 (40:11 Eng.); 51:3 (51:1 Eng.); 69:17 (69:16 Eng.); 103:4; Isa. 63:7; Jer. 16:5; Lam. 3:22; Hosea 2:21; Zech. 7:9 (cf. Dan. 1:9). Also notice Neh. 9:17–19, 31.

36. Hamilton, *Exodus*, 573, notes the "assonance" between these two words, which not only binds them closely together as a word pair but expresses "emphasis."

37. The OG translates it as ἐλεήμων (merciful).

38. Also note the regular combination of terms from the two basic parts of Exod. 34:6: רחם (compassionate) and חסד (steadfast love): Neh. 13:22; Pss. 25:6; 40:12 (40:11 Eng.); 51:3 (51:1 Eng.); 69:17 (69:16 Eng.); 103:4; Isa. 54:8, 10; 63:7; Jer. 16:5; Lam. 3:22, 32; Hosea 2:19.

39. Notice the contrasting quality: "short of anger" (קְצַר־אַפַּיִם), short-tempered, Prov. 14:17.

This emphasizes his patience with his people. At the same time he is "abundant in steadfast love and truth." These two terms appear regularly together throughout the OT: Gen. 24:27, 49; 32:11; 47:29; Josh. 2:14; 2 Sam. 2:6; 15:20; Pss. 25:10; 40:11; 57:4; 61:8; 85:11; 86:15; 89:15; 115:1; 138:2; Prov. 3:3; 14:22; 16:6; 20:28.[40] Especially important here again is the key Hebrew term חֶסֶד (steadfast love), which refers not only to Yahweh's faithfulness but also to his gracious mercy experienced by those who enter into relationship with him.[41] This divine steadfast love "involves acts of beneficence, mutuality, and often also obligations that flow from a legal relationship,"[42] and "depending on the context, it can express conduct conditioned by intimate relationship, covenantal obligation, or even undeserved magnanimity."[43] The term with which it is linked in Exod. 34:6, אֱמֶת (truth), "encompasses reliability, durability, and faithfulness. The combination of terms expresses God's absolute and eternal dependability in dispensing His benefactions."[44]

It is clear that the core of this creedal tradition is dominated by positive features of God's character.[45] However, the phrase "long of anger" reminds us that anger remains as a possible response and may be the appropriate response from a God who is truly loyal to his covenant agreements, as becomes evident in the "functional" qualities or activities found in Exod. 34:7 (see above).[46] Also, God's anger should not be placed in conflict with his gracious and merciful character. God's anger toward injustice is designed to express mercy, grace, and

40. Sarna, *Exodus*, 216.
41. Cf. Sakenfeld, *Faithfulness*; Clark, *Hesed*.
42. Sarna, *Exodus*, 216.
43. Ibid., 80.
44. Ibid., 216.
45. As noted by Hamilton, *Exodus*, 576: "Nowhere in the litany does the Lord draw attention to his attributes of power, perfection, or holiness. Everything the Lord says autobiographically is something that God is or does for the benefit of others, especially his chosen people."
46. See Knowles, *Unfolding Mystery*, 104, who wisely notes: "This affirms, on the one hand, the reality of divine wrath, with its implications of divinely sanctioned religious or ethical norms and boundaries, together with the prospect of judgment and condemnation for those who transgress them. On the other hand, it suggests a temperate wrath and tempered judgment—precisely what Habakkuk's finely balanced prayer envisages: 'In wrath, remember mercy' (Hab. 3:2)."

loyalty to those who are experiencing that injustice. However, the list of core attributes of Yahweh here in Exod. 34:6 does emphasize God's mercy and compassion over his wrath and discipline. It reveals God's desire for normative relationship with his people, enjoying one another in covenantal harmony.

This initial set of attributes is a fulfillment of God's promise during the passing of his goodness and proclamation of his name in Exod. 33:19: "I will be gracious (חנן) to whom I will be gracious (חנן), and I will show compassion (רחם) on whom I will show compassion (רחם)."[47] This statement in Exod. 33:19 fills in details in his earlier revelation of the divine name, "I am who I am," in Exod. 3:13–14, now focusing on his gracious and compassionate nature, the first two attributes he declares in Exod. 34:6.[48]

The functional statements about Yahweh in Exod. 34:7 are linked with ontological statements in Exod. 34:6 that emphasize God's mercy and compassion. However, elsewhere in the OT these functional statements about Yahweh appear with ontological statements that draw in other aspects of God's character that should not be ignored.[49]

Within the Decalogue, Exod. 20:5–6 comes immediately to mind:

For I, Yahweh, your God, am a jealous God, visiting the punishment for the iniquity of parents on the children, on the third and the fourth generations of those who hate Me, but showing steadfast love to thousands, to those who love Me and keep My commandments. (AT)

One key difference between Exod. 20:5–6 and Exod. 34:6–7 is the order of the functional statements.[50] Whereas Exod. 34:7 begins by

47. Gentry and Wellum, *Kingdom through Covenant*, 144.
48. Janzen, *Exodus*, 401.
49. See also the helpful chart in Kelly, "Joel, Jonah, and the YHWH Creed," 807.
50. See Sarna, *Exodus*, 216, who notes regarding Exod. 34:6–7, "emphasis and priority here are given to God's magnanimous qualities rather than to His judgmental actions." Cf. Hamilton, *Exodus*, 576, on the contrast between Exod. 20 and 34. See Dozeman (*Commentary on Exodus*, 736) on Exod. 34:6–7 as "an innerbiblical transformation of the Decalogue" that introduces "a change into the character of God which is necessary if covenant with the Israelites is to continue after the sin of the Golden Calf.... Yahweh the jealous God ... now becomes Yahweh, the merciful and gracious God."

Character Creed	Exod. 34:6–7	Num. 14:18	Exod. 20:5–6; Deut. 5:9–10	Deut. 7:9–10	1 Kings 8:23; 2 Chron. 6:14	Neh. 1:5	Neh. 9:32	Jer. 32:18	Dan. 9:4
merciful (רַחוּם)	●								
gracious (חַנּוּן)	●								
slow to anger (אֶרֶךְ אַפַּיִם)	●	●							
abundant in steadfast love (וְרַב־חֶסֶד)	●	●							
and faithfulness (וֶאֱמֶת)	●								
keeping/showing (covenant and) steadfast love for thousands (נֹצֵר/עֹשֶׂה/שֹׁמֵר [הַבְּרִית וְ]חֶסֶד לַאֲלָפִים)	●		●	●	●	●	●	●	●
forgiving iniquity, transgression, and sin (נֹשֵׂא עָוֹן וָפֶשַׁע וְחַטָּאָה)	●	●							
by no means clearing the guilty (וְנַקֵּה לֹא יְנַקֶּה)	●	●							
visiting (or repaying) punishment for the iniquity of the parents on the children and the children of children to the third and the fourth generation (פֹּקֵד/מְשַׁלֵּם) פֹּקֵד עֲוֹן אָבוֹת עַל־בָּנִים וְעַל־בְּנֵי בָנִים עַל־שִׁלֵּשִׁים וְעַל־רִבֵּעִים*			●	●				●	
jealous (קַנָּא)			●						
no God like you (אֵין־כָּמוֹךָ אֱלֹהִים)					●				
faithful (הַנֶּאֱמָן)				●					
great (גָּדוֹל)						●	●	●	●
mighty (גִּבּוֹר)							●	●	
awesome (נוֹרָא)						●	●	●	●

*See also Deut. 7:10: "but repays those who hate him to their faces, to destroy them; he will not delay with him who hates him, he will repay him to his face" (וּמְשַׁלֵּם לְשֹׂנְאָיו אֶל־פָּנָיו לְהַאֲבִידוֹ לֹא יְאַחֵר לְשֹׂנְאוֹ אֶל־פָּנָיו יְשַׁלֶּם־לוֹ).

focusing on God showing steadfast love and then shifts to God visiting punishment for iniquity, Exod. 20:5–6 reverses the order. Another
key difference, which matches the reversal in functional statements,
is the dramatic shift in ontological statements. Rather than focusing
on God's gracious and merciful nature (ontological statements) prior
to the recitation of the participles (functional statements), Exod.
20:5 begins with the ontological statement that Yahweh is "a jealous
God" (אֵל קַנָּא). This focus on God's jealousy is not antithetical to
his character expressed in Exod. 34:6–7, for it appears later in the
covenant renewal in 34:14: "for you shall not worship any other god,
for Yahweh, whose name is Jealous, is a jealous God."

The contrast between mercy and jealousy is found not only in
Exodus but also in Deuteronomy. Deuteronomy 5:9–10 depicts Moses
rehearsing the Decalogue and with it the reason for rejecting false
worship:

> For I, Yahweh, your God, am a jealous God, visiting punishment for
> iniquity of parents on the children, and on the third and the fourth
> *generations* of those who hate Me, but showing steadfast love to thou-
> sands, to those who love Me and keep My commandments. (AT)

The counterpart to Exod. 34:6–7, again flipping the order of the
functional statements and here replacing the ontological statement
that Yahweh is "a jealous God," is Deut. 7:9–10 (AT):

> Yahweh your God, He is God, the **faithful** God [הָאֵל הַנֶּאֱמָן], *keeping*
> *His covenant and His steadfast love to a thousandth generation with*
> *those who love Him and keep His commandments; but repaying those*
> *who hate Him to their faces, to destroy them; He will not delay with*
> *him who hates Him, He will repay him to his face.*

Nelson has helpfully noted the shift that occurs between Deut. 5 and 7:

> Yahweh's character is expressed through a restatement of the traits
> described in [Deut.] 5:9b–10. These are set forth in a hymnic, parti-
> cipial style with a confessional echo. . . . The "jealous God" (. . . 5:9)
> is replaced by "the faithful God." . . . The parity in 5:9b–10 between
> divine punishment and divine steadfast love is rebalanced in favor of

divine grace. Punishment is moved back to last place, while steadfast love applies unambiguously to a thousand generations.[51]

Thus, in both Exodus and Deuteronomy we see a revelation and confession of Yahweh's active character as the merciful/faithful God who is also a jealous God (אֵל קַנָּא). Similar to this is the phrase "a jealous God" (אֵל־קַנּוֹא) in Josh. 24:19 and Nah. 1:2. These terms are used only in connection with God and always in contexts where there is a danger of God's people worshiping another god (Exod. 20:5; 34:14; Deut. 4:23–24; 5:9; 6:15; Josh. 24:19–20) or being abused by a foreign nation (Nah. 1:2). Both of these terms refer to the quality in Yahweh that demands or enjoys exclusive relationship with his people. Of course, this quality is intricately linked with God's gracious and merciful nature since his love for his people involves passionate pursuit of exclusive relationship with them. In this way it is linked to disciplinary response, including God acting as a "consuming fire" (Deut. 4:24), as one provoked to anger (Deut. 4:25; 6:15), leading to the people's perishing, destruction (4:26; 6:15), and scattering to the nations (4:27). For Assyria, God's jealousy for his people prompts vengeance and wrath (Nah. 1:2). Joshua 24:19 links God's jealousy with God's holiness.

Other passages in the OT connect the functional statements we encountered in Exod. 34:7 to Yahweh's power:

Jer. 32:18	who *shows steadfast love to thousands, but repays the iniquity of parents into the bosom of their children after them*, O **great** and **mighty** God. Yahweh of hosts is His name. (AT)
Neh. 1:5	O Yahweh God of heaven, the **great** and **awesome** God, *who preserves the covenant and steadfast love for those who love Him and keep His commandments,*
Neh. 9:32	Now therefore, our God, the **great**, the **mighty**, and the **awesome** God, *who keeps covenant and steadfast love,*
Dan. 9:4	O Lord, the **great** and **awesome** God, *who keeps His covenant and steadfast love for those who love Him and keep His commandments,*

51. Nelson, *Deuteronomy*, 101. Notice, however, the lack of reference to the third and fourth generations, bringing greater focus on the offending generation. This does not contradict Exod. 20; 34; and Deut. 5 but rather makes explicit what is meant in those other passages. Retribution comes upon a family unit (three–four generations) until the death of the offending party, which is precisely what is showcased in the narratives of Exodus–Numbers; cf. Boda, *Severe Mercy*, 45n30.

These references to Yahweh as the great (גָּדוֹל), awesome (נוֹרָא), and/or mighty (גִּבֹּר) God play a key role in the book of Deuteronomy (Deut. 7:21; 10:17, 21; cf. 2 Sam. 7:23). The praises of Israel reveal the importance of these descriptions of Yahweh as powerful (Exod. 15:11–13; 1 Chron. 16:25; Pss. 47:3; 89:7; 96:4; 99:3; 145:6).[52] Exodus 15:11 and Ps. 99:3 connect God's power with God's holiness.

The two characteristics identified from those passages distinct from the character creed, God's jealousy and power, have evidenced a link with God's holiness (קָדוֹשׁ ,קֶדֶשׁ):

Exod. 15:11	Who is like You among the gods, O Yahweh? Who is like You, majestic in holiness, Awesome in praises, working wonders?
Josh. 24:19	Then Joshua said to the people, "You will not be able to serve Yahweh, for He is a **holy** God. He is a **jealous** God; He will not forgive your transgression or your sins."
Ps. 99:3	Let them praise Your **great** and **awesome** name; **Holy** is He.

Isaiah 6 makes clear that holiness is a key descriptor for Yahweh since it is the content of the praise of the seraphim in the heavenly throne room. Yahweh is identified as "holy, holy, holy," a superlative that distinguishes him from all people or items designated as "holy" in the OT. God's holiness refers to God's divine quality that distinguishes him from the created order.[53] Those people or items designated as "holy" or "holy of holies" belong "to the sphere of God's being or activity."[54] The opposite of "holy" is "common" (cf. Lev. 10:10, 11), or that which is created and has not been ritually set apart for contact with Yahweh.[55] It is not surprising that the most common characteristic for Yahweh within the priestly writings of the OT is his holiness, expressed in the phrase: "You shall be holy, for I am holy" (Lev. 11:44–45; 19:2; 20:7; 21:6–8). The call for the priests as well as

---

52. Notice in prophetic literature how the Day of Yahweh is described using these descriptors: Joel 2:11; 3:4 (2:31 Eng.); Mal. 3:23 (4:5 Eng.).

53. Levine, *Leviticus*, 257; Jenson, *Graded Holiness*, 48; Brueggemann, *Theology of the Old Testament*, 208; Goldingay, *Israel's Faith*, 23.

54. Jenson, *Graded Holiness*, 48.

55. Boda, *Severe Mercy*, 49–52.

the nation as a whole (Exod. 19:6) to be holy, set apart to the one who is holy, holy, holy, makes demands on behavior as expressed through the Decalogue and priestly legislation. When Isaiah encounters the thrice-holy deity in Isa. 6, it is natural that he would be overwhelmed by the uncleanness (6:5) as well as iniquity and sin (6:7) of himself and his people. So also the holiness of Yahweh is used in connection with the passionate jealousy and the awesome power of God.

Integrating the Active Characteristics

While the character creeds in Exod. 34:6–7 and Deut. 7:9–10 focus attention on God's gracious mercy, the character creeds revealing the holiness of God focus on God's severe mercy. Both of these are key to God's character and should not be juxtaposed. Exodus 15:13 celebrates both as key to God's act of salvation in the exodus and conquest:

> In Your steadfast love [חֶסֶד] You have led the people whom
> You have redeemed;
> In Your strength [עֹז] You have guided *them* to Your holy
> habitation.

God is strong enough to save Israel in its moment of need; God is merciful enough to notice Israel in its moment of need. God is also zealous for his holiness and jealous in his relationship with his people, but God's mercy and faithfulness ensure that his people will experience grace when they fail.

At the core of the character creed tradition in the OT is the declaration of Yahweh's typical redemptive activity in relation to his people, activity expressed through nonperfective verbs that focus on God's steadfast love, which entails forgiveness but also justice. These two dimensions of God's steadfast love point to his key characteristics of mercy and holiness.

Function

While the foundational passages of the character creed identify this summary as divine revelation (Exod. 20:5–6//Deut. 5:9–10; Exod.

34:6–7; Num. 14:18), it is clearly employed as human confession elsewhere in the OT (Deut. 7:9–11; 1 Kings 8:23//2 Chron. 6:14; 2 Chron.
30:9; Neh. 1:5; 9:17, 32; Pss. 86:15; 103:8; 111:4; 145:8; Jer. 32:18;
Dan. 9:4; Joel 2:13; Jon. 4:2; Nah. 1:3; cf. Ps. 111:4; 2 Chron. 30:9).[56]
Like the narrative creed, the character creed is a reflection of both
the faith of Israel and the revelation of their God.

Also like the narrative creed, the rhythm of the character creed
can be felt throughout the OT. It is used in contexts ranging from
praise (1 Kings 8:23//2 Chron. 6:14; Pss. 111:4; 145:8), to prayer for
help (Jer. 32:18), to repentance and renewal (2 Chron. 30:9; Neh. 1:5;
9:32; Dan. 9:4; Joel 2:13), to forgiveness (Exod. 34:6–7; Num. 14:18;
Neh. 9:17; Pss. 86:15; 103:8; Jon. 4:2), to warnings to remain faithful
(Exod. 20:5–6//Deut. 5:9–10; Deut. 7:9–11), to prophetic judgment
(Nah. 1:3). This broad spectrum of texts and traditions reveals its
dominant role in OT theological expression.

Just as the narrative creed, the character creed at times focuses on
God's redemptive character for a people in need without reference
to their sin, but it plays an essential role in those situations where
humanity's sin has created a crisis. Just as we see different strategies for the form of the narrative creed based on human rebellious
response (see above), so we see different strategies for the recitation
of the character creed.

For instance, we noticed above key distinctions between the use
of the character creed in the Decalogue and Exod. 34. The version in
the Decalogue (Exod. 20//Deut. 5) places the disciplinary character
of Yahweh in first position because it stands as a warning to those
who might consider idolatry as God makes covenant with Israel.
The version in Exod. 34 is declared in the wake of the golden calf
incident, a time when God's mercy was desperately needed and thus
placed in first position. Furthermore, the objects of discipline and
mercy are defined more carefully in the Decalogue as "those who hate
Me" and "those who love Me and keep My commandments," thus,
emphasizing the importance of human response to both discipline
and mercy. Since the Decalogue is calling for obedient response to

---

56. On the use of the character creed elsewhere in the OT, see Dozeman, "Innerbiblical Interpretation"; House, "Character of God"; Bosman, "Paradoxical Presence"; Boda, "Penitential Innovations"; Kelly, "Joel, Jonah, and the YHWH Creed."

Yahweh's covenant demands, it emphasizes human response. In the wake of the infamous failure of Israel in the golden calf incident, human response is emphasized less.

At times Israel will struggle with the character creed. Jonah expresses this in the prophet's final outburst against God, in Jon. 4. There Jonah explains his flight from God's call to prophesy to Nineveh as based on his belief in the character creed in Exod. 34:6:

> But it greatly displeased Jonah and he became angry. He prayed to Yahweh and said, "Please Yahweh, was not this what I said while I was still in my *own* country? Therefore in order to forestall this I fled to Tarshish, for I knew that You are a gracious and compassionate God, slow to anger and abundant in steadfast love, and one who relents concerning calamity. Therefore now, O Yahweh, please take my life from me, for death is better to me than life." (Jon. 4:1–3 alt.)

Jonah, however, is creative with his citation of Exod. 34:6, adding to the end a different functional statement: "one who relents concerning calamity," employing the term נחם (Niphal), which means to change one's mind, and רָעָה, which can mean evil or calamity. In the place of the statements on God's patterns of forgiving and punishing in Exod. 34:7, the prophet portrays God as fickle. The same recitation, however, is used to the advantage of God's people in Joel 2:13–14. They deserve enduring punishment but look in hope to a shift in their divine covenant partner based on his gracious character.

As with the narrative creed, so with the character creed, we have once again discerned a key rhythm in the heartbeat of OT theology. But are these the only two rhythms we can hear? Again, I would say not. There is yet another rhythm felt throughout OT revelation and faith that cannot be ignored. This rhythm does not compete with either the narrative creed or character creed, but rather provides another theological complement in a vastly different form. It is the relational creed.

4

The Relational Rhythm

God's Relational Identity

So far we have discerned two rhythms in the heartbeat of OT theology: the narrative and character creeds. The narrative creed describes Yahweh as the redemptive God through finite past action, while the character creed describes Yahweh as the redemptive God through regular activity utilizing nonperfective/nonpreterite verbal forms (participle, imperfect), as well as personal attributes utilizing adjectives and nouns. But careful attention to the pulse reveals another rhythm in the heartbeat of OT theology, one that can be discerned again in all the major sections of the OT: the relational creed.

Relationship as Creed

The importance of the relational creed has been highlighted by nearly all major scholars working on the OT throughout the history of interpretation, and for many it points to the one topic that can organize OT as well as Biblical Theology (OT and NT). In the modern era it was Eichrodt who championed its cause for understanding the OT.[1] The relational creed is often understood with reference to the common English translation of the Hebrew word *bərît* (בְּרִית): "covenant." However, while *bərît* will play a role in articulating the nature of the relationship between Yahweh and humanity, I want to focus attention on a phrase even more fundamental.[2] Rendtorff notes its importance when he writes:

> That Yhwh is Israel's God, and Israel Yhwh's people is one of the central statements in the OT. It is expressed in a variety of linguistic forms. Among these one characteristic phrase, almost formula-like in character, stands out clearly: "I will be God for you and you shall be a people for me."[3]

Leviticus 26:12 provides an exemplar expression of this theological statement:

> I will also walk among you and be your God and you shall be My people.

Echoes of this statement can be discerned throughout the OT, examples of which include: Exod. 6:7; Deut. 4:20; 7:6; 14:2; 26:16–19; 27:9; 29:13; 2 Sam. 7:22–24; 2 Kings 11:17; Pss. 95:7; 100:3; Jer. 7:23; 11:4; 13:11; 24:7; 30:22, 25; 31:1, 32, 33; 32:38; Ezek. 11:20; 14:11;

---

1. Eichrodt, *Theologie des Alten Testaments*; Eichrodt, *Theology of the Old Testament*; cf. Mendenhall, *Law and Covenant*; Kline, *Treaty of the Great King*; McCarthy, *Treaty and Covenant*; Clements, *Prophecy and Covenant*; Hillers, *Covenant*; Baltzer, *Covenant Formulary*; Kalluveettil, *Declaration and Covenant*; McComiskey, *Covenants of Promise*; Nicholson, *God and His People*; Dumbrell, *Covenant and Creation*; Hugenberger, *Marriage as a Covenant*; Rendtorff, *Covenant Formula*; McKenzie, *Covenant*; Williamson, *Sealed with an Oath*; Mason, *"Eternal Covenant"*; Hahn, *Kinship by Covenant*; Gentry and Wellum, *Kingdom through Covenant*. For a review of research, see Bartholomew, "Covenant and Creation"; Barton, "Covenant"; Hahn, "Covenant."

2. Hasel, *Basic Issues*, 40, writes: "It is surprising that this 'covenant formula,' which is conceived by J. Wellhausen, B. Duhm, B. Stade, M. Noth, and most recently by R. Smend as the center of the Old Testament and by Smend as 'the material framework for organizing the [OT] materials' into an Old Testament theology, remains unrecognized as providing the framework for the structure of an Old Testament theology."

3. Rendtorff, *Covenant Formula*, 11. Extremely important is the earlier work of Smend, *Bundesformel*.

34:30–31; 36:28; 37:23, 27; Hosea 1:9–10; 2:23; Zech. 2:11; 8:8; 13:9; cf. Gen. 17:7–8; Lev. 11:45; 22:33; 25:38; Num. 15:41; 2 Sam. 7:14; Ps. 89:27–28; 1 Chron. 17:13; 22:10.

Like its narrative and character counterparts, the relational creed is an encapsulation of theology, only utilizing a different form.

Elements

In this creedal tradition in ancient Israel, theology is expressed in terms of Yahweh's relational identity, described typically by utilizing copular syntactical constructions (היה as copula, verbless clauses, third-person pronoun copula), usually translated into English as "I am/you are," "I will be/you will be" or "He is/they are," "He will be/they will be."[4] Yahweh is usually described in this creedal tradition as "God," but in the royal appropriation of this tradition Yahweh is identified as "Father." Just as with the other creedal traditions, humanity plays an important role, assuming the identity of "people" in most cases but also as "son" in the case of the royal tradition.

Some of the most common expressions used within this creedal tradition include the following:

Formula	Type	Reference
I will be your God and you will be my people	Sinai	Exod. 6:7; Lev. 26:12; Deut. 29:12 (29:13 Eng.)
To be your God	Sinai	Lev. 11:45; 22:33; 25:38; Num. 15:41
To be your God and the God of your descendants after you. . . . I will be their God	Abraham	Gen. 17:7–8
I will be for him as a father and he will be for me as a son	David	2 Sam. 7:14; cf. Ps. 89:27–28; 1 Chron. 17:13; 22:10
I will be their God and they will be my people	New	Jer. 31:33

Tracing this ubiquitous formula throughout the OT, Rendtorff concludes:

---

4. See *IBHS* chap. 8.

The covenant formula is an element of theological language which is introduced in a *highly conscious manner*. It expresses in an extremely pregnant way God's relationship to Israel and Israel's to God.[5]

Focusing attention on the Torah, one only finds the full reciprocal formula (I will take you for my people and I will be your God) twice in Genesis–Numbers (Exod. 6:7; Lev. 26:12) and twice in Deuteronomy (26:17–19; 29:11–12 [29:12–13 Eng.]).[6] Elsewhere in Genesis–Numbers the divine part of the formula is used (I will be their God; e.g., Gen. 17:7–8), while elsewhere in Deuteronomy the human part of the formula is used (you are a holy people to Yahweh your God; e.g., Deut. 14:2). In Jeremiah and Ezekiel the full reciprocal formula dominates (Jer. 31:33; Ezek. 36:28), with a single exception in Ezekiel focusing on the divine part of the formula (Ezek. 34:24) and a single exception in Jeremiah focusing on the human part of the formula (Jer. 13:11).[7] Notwithstanding emphasis on one or other parts of the formula in the relational creed, this theological tradition highlights the relational identity of Yahweh and his people.

Core Relational Identity: God and Father

Yahweh's core relational identity is that of "God," and this is expressed in the context of a group that is identified as "people."[8] What does it mean to be "God" and "people"?[9] These identities, along with the relational identities of "Father" and "son" within the royal relational tradition, were identified long ago by Weinfeld as "legal terminology used in connection with marriage and adoption."[10] Such social contexts involve the joining of a non-family member into

5. Rendtorff, *Covenant Formula*, 92.

6. Smend, *Bundesformel*, 34–35; Rendtorff, *Covenant Formula*, 11–37.

7. In this Ezekiel aligns with the Genesis–Numbers corpus, which is dominated by the Priestly tradition as is Ezekiel, and Jeremiah aligns with the Deuteronomy corpus, which is dominated by the Deuteronomistic tradition as is Jeremiah.

8. See esp. Martens (*God's Design*, 65–79), who considers the issue of covenant but keeps the focus on what he calls the covenant formula: "I will take you for my people, and I will be your God."

9. For "people" (עַם) as a kinship term, see Gottwald, *Tribes of Yahweh*, 240.

10. Weinfeld, *Deuteronomy and the Deuteronomic School*, 81.

a family unit. Echoes of the relational creed can be discerned, for instance, in Ruth's declaration to Naomi, "Your people *shall be* my people, and your God, my God" (Ruth 1:16), as she seeks entrance into Naomi's family after the death of her husband, her only legitimate link to the family unit. The familial link is explicit in the royal relational tradition (father/son), but so also the term "people" should be understood in familial terms.

Exodus 6:7, for instance, expresses the relational creed in the following way: "I will take (לקח) you to (ל) myself as (ל) my people and I will be (היה) to (ל) you as (ל) God." The vocabulary and syntax here are reminiscent of marriage[11] and in Esther 2:7 of adoption. We have uncovered an important nuance to the relational creed found throughout the OT. It expresses the status of those who once were not part of a family unit who have attained that status through agreement. "People" then refers to one's "kindred," and the relational creed represents a declaration that establishes kinship relations.[12] Such a declaration, thus, would be considered unnecessary for a natural kin relationship.[13]

Further evidence of the relational creed as evidence of the establishment of kin relations with non-kin is available from close attention to the use of the Hebrew term *bərît* (בְּרִית), typically translated into

---

11. Cf. Sarna, *Exodus*, 32, who notes the use of לקח (take) for marriage in Gen. 4:19; 6:2; 11:29; 12:19; 24:4; 25:1; 34:16; and seventy other times in the Hebrew Bible; as well as היה (be) in Lev. 21:3; Num. 30:7 (30:6 Eng.); Judg. 14:20; 15:2; 2 Sam. 12:10; Jer. 3:1; Ezek. 16:8; Hosea 3:3; cf. Ruth 1:12–13.

12. The foundational study on people as kin and covenant as establishing kinship relations with non-kin is Cross, "Kinship and Covenant"; cf. McCarthy, *Treaty and Covenant*; Kalluveettil, *Declaration and Covenant*; Hugenberger, *Marriage as a Covenant*; Sohn, "'I Will Be Your God and You Will Be My People'"; McKenzie, *Covenant*, 11–12. Hugenberger points to the dominance of the kinship sphere in covenantal texts in the ancient Near East and Hebrew Bible (father/son; husband/wife; siblings) but is also aware of the lord/servant sphere and friend/companion sphere (*Marriage as a Covenant*, 177–78); cf. Williamson, *Sealed with an Oath*, 39.

13. Once established, this parent/child motif is used regularly throughout the OT. Foundational is Yahweh's message for Moses to declare to Pharaoh: "Thus says Yahweh, 'Israel is My son, My firstborn. So I said to you, "Let my son go that he may serve Me"'" (Exod. 4:22–23). Deuteronomy assumes a parent/child relationship at various points (Deut. 1:31; 8:5; 14:1; 32:6). The prophetic literature draws on this relational motif regularly (Isa. 1:2; 63:16; 64:8; Jer. 3:4, 19, 22; 31:9, 20; Hosea 1:10; 11:1–4; Mal. 1:6; 2:10; 3:17) as do the Psalms (Pss. 68:5; 103:13), Chronicles (1 Chron. 29:10), and Proverbs (Prov. 3:12).

English as "covenant."[14] The "new covenant" in Jer. 31–32 showcases the close link between the relational creed and this Hebrew term:

"But this is the *covenant* [בְּרִית] which I will make with the house of Israel after those days," declares Yahweh, "I will put My law within them and on their heart I will write it; and *I will be their God, and they shall be My people.*" (Jer. 31:33, emphasis added)

"*They shall be My people, and I will be their God.* . . . I will make an everlasting *covenant* [בְּרִית] with them that I will not turn away from them, to do them good; and I will put the fear of Me in their hearts so that they will not turn away from Me." (Jer. 32:38, 40, emphasis added)

For this reason *bərît* (בְּרִית) is connected with each of the major relationships established between God and humanity in the OT, whether that established between Yahweh and Abraham/Sarah (Gen. 15:18; 17:2, 4, 7, 9, 10, 11, 13, 14, 19, 21; Exod. 6:4–5; Lev. 26:42), Yahweh and Israel at Sinai (Exod. 19:5; 24:7–8; 31:16; 34:10, 27–28; Lev. 24:8; 26:9, 15, 25, 44–45; Deut. 4:13, 23, 31; 5:2, 3; 7:2, 9, 12; 8:18; 9:9, 11, 15; 10:8; 17:2; 28:69 [29:1 Eng.]; 29:8, 11, 13, 20, 24 [29:9, 12, 14, 21, 25 Eng.]; 31:16, 20; 33:9), Yahweh and the priestly caste (Num. 18:19; 25:12–13; Neh. 13:29; Jer. 33:21; Mal. 2:4–5, 8), and Yahweh and the royal house (2 Sam. 23:5; Pss. 89:35 [89:34 Eng.]; 132:12; Jer. 33:21; 2 Chron. 21:7; cf. 2 Chron. 7:18; Isa. 55:3).[15]

A closer look at the use of the term *bərît* (בְּרִית) to describe relational agreements between human beings confirms that the relational agreements in view in the relational creed involve establishing kin relationships with non-kin. Genesis 14:13 tells us that Abram

---

14. See esp. Rendtorff, *Covenant Formula*, 3, who after noting the way election (בחר) and covenant (בְּרִית) are intertwined in Neh. 9:7–8, while often not discussed together in OT scholarship, then notes the interconnectedness of these two words and themes with the covenant formula, mentioning especially Gen. 17:7; Deut. 7:6; 14:2. For Gen. 17:7, he states: "Here, 'covenant' and 'covenant formula' cannot be separated." Yet he is aware that "this formula is by no means linked directly in every instance with the Hebrew word *bᵉrît*" (p. 11). Key passages of connection between covenant and the formula include: Gen. 17; Exod. 6; Lev. 26:12, 45. On the close relationship between covenant and this relational formula see Gentry and Wellum, *Kingdom through Covenant*, 271.

15. On the Noachic, see below (cf. Gen. 6:18; 9:9–17).

and the Amorites enjoyed covenantal relations. This explains why when Abram's relative Lot is taken captive in the clash between two royal coalitions, the Amorite clans of Aner, Eshcol, and Mamre join Abram's armed pursuit to rescue Lot (14:13–24). This covenant entailed a relational agreement of mutual obligations, here the obligation to assist one another in battle. Abraham makes other agreements with gentiles, in particular Abimelech (Gen. 21:22–34), to whom he gave gifts of sheep and oxen and swore an oath. Similarly, his son Isaac would make a covenant with Abimelech (Gen. 26:26–33), which entailed swearing an oath and feasting together (26:29–31). The covenant established between Jacob and Laban in Gen. 31 follows Jacob's flight from Laban, a clear indication that Jacob was setting out as a distinct family from Laban, even though Laban contests this (Gen. 31:43). Here we see key rituals related to covenant making, including setting up a stela (stone) as a sign of the treaty between two households (31:44–48, 51–52), appeal to the deity as witness (31:49–50, 53), a sacrificial meal on a mountain (31:54), and blessing (31:55). In Josh. 9 a covenant is established between Israel and the Gibeonites, promising peaceful relations, which meant the Gibeonites would not be exterminated (vv. 15–16). This entailed swearing an oath to the other party with the deity as witness (vv. 15b, 19). The seriousness of this agreement becomes clear in verses 19–20, as the Israelites express fear over the "wrath," presumably from the deity if they were to break their oath (cf. 2 Sam. 21). First Kings 9:16 showcases a covenantal arrangement between royal houses, sealed by marriage. Similarly, 1 Samuel regularly depicts a covenantal relationship between David and Jonathan, a compact established between individuals who also were royal figures (1 Sam. 18:3; 20:8; 23:18; 2 Sam. 9:1; 21:7). This relationship is called "a covenant of/before Yahweh" (20:8; 23:18; cf. 20:12–16, 42),[16] pointing to the deity's role as witness to and protector of the agreement. This covenant entailed the transfer of a gift (1 Sam. 18:4) and swearing of an oath (1 Sam. 20:17, 42; 2 Sam. 21:7). One final example of human covenantal relationships is seen in the compacts established between the people

---

16. Compare 2 Sam. 9:1, 3, where the covenant loyalty of David to Jonathan's family is identified as the covenant loyalty of Yahweh.

and the king in Israel (2 Sam. 3:21; 5:3; 1 Chron. 11:3; 2 Chron. 23:3, 16; Jer. 34:8–9). According to 2 Sam. 5:3 (//1 Chron. 11:3) such a covenant was established "before Yahweh" and involved the ritual of anointing with oil (cf. 2 Sam. 2:4). Second Chronicles 23:11–16 depicts other rituals, including crowning, giving of the covenantal agreement (the testimony), anointing with oil, and shouting "Long live the king" at a special location ("his pillar at the entrance").[17] Covenants could also be made on an ad hoc basis between a king and the people, as indicated in Zedekiah's covenantal agreement with the people of Jerusalem in the face of the Babylonian threat (Jer. 34:8–9).

It must be remembered, however, that "covenant" is not the relationship itself[18] but rather an agreement that articulates the nature of the relationship and structures it.[19] In most cases the relationship already exists (e.g., 1 Sam. 18:1–3), so the covenant agreement represents a formalization of the relationship.[20]

These examples of human-human covenants show that covenant refers to an agreement with obligation between two parties. Common is some form of public ritual as well as appeal to the deity for

17. See also 1 Kings 1 for rituals associated with the installation of a king.

18. As Hugenberger (*Marriage as a Covenant*, 168) wisely argues concerning "the now-discredited notion that 'covenant [בְּרִית]' is essentially a synonym for 'relationship.'" Cf. Naylor, "Language of Covenant."

19. See Dumbrell, *Covenant and Creation*, 16–20. Relationship, though, remains in the forefront; this is truly covenant and not contract; cf. McCarthy, *Treaty and Covenant*, 297, who notes, "The relationship comes first"; and Kalluveettil, *Declaration and Covenant*, 51, who writes, "Covenant is relational, in one way or other it creates unity, community." See Bartholomew, "Covenant and Creation," 24–25, who notes how covenants "articulate and solemnize the contours of Yahweh's relationship with his people as it develops in history," but then qualifies this: "The divine covenants thus do more than formalize relationships, they also constitute them and in the process become metaphors for God's relationship with his people." The truth is that the formalization of relationship impacts the relationship significantly and provides an external symbol of the intimacy enjoyed in the relationship.

20. As Hugenberger, *Marriage as a Covenant*, 169: "far from creating a relationship *de novo*, the making of a covenant seems to presuppose an existing relationship, to which explicit appeal is made during the negotiations to make the covenant"; cf. McCarthy, *Treaty and Covenant*, 19–20; Williamson, *Sealed with an Oath*, 43. Sometimes this is not the case, such as the covenant with the Gibeonites, although the exception (and its problems) may be proving the rule. In the case of Isaac with Abimelech it may be that the earlier covenant between Abraham and Abimelech is assumed.

accountability to the agreement. Initial examples reveal agreements between two families or clans, which extend into the royal realm as royal families establish agreements. Marriage was considered a covenant in the OT (Mal. 2:14; cf. Prov. 2:17); it is an example of an agreement between two families or clans. The final examples of agreements between a royal house and the nation as a whole probably are best understood in this familial context, showcased in the foundational case of David, with whom first his own tribal entity with its clans establishes a covenant for royal rule, and then further tribes and clans, such as the northern tribes, establish a covenant with him. This interfamilial dimension for human-human covenants provides evidence for Hugenberger's conclusion, "The predominant sense of בְּרִית in Biblical Hebrew is an elected, as opposed to natural, relationship of obligation established under divine sanction."[21] A "natural relationship" is one within the family unit (parent/child). Covenants are unnecessary in those contexts because of the natural relationship of trust between family members.[22] Covenant and the relationships to which it points are thus redemptive in nature: they assume a sinful world where humans are distant from God. Through relational agreements and expressions God takes the initiative to draw them into his family unit.[23]

These various texts provide insight into the nature of the covenantal relationships established between Yahweh and Israel throughout the OT, which involve obligations placed on both parties (see below). Accountability with the deity is, of course, unavoidable since one of the covenant partners is Yahweh. Rituals are evident in, for example, Gen. 15 (covenant with Abraham/Sarah), Exod. 19–20; 24 (covenant with Israel at Sinai), Ps. 2 (covenant with the royal house), and Lev. 8–9; Num. 18 (covenant with priestly caste). While *bərît* (בְּרִית) is not the only term used, nor covenant the only way of expressing

---

21. Hugenberger, *Marriage as a Covenant*, 171.

22. Thus, Hugenberger's "four essential ingredients in the Old Testament understanding of בְּרִית . . . that it is used of (1) a relationship (2) with a nonrelative (3) which involves obligations and (4) is established through an oath" (ibid., 11). See also John A. Davies (*A Royal Priesthood*, 177), who finds in *bərît* "the use of familial categories for those who are not bound by ties of natural kinship," with thanks to Gentry and Wellum, *Kingdom through Covenant*, 132–33.

23. With Stek, "'Covenant' Overload."

the nature of the relationship between God and humanity,[24] it does dominate the biblical corpus.

Foundational to the relational creed, however, is not the word *bərit* (בְּרִית), but rather reciprocal expressions that articulate the relational identity of the divine and human partners. Exemplary is the relational agreement found in Deut. 26:16–19:

> This day Yahweh your God commands you to do these statutes and ordinances. You shall therefore be careful to do them with all your heart and with all your soul. You have today declared Yahweh to be your God, and that you would walk in His ways and keep His statutes, His commandments and His ordinances, and listen to His voice. Yahweh has today declared you to be His people, a treasured possession, as He promised you, and that you should keep all His commandments; and that He will set you high above all nations which He has made, for praise, fame, and honor; and that you shall be a consecrated people to Yahweh your God, as He has spoken.

At its core this relational agreement involves reciprocity. This is not a unilateral agreement but rather a bilateral, reciprocal agreement that involves both parties.[25] While Yahweh is clearly the initiator in the relationship, the people's response is essential. This relational agreement focuses on a clear declaration of the identity of the two partners in this relationship: God and people. Not surprisingly, the people's identity is attained through a declaration of Yahweh, but possibly surprising to some, Yahweh's identity is attained through a declaration of the people. There are responsibilities for both part-

---

24. See Boda, "Reenvisioning the Relationship."

25. Much has been made of the distinction between royal grant and suzerainty treaty in the ancient world in order to distinguish between the Abrahamic/Davidic covenants and the Sinai covenant; Weinfeld, "Covenant of Grant"; Hahn, *Kinship by Covenant*. However, see the critique in Knoppers, "Ancient Near Eastern Royal Grants"; and note the conclusion of Gentry and Wellum (*Kingdom through Covenant*, 133–35), who resist placing OT covenants in a particular category. In this present study I am seeking to move away from the fixation of OT studies with the broader imperial and royal covenant forms and focus more attention on the familial/ kinship base of the relational creed and agreements; cf. Hugenberger, *Marriage as a Covenant*, 172. This focus on kinship was also key to the works on the broader covenant forms; see McCarthy, *Treaty and Covenant*; and Kalluveettil, *Declaration and Covenant*.

ners in this reciprocal relationship. For Yahweh this means that he will fulfill his promise to exalt Israel above all nations and to set them apart as a special community: exaltation and consecration. For Israel this means that they will fulfill their promise to keep the law and obey him.

Deuteronomy 26:16–19	God: Yahweh	People: Israel
reciprocity	Yahweh has today declared	You have today declared
identity	Yahweh to be your God	you to be his people, a treasured possession
responsibility	He will set you high above all nations which He has made, for praise, fame, and honor; and that you shall be a consecrated people to Yahweh your God, as He has spoken.	you would walk in His ways and keep His statutes, His commandments and His ordinances, and listen to His voice . . . you should keep all His commandments

This same basic structure of relationship can be discerned in other relational agreements throughout the OT. Key is the relational agreement between Yahweh and Abraham and Sarah in Gen. 17. Reciprocity is clearly articulated, with the basic structure of the passage signaled by fronted personal pronouns in 17:4 (me, אֲנִי) and 17:9 (you, אַתָּה) and Sara(i/h)'s name in 17:15.[26] Again Yahweh takes the initiative in this reciprocal relationship, but essential to this agreement is the fulfillment of the responsibilities of each covenant partner. Yahweh's responsibilities entail the fulfillment of promises of seed, covenant with that seed, and land. Abraham's responsibilities include walking blamelessly and circumcising his seed. Both partners attain a new identity, with Yahweh assuming the identity of "God" and Abram and Sarai the new identities of Abraham and Sarah, indicating Abraham (father of a multitude) as father of a multitude of nations and Sarah (princess) as mother of royalty, reflecting the core promise of descendants in 17:6 ("nations . . . kings").[27]

26. Sara(i/h) is mentioned in third person by name because the encounter is between Abra(m/ham) and Yahweh, but she is clearly included in this covenantal agreement.

27. Genesis 17:5 refers to אַב־הֲמוֹן גּוֹיִם, which sounds like אַבְרָהָם. אַבְרָם means exalted father (אָב + רוֹם). Genesis 17:15 refers to שָׂרִי, which is changed to שָׂרָה, which means queen/princess.

Genesis 17:1–15	God: Yahweh/God Almighty	People: Abra(m/ham), Sara(i/h)
reciprocity	As for Me, behold, My covenant is with you. (17:4)	Now as for you (17:9)
		As for Sarai, your wife (17:15)
identity	I am God Almighty (17:1)	No longer shall your name be called Abram, But your name shall be Abraham (17:5)
	to be God to you and to your descendants after you (17:7)	
	I will be their God (17:8)	You shall not call her name Sarai, but Sarah *shall be* her name (17:15)
responsibility	I will establish My covenant between Me and you, And I will multiply you exceedingly (17:2)	Walk before Me, and be blameless (17:1)
	My covenant is with you, and you will be the father of a multitude of nations (17:4)	You shall keep My covenant, you and your descendants after you throughout their generations. This is My covenant, which you shall keep, between Me and you and your descendants after you: every male among you shall be circumcised. (17:9–10)
	for I will make you the father of a multitude of nations (17:5)	
	I will make you exceedingly fruitful, and I will make nations of you and kings will come forth from you (17:6)	And you shall be circumcised in the flesh of your foreskin, and it shall be the sign of the covenant between Me and you. And every male among you who is eight days old shall be circumcised throughout your generations, a *servant* who is born in the house or who is bought with money from any foreigner, who is not of your descendants. A *servant* who is born in your house or who is bought with your money shall surely be circumcised; thus shall My covenant be in your flesh for an everlasting covenant (17:11–13)
	I will establish My covenant between Me and you and your descendants after you throughout their generations for an everlasting covenant (17:7)	
	I will give to you and to your descendants after you, the land of your sojournings, all the land of Canaan, for an everlasting possession; and I will be their God (17:8)	
	I will bless her, and indeed I will give you a son by her. Then I will bless her, and she shall be *a mother of* nations; kings of peoples will come from her (17:16)	

While the relational agreements between Yahweh and Abraham/ Sarah and between Yahweh and Israel are foundational within the OT, two other relational agreements should not be overlooked. These relational agreements are those established between Yahweh and the two key leadership groups within Israel: priests and kings.

Numbers 18 showcases the relational agreement between Yahweh and the priestly groups, focusing on their responsibilities for offerings at the sanctuary.[28] The priestly groups in view are the Aaronic priests and the broader group of Levites. Their identity is obviously priestly and Levitical, but their function within the broader identity of "the sons of Israel" is important to note (18:5, 8, 11, 14, 19, 20 for priests; 18:6, 21, 22, 23, 24, 26, 28, 32 for Levites). Interestingly, Yahweh identifies himself as the priests' portion and inheritance, and his main responsibility is his provision of priestly needs through the offerings of the people.

Numbers 18	God: Yahweh	People: Priest/Levites
reciprocity	As for me, behold (18:6) As for me, behold (18:8)	As for you and your sons with you (18:7; cf. 18:1) And to the sons of Levi, behold (18:21)
identity	I am your portion and your inheritance (18:20)	Priesthood as a bestowed service (18:7) sons of Levi (18:21)
responsibility	I have taken your fellow Levites from among the sons of Israel; they are a gift to you, dedicated to Yahweh, to perform the service for the tent of meeting (18:6) all the holy gifts of the sons of Israel I have given them to you as a portion and to your sons as a perpetual allotment. (18:8; cf. 18:9–18) All the offerings of the holy *gifts*, which the sons of Israel offer to Yahweh, I have given to you and your sons and your daughters with	You and your sons and your father's household with you shall bear the guilt in connection with the sanctuary, and you and your sons with you shall bear the guilt in connection with your priesthood. (18:1) So you shall attend to the obligations of the sanctuary and the obligations of the altar, so that there will no longer be wrath on the sons of Israel (18:5) I Myself have given you charge of My offerings (18:8) in return for their service which they perform, the service of the tent of meeting. The sons of Israel shall not come near the tent of meeting again, or they will bear sin and die. Only the Levites shall perform the service of the

28. The priestly covenant is developed elsewhere in the OT and is reflected in: Exod. 29:9; 40:15; Num. 25:12–13; 1 Sam. 2:35; 1 Kings 2:26–27, 35; Neh. 13:29; Ps. 106:30–31; Jer. 33:20–22; Ezek. 40:46; 43:19; 48:11; Zech. 3; 6:9–15; Mal. 2:1–9. Figures associated with this relational tradition include: Levi, Aaron, Phinehas, Eli, Zadok, Joshua. On the priestly covenant, see further Busenitz, "Introduction to the Biblical Covenants"; Williamson, "Covenant," 425.

Numbers 18	God: Yahweh	People: Priest/Levites
	you, as a perpetual allotment. It is an everlasting covenant of salt before Yahweh to you and your descendants with you. . . . You shall have no inheritance in their land nor own any portion among them; I am your portion and your inheritance among the sons of Israel (18:19–20) I have given all the tithe in Israel for an inheritance (18:21a) it shall be a perpetual statute throughout your generations, and among the sons of Israel they shall have no inheritance. For the tithe of the sons of Israel, which they offer as an offering to Yahweh, I have given to the Levites for an inheritance; therefore I have said concerning them, "They shall have no inheritance among the sons of Israel" (18:23b–24)	tent of meeting, and they shall bear their iniquity (18:21b–23a) Moreover, you shall speak to the Levites and say to them, "When you take from the sons of Israel the tithe which I have given you from them for your inheritance, then you shall present an offering from it to Yahweh, a tithe of the tithe. Your offering shall be reckoned to you as the grain from the threshing floor or the full produce from the wine vat. So you shall also present an offering to Yahweh from your tithes, which you receive from the sons of Israel; and from it you shall give Yahweh's offering to Aaron the priest. Out of all your gifts you shall present every offering due to Yahweh, from all the best of them, the sacred part from them." You shall say to them, "When you have offered from it the best of it, then *the rest* shall be reckoned to the Levites as the product of the threshing floor, and as the product of the wine vat. You may eat it anywhere, you and your households, for it is your compensation in return for your service in the tent of meeting. You will bear no sin by reason of it when you have offered the best of it. But you shall not profane the sacred gifts of the sons of Israel, or you will die" (18:26–32)

The relational agreement between Yahweh and the royal house is reflected in various texts throughout the OT. Foundational to this agreement is the identity of Yahweh as father and the king as son, as seen in 2 Sam. 7:14 ("I will be a father to him and he will be a son to Me"); 1 Chron. 22:10 ("he shall be My son and I will be his father"), Ps. 2:7 ("You are my son, today I have begotten You"), and Ps. 89:26–27 ("You are my father . . . I also shall make him firstborn"). While the covenant is made with David in 2 Sam. 7, it is only fully realized in the reign of Solomon since the core of the agreement is related to the dynasty that will follow David. However, even in the initial relational agreement text in 2 Sam. 7, Yahweh reveals not only his own responsibility to David and his dynasty but also the dynasty's responsibility to Yahweh, including building the temple and avoiding sin (2 Sam. 7:13–14).

This relational agreement is confirmed with Solomon, and one can discern the reciprocity evident in OT relational agreements in the two interactions between Yahweh and Solomon in 1 Kings 3:6–15 and 9:1–9, linked by their reference to Yahweh's appearance to Solomon at Gibeon (3:5; 9:2; cf. 11:9). The relational identity for God is "Yahweh, my God," while for Solomon it is "your servant, king" (3:7). As the priestly identity, so the royal identity is carefully placed in the context of the people as a whole (3:8; 9:5). The responsibilities of the two relational partners are also clearly laid out, with Yahweh providing a perpetual dynasty along with the wisdom to rule, material blessings, and social honor, and the dynasty is called to walk "in integrity of heart and uprightness, doing according to all that I have commanded you *and* will keep My statutes and My ordinances" (9:4).

1 Kings 3; 9	God: Yahweh	People: Servant King
reciprocity	You (3:6) You (3:7)	you (9:4)
identity	Yahweh, my God (3:7)	You have made Your servant king (3:7) Your servant is in the midst of Your people which You have chosen, a great people who are too many to be numbered or counted (3:8) Your servant (3:9)
responsibility	You have shown steadfast love to Your servant David my father. . . . You have reserved for him this great steadfast love, that You have given him a son to sit on his throne, as *it is* this day (3:6) behold, I have done according to your words. Behold, I have given you	Your servant David my father, according as he walked before You in truth and righteousness and uprightness of heart toward You (3:6) If you walk in My ways, keeping My statutes and commandments, as your father David walked (3:14) if you will walk before Me as your father David walked, in integrity of heart and uprightness, doing according to all that I have commanded you *and* will keep My statutes and My ordinances (9:4)

1 Kings 3; 9 God: Yahweh	People: Servant King
a wise and discerning heart, so that there has been no one like you before you, nor shall one like you arise after you. "I have also given you what you have not asked, both riches and honor, so that there will not be any among the kings like you all your days" (3:12–13) I will prolong your days (3:14) then I will establish the throne of your kingdom over Israel forever, just as I promised to your father David, saying, "You shall not lack a man on the throne of Israel" (9:5)	But if you or your sons indeed turn away from following Me, and do not keep My commandments and My statutes which I have set before you, and go and serve other gods and worship them, then I will cut off Israel from the land which I have given them, and the house which I have consecrated for My name, I will cast out of My sight. So Israel will become a proverb and a byword among all peoples. And this house will become a heap of ruins; everyone who passes by will be astonished and hiss and say, "Why has Yahweh done thus to this land and to this house?" And they will say, "Because they forsook Yahweh their God, who brought their fathers out of the land of Egypt, and adopted other gods and worshiped them and served them, therefore Yahweh has brought all this adversity on them." (9:6–9)

This evidence highlights the key principles of reciprocity and identity that are foundational to the relational creed. Yahweh initiates each of these relational agreements reviewed above, but this does not mean they are merely unilateral, for each makes considerable demands on the human and divine partners.

Reciprocity is evident in each of these relational agreements found throughout the OT, and each one of them is also described multiple times using the word *bərît* (בְּרִית). Furthermore, the word *ôlām* (עוֹלָם) is used alongside *bərît* (בְּרִית) to describe each of the relational agreements.[29] Whether one understands the word *ôlām* (עוֹלָם) as meaning "eternal," "everlasting," "in perpetuity," or "enduring," each of the relational agreements in the OT receives the same designation, whether Yahweh's agreement with Abraham/Sarah (Gen. 17:7, 13, 19; Ps. 105:10), Israel at Sinai (Exod. 31:16; Lev. 24:8),[30] the priestly caste (Num. 18:19; 25:12–13; cf. Jer. 33:21–22), or the royal house (2 Sam.

29. See Mason, *"Eternal Covenant" in the Pentateuch*, for a study of the phrase בְּרִית עוֹלָם in the Torah.

30. Contra Gentry and Wellum, *Kingdom through Covenant*, 476.

23:5; 2 Chron. 13:5; cf. Jer. 33:21–22).[31] These relational agreements are all described as having enduring relevance throughout the OT.

Extending the Relational Identity

While we have focused on certain key texts to highlight the principles of reciprocity and identity, it is important to provide a macro view of the development of these relational agreements throughout the biblical corpus. Each of the relational agreements begins with a promise that later is fulfilled in multiple scenes of relational agreement and then renewed in later generations.

The relational agreement between Yahweh and Abraham/Sarah is first promised in Gen. 12 (vv. 1–3, 7),[32] then formalized for the first time in Gen. 15, a second time in Gen. 17, and even a third time in Gen. 22:15–18.[33] The relational promises are then relayed on to Isaac in Gen. 26:3–5 and Jacob in 35:11–12; 48:3–4. In this way the covenant initiated with Abraham/Sarah is also identified as the "covenant with Abraham, Isaac, and Jacob" (Exod. 2:24; 2 Kings 13:23).

Similarly, the agreement between Yahweh and Israel at Sinai is first promised in Gen. 17:7 to Abraham and in Exod. 6:6–8 to Moses before being formalized in the encounter at Sinai (Exod. 19–20) and confirmed in Exod. 24:3–7. Renewal of covenant is needed in Exod. 34 after the golden calf incident and on the plains of Moab (Deut. 29–31) after the failure at Kadesh Barnea. Further examples include the confirmation of the covenant at Gerizim/Ebal after Israel had entered the land (Josh. 8:30–35), at Shechem after the conquest of the land (Josh. 24), and during King Josiah's reign (2 Kings 22–23).

The priestly agreement is first promised in the tabernacle instructions in Exod. 28–29 but formalized only in Lev. 8–9 and Num. 18.[34]

31. Notice the tendency to translate this word when related to the priestly covenant as "perpetual" in the NASB (Exod. 29:9; Num. 18:19 [1×]; 25:13); similarly for the Sinaitic covenant (Exod. 31:16).

32. With Bartholomew, "Covenant and Creation," 23; contra Dumbrell, *Covenant and Creation*, 55–72.

33. See Williamson, "Covenant," 422, for Gen. 15 and 17 as two distinct covenants between God and Abraham, one focused on land and the other on seed.

34. Also note Deut. 32:8–10; Jer. 33:21–22; Mal. 2:1–9 for evidence of a Levitical covenant.

Phinehas certainly confirms this agreement with his violent act in Num. 25 (cf. Ps. 106:30–31). Evidence of later developments in the priestly agreement can be discerned in 1 Sam. 2:35; 1 Kings 2:26–27, 35; Ezek. 40:46; 43:19; 48:11; Zech. 3; 6:9–15 (cf. Neh. 13:29).

The royal agreement is first promised in general for the line of Abraham/Sarah in Gen. 17:6, 16; Jacob in 35:11; and Judah in 49:8–12 and then specifically for David in 1 Sam. 16:1, 12–13. This agreement is formalized only in 2 Sam. 7 together with 1 Kings 3; 8–9. The regular rehearsal of the royal agreement can be discerned in coronation in Ps. 2 and renewal of the agreement in Hag. 2:20–23; Zech. 3; 6:9–15.

Tracing the phases in relational agreements has highlighted the enduring relevance of these agreements throughout Israel's history, showcasing that relationships develop over time as God pursues redemptive priorities but also as humanity fails in relationship, prompting encounters of renewal in that relationship.

Integrating the Relational Identities

These major relational agreements are not isolated from one another but rather are integrated as each builds on the other. The relational agreement between Yahweh and Abraham/Sarah is foundational, functioning as a relational agreement of promise fulfilled in the relational agreement forged between Yahweh and Israel at Sinai.[35] Evidence for this can be discerned in both Genesis (Abraham/Sarah) and Exodus (Israel at Sinai). Reference is made to the future nation of Israel in the two key relational agreement texts in Gen. 15 and 17 (15:13–21; 17:7–8). Similarly, as Moses sets out to lead Israel, his mission is founded on the covenantal relationship established with Abraham, Isaac, and Jacob (Exod. 6:3–8). These two relational agreements are intricately related and should not be pitted against each other, as the later prayer in Neh. 9 shows quite clearly when it identifies the covenant with Abraham before rehearsing the Sinai experience.

---

35. Their foundational nature may explain why they both have a sign or symbol (אות) associated with them, while such a sign/symbol is not provided for the priestly and royal agreements. For the relational agreement between Yahweh and Abraham/ Sarah it is circumcision (Gen. 17:11), while between Yahweh and Israel at Sinai it is the Sabbath (Exod. 31:13–17; Ezek. 20:12, 20).

The priestly and royal relational agreements are subsumed within the relational framework of the nationally focused agreements with Abraham/Sarah and Israel at Sinai. Evidence for this comes from the fact that the priestly relational agreement is embedded within the legislation delivered at Sinai (cf. Mal. 2:4–7), and the priest's role was to facilitate the fulfillment of much of the law, including its sacrificial, festal, moral, ritual, and ceremonial requirements (Exodus–Numbers).[36] Not only is the royal relational agreement traced back to promises (Gen. 17:6) and instructions (Deut. 17:14–20) in the two foundational relational agreements, but the standard for royal rule is clearly linked to the legal revelation at Sinai (e.g., 1 Kings 9:4–9), which kings were to consult (Deut. 17:18–19).[37]

New Covenant

Another relational agreement, expressed almost exclusively in the prophetic literature, can be discerned in the OT. Jeremiah 31–32 showcases this relational agreement, referred to as the "new covenant" (בְּרִית חֲדָשָׁה) in 31:31 and identified as an everlasting or enduring covenant (בְּרִית עוֹלָם) in 32:40 (cf. 50:4–5). The core relational formula, "I will be their God, and they shall be My people," occurs in both 31:33 and 32:38. The timing of this future relational agreement is linked to the period of restoration after the fall of Israel and Judah and exile of the community ("I will gather them out of all the lands . . . I will bring them back," 32:37). Key to this new, enduring covenant is the emphasis on divine influence on the human partners, as God declares: "I will put My law within them and on their heart I will write it" (31:33) and "I will give them one heart and one way" (32:39). And yet human response is still essential, as seen in the phrases "for they

36. See Williamson, "Covenant," 425, for the close relationship between the Sinai and priestly covenants: "Thus the priestly and Mosaic covenants, while remaining distinct, run in parallel with one another, and are closely related in purpose: the perpetuity of the relationship between God and Israel."

37. Williamson (ibid., 425) focuses more on the close relationship between the Davidic and Abrahamic covenants: "In the Davidic covenant the promises made to Abraham become more focused. The Davidic dynasty inherits the promises of the patriarchal covenant; the special divine-human relationship and attendant blessings now belong primarily to the Davidic royal lineage."

will all know me" (31:34), "that they may fear Me always" (32:39), and "so that they will not turn away from Me" (32:40).

The new, enduring covenant in Jer. 31–32 is defined in relation to the Sinai covenant, first in terms of contrast ("not like the covenant which I made with their ancestors in the day I took them by the hand to bring them out of the land of Egypt," 31:32), and then in terms of similarity ("I will put My law within them," 31:33). This new, enduring covenant includes the same stipulations as the Sinai covenant but involves a new means through which the covenant relationship is sustained. This covenant still involves reciprocity, identity, and responsibility, and thus echoes the core values of the other relational agreements.

Jeremiah 32	God: Yahweh	People: Restoration Community
reciprocity	I (32:37–42)	They (32:38, 39, 40)
identity	I will be their God (32:38)	They shall be my people (32:38)
responsibility	Behold, I will gather them out of all the lands to which I have driven them in My anger, in My wrath and in great indignation; and I will bring them back to this place and make them dwell in safety (32:37)	they may fear Me always, for their own good and for *the good of* their children after them. (32:39)
	and I will give them one heart and one way (32:39)	so that they will not turn away from Me (32:40)
	I will make an everlasting covenant with them that I will not turn away from them, to do them good; and I will put the fear of Me in their hearts (32:40)	
	I will rejoice over them to do them good and will faithfully plant them in this land with all My heart and with all My soul. (32:41)	
	For thus says Yahweh, "Just as I brought all this great disaster on this people, so I am going to bring on them all the good that I am promising them" (32:42)	

While the new, enduring covenant of Jer. 31–32 is most directly defined in relation to the Sinai covenant, it is carefully linked to the

Noachic covenant in 31:35–37, the first indication that the future relational agreement(s) envisioned by the prophet should not be limited to the earlier Sinai tradition.

The book of Ezekiel also creates expectation for a future "everlasting covenant" that will occur after the community has broken the covenant (16:59–63). This everlasting covenant, also called "a covenant of peace" (37:26), involves, as with Jeremiah, the relational identity formula: "they will be My people, and I will be their God" (37:23). Again Ezekiel defines this covenant in terms of the Sinai relational agreement, as seen in the expectation expressed in 37:24 that "they will walk in My ordinances and keep My statutes and observe them," and the promise in 37:26–28 to "set My sanctuary in their midst forever. My dwelling place also will be with them. . . . My sanctuary will be in their midst forever." However, 37:24–25 makes clear that the Davidic covenant ("My servant David . . . David my servant") and the covenant with the patriarchs ("the land that I gave to Jacob My servant") will also play a key role.

A future covenant is also featured in the book of Isaiah, especially Isa. 54–55 (see also 59:21; 61:8). Explicit reference to a future "everlasting covenant" with the people can be found in Isa. 55:3 ("I will make an everlasting covenant with you"). This covenant is linked to "the faithful mercies shown to David" (55:3). Thus, the making of covenant with the community is related to the Davidic covenant. Furthermore, the agreement with Abraham and Sarah can be discerned at the outset of Isa. 54 with its allusion to the "barren one" who will "spread out" (פרץ), along with her "descendants" (זֶרַע), to possess nations and cities.

This evidence highlights the fact that future expectation for covenant in the Prophets looks for renewal of the entire covenant tradition in the OT.[38]

Functional Contexts

As with the narrative and character creeds, so also the rhythm of the relational creed can be sensed in every section of the OT canon,

38. See Williamson (ibid., 427) for "the new covenant's continuity with previous divine covenants"; cf. Williamson, *Sealed with an Oath*, 146–81.

where it functions in a variety of ways. Fundamentally it grounds the relationship between God and his people, and this explains why it features so prominently in Israel's historical traditions (Gen. 17:7–8; Exod. 6:7; Lev. 11:45; 22:33; 25:38; 26:12; Num. 15:41; Deut. 4:20; 7:6; 14:2; 26:16–19; 27:9; 29:13; 2 Sam. 7:14, 22–24; 2 Kings 11:17; 1 Chron. 17:13; 22:10). Israel's identity is inextricably linked with their fundamental relationship and relational agreements with Yahweh, and Yahweh's identity is also expressed in terms of this relationship. But the appeal to relationship is also key to the message of the prophets, whether they are calling the people back to relationship with God or providing a hopeful vision of the future of that relationship (Jer. 7:23; 11:4; 24:7; 30:22, 25; 31:1, 32, 33; 32:38; Ezek. 11:20; 14:11; 34:30–31; 36:28; 37:23, 27; Hosea 1:9–10; 2:23; Zech. 2:11; 8:8; 13:9; cf. Ps. 50:7). Finally, the relational creed is found regularly on the lips of Yahweh's people as they lift their voices to praise their God (Pss. 33:12; 46:11 [46:10 Eng.]; 95:7; 100:3; 144:15) or cry out for help (Ps. 79:13).

Certainly God dominates the revelation and confession found in the relational creed, as he did in the narrative and character creeds, justifying our identification of these creeds as core to the "theology" of the OT. But just as with the narrative and character creeds, the relational creed emphasizes humanity. God's relational identity is consistently cast in terms of the redemption of human partners and in particular overcoming the sin problem. The relational creeds anticipate human failure and provide ways forward for renewal of relationship. At the same time the relational creeds look to the opportunity for passionate human response to God.

Conclusion

In this chapter we have again taken the pulse of the OT, discerning a third and final rhythm to this heartbeat of OT theology. Here we have seen how the revelation and confession of God are expressed in relational terms. Through this we are reminded that God's identity is linked with humanity and his redemptive purposes for humanity. This identity is fundamentally a kinship identity as God invites a people into covenant relationship as family members. While to this point we have discerned three rhythms in the heartbeat of OT theology independent of one another, these three rhythms are interconnected. The following chapter will showcase passages that interlink the narrative, character, and relational creeds, those three distinct rhythms that constitute the heartbeat of OT theology.

5

Integrating the Creedal Rhythms

To this point I have identified three rhythms within the heartbeat of
OT theology, each of which unpacks the basic self-declaration of God
in the OT and its echoes in the NT: "I am Yahweh."[1] One focuses on
Yahweh's historical action, a second on Yahweh's active character,
and a third on Yahweh's relational identity. Of course, these do not
exhaust OT theology any more than the Apostles' Creed (or any
creed) is able to exhaust Christian theology, but they are core values
of Biblical Theology that pump life into every part of the OT. In the
Hebrew tradition these three rhythms originate in the foundational
canonical division, the Torah, but they can be discerned in all other
sections of the canon. One may be tempted to see here a competition
between three contrasting visions of God, but this is inappropriate.
All three emphasize the positive aspects of God's grace and sometimes exclude the negative tone of discipline. It is grace that stands
forefront in all three presentations, although they are not ashamed of
the disciplinary character and action of Yahweh. Even though George
Ernest Wright collapsed the character creed into the narrative creed,
he did acknowledge: "The emphasis in this confession [Exod. 34:6–7]

1. See Zimmerli and Brueggemann, *I Am Yahweh*.

is upon the gracious, loyal and forgiving nature of God, an emphasis which lies at the centre of the biblical kerygma."[2] Unquestionably, in Yahweh's redemptive story, character and relationship are essential to the spiritual rhythms of OT revelation and response.

Although we have isolated these three redemptive rhythms in order to focus attention on each one individually, it is important to consider passages that combine them.

Exodus 5:22–6:8

Our first passage comes early in the book of Exodus:

> Then Moses returned to Yahweh and said, "O Lord, why have You brought harm to this people? Why did You ever send me? Ever since I came to Pharaoh to speak in Your name, he has done harm to this people, and You have not delivered Your people at all."
>
> Then Yahweh said to Moses, "Now you shall see what I will do to Pharaoh; for under compulsion he will let them go, and under compulsion he will drive them out of his land." God spoke further to Moses and said to him, "I am Yahweh; and I appeared to Abraham, Isaac, and Jacob, as God Almighty, but **My name, Yahweh**, I did not reveal to them. *I also established My covenant with them*, to give them the land of Canaan, the land in which they sojourned. Furthermore I have heard the groaning of the sons of Israel, because the Egyptians are holding them in bondage, and I have remembered My covenant.
>
> "Say, therefore, to the sons of Israel, 'I am Yahweh, and <u>I will bring you out from under the burdens of the Egyptians, and I will deliver you from their bondage. I will also redeem you with an outstretched arm and with great judgments.</u> Then *I will take you for My people, and I will be your God*; and you shall know that I am Yahweh *your God*, <u>who brought you out from under the burdens of the Egyptians. I will bring you to the land which I swore to give to Abraham, Isaac, and Jacob, and I will give it to you for a possession;</u> I am Yahweh.'" (Exod. 5:22–6:8 alt.)

Exodus 5:22–6:8 is set at a key moment in redemptive and revelatory history, that important transition as the descendants of Abraham

2. G. Wright, *God Who Acts*, 85.

and Sarah, a small family unit at the end of Genesis, have now at the beginning of Exodus grown to a great people, a nation. Yahweh signals the shift in redemptive history in 5:22–6:1 as he states unequivocally that Pharaoh will let the people go. This assumes not only the fulfillment of God's promise of a nation through Abraham and Sarah (and Isaac and Jacob; Gen. 17) but also a fulfillment of the promise that this nation would be released from bondage in Egypt (cf. Gen. 15:13–14). Yahweh next signals the shift in revelatory history in Exod. 6:2–3 as he announces an unveiling of fuller revelation than that experienced by Abraham, Isaac, and Jacob. While Yahweh appeared to their ancestors as God Almighty (El-Shaddai), he now declares that he will reveal his name Yahweh (6:3). Many have struggled with this statement because the book of Genesis depicts Yahweh speaking to the ancestors and the ancestors using that name (e.g., Gen. 13:4). Solutions have ranged from seeing contradiction (either due to different sources or error), to seeing Yahweh as referring to his dominant name in Genesis, to anachronisms in the text of Genesis. It is possible that here God is referring to the covenant-making name he is employing (contrast Gen. 17:1; 35:11–12, where he introduces himself as El-Shaddai),[3] but better is to understand Yahweh here as referring to his revelation of the significance of the name. Thus, Yahweh is saying that he revealed himself to Abraham, Isaac, and Jacob with the name El Shaddai, but (notice no preposition *bet* here) the name of Yahweh he did not reveal to them. Yahweh did not reveal the significance of the name of Yahweh, something he had begun to reveal to Moses in Exod. 3:13–15.[4]

So at this key juncture in redemptive and revelatory history we see the intertwining of the three fundamental creedal statements in the OT. The declaration, I am Yahweh, occurs at regular intervals (6:2–3, 6a, 7b, 8b) and structures this entire passage. The three creedal expressions are fundamentally a self-revelation of Yahweh. First, already clear has been the focus on the character creed ("**My name, Yahweh**"), which is fundamentally an unpacking of the name of

3. Cf. Gen. 17:1; 28:3; 35:11; 43:14; 48:3; 49:25.
4. Notice the similar language in Exod. 3:13–15, where Moses speaks of "the God of your fathers" and wants to know Yahweh's name, to which Yahweh responds: "I am who I am. . . . 'I am has sent me to you.'"

Yahweh, which will reach a heightened state in Exod. 33–34. Second, we also hear the narrative creed and its core rehearsal of the deliverance from Egypt through miracle ("I will bring you out from under the burden of the Egyptians, and I will deliver you from their bondage. I will also redeem you with an outstretched arm and with great judgments") and safe delivery into the land sworn to the ancestors and provided as a gift ("I will bring you to the land which I swore to give to Abraham, Isaac, and Jacob, and I will give it to you for a possession"). Finally, we hear the relational creed and its declaration of the relational identity of both Yahweh and Israel ("*I will take you for My people, and I will be your God*"), as well as reference to making covenant ("*I also established My covenant with them*").

Nehemiah 9

While our first integrated passage comes at the beginning of the canon and in the form of Yahweh's revelation to Israel, our second integrated passage comes at the end of the Hebrew canon and in the form of Israel's response to Yahweh. Exodus 6 looks forward to the history of Israel's experience with Yahweh through the tragic experience of bondage in Egypt, but our second passage, Neh. 9, looks back over this history through the tragic experience of exile. Once again, however, we hear the distinct triple beat of all three creedal traditions.

Obvious to all is the presence of the narrative creed. As already noted in chapter 2 above, Neh. 9 is one of the most developed of von Rad's short historical creeds. We find here not only God's delivering Israel from Egypt by miracle (9:9–11) and bringing them into the promised land (9:23–25) but also God's interactions with Abraham (9:7–8), Israel in the wilderness (9:12–22), and Israel in the land (9:26–31). The narrative creed reminds the people of Yahweh's gracious actions throughout their history as well as their own failures and in this way functions perfectly as both a penitential confession of culpability and the foundation for the community's cry for mercy in 9:32–37.

Nehemiah 9, however, also bears witness to the character creed. After depicting the rebellion at Kadesh Barnea in 9:16–17a, the supplicants declare the character creed from Exod. 34: "You are a God of forgiveness, gracious and compassionate, slow to anger and abundant in steadfast love; and You did not forsake them" (9:17b). After the description of the rebellion of the golden calf in 9:18, the supplicants again declare, "You, in Your great compassion, did not forsake them in the wilderness" (9:19a). The compassion of Yahweh is celebrated in 9:27 ("Your great compassion"), 9:28 ("Your compassion"), and 9:31a ("Your great compassion"), followed by an abbreviated version of the character creed in 9:31b ("You are a gracious and compassionate God"). As the prayer shifts to request in 9:32, we hear the other character creed tradition as the people appeal to "our God, the great, the mighty, and the awesome God, who keeps covenant and steadfast love." The character creed is essential to this prayer in Neh. 9, reminding Yahweh of his mercy, which is Israel's only hope in this time of national crisis, but also of his power, which will make possible their salvation.

The relational creed is evident near the beginning of the prayer as the Abra(m/ham) tradition is rehearsed. In 9:7–8 we hear the declaration "You are Yahweh God," followed immediately by the depiction of Yahweh choosing Abram and giving him a new identity: "the name Abraham." The term "covenant" (בְּרִית) is only found in Neh. 9 in connection with Abraham, not with Israel at Sinai. The focus is on the faithful response of Abraham, which prompts Yahweh's relational invitation, which focuses on the gift of land and seed. The declaration in 9:8 that "You have fulfilled Your promise" refers to the gift of the land to Abraham's descendants, a gift on which the generation that prayed Neh. 9 was relying as they cried out for help (9:32–37). The relational agreement with Israel at Sinai is not ignored (9:13–14), but it is carefully fused or possibly subordinated to the relational agreement forged with Abraham, whose obedience secured the land.[5] It is not an accident that Neh. 9 transitions into a signing of a new agreement document in Neh. 10, which is introduced in Neh. 10:1 [9:38 Eng.] with these words: "We are making an agreement in writing." Here we find the typical verb for covenant making (making = כרת) followed not by the expected word, בְּרִית (covenant, used of Abraham in 9:8), but

---

5. Rendtorff, *Covenant Formula*, 2, also highlights the focus on the choosing (בחר) of Abra(m/ham) in Neh. 9:7 instead of the choosing of Israel, as is common in Deuteronomy. This would fit the shift from Israel at Sinai to Abraham seen in the use of the term בְּרִית.

rather the word אֲמָנָה (an agreement). While this may signal something about the changing nature of covenantal documents in the Persian period,[6] one should not miss the play on words here, alluding back to Abraham, the faithful one (נֶאֱמָן) whose covenant is foundational to the hoped-for freedom in the promised land that would emerge from this community undertaking this agreement (אֲמָנָה).[7]

Once again, all three creeds can be heard, now not in the voice of Yahweh but rather on the lips of the community crying for help. At the moment of greatest need the community of God reaches for these key theological creeds as they grapple with the realities of pain in their present time.

Compact Form

These two passages that envelop the OT canon as a whole, and certainly the OT story of redemption, highlight the integration of these three creedal traditions within the theological framework of those responsible for the OT.[8] If we were to collapse this integration into its most compact form, it would be the phrase that occurs at the beginning of the Decalogue as Yahweh makes covenant with Israel and provides a manifesto that will shape their ethical response to this covenant relationship for millennia to come (Exod. 20:2//Deut. 5:6):

> I am Yahweh your God who brought you out from the land
>   of Egypt.

אָנֹכִי יהוה אֱלֹהֶיךָ אֲשֶׁר הוֹצֵאתִיךָ מֵאֶרֶץ מִצְרָיִם[9]

6. Sperling, "Rethinking Covenant"; cf. Boda, "Reenvisioning the Relationship."
7. Holmgren, "Faithful Abraham." These two words are cognates, sharing the same root letters (אמן).
8. These examples from Exodus and Nehemiah remind us that the rhythms of these foundational creeds can be felt throughout the length of the canon, from the Law (Torah) to the Writings (Ketuvim). While it is important to note the foundational role of the Law (Torah), in which all three creeds are given first canonical expression, all the creeds develop significantly in the Prophets and Writings as the action of the story, revelation of the character, and development of the relationship continue.
9. See esp. the more diachronic work of Zimmerli and Brueggemann, *I Am Yahweh*, 17, who mine the data for the phrase "I am Yahweh" and write of "I am Yahweh, your

Here we see allusions to the character creed (I am Yahweh), the relational creed (I am . . . your God), and the narrative creed (I brought you out from the land of Egypt). Integrated expressions like this are ubiquitous in the OT, with similar expressions found in Exod. 6:7; 20:2; 29:46; Lev. 11:45; 19:36; 22:33; 23:43; 25:38, 55; 26:13, 45; Num. 15:41; Deut. 5:6, 15; 7:19; 8:14; 13:5, 10; 16:1; 20:1; 29:25; Josh. 24:17; Judg. 2:12; 6:8; 1 Sam. 10:18; 1 Kings 9:9; 2 Kings 17:7; 1 Chron. 11:2; 2 Chron. 7:22; Ps. 81:11 [81:10 Eng.]; Jer. 34:13; Dan. 9:15. Here we see all three creedal traditions in their most compact form, articulating the identity of the God whom Israel worshiped.

These three creeds are thus core to the faith of Israel and the revelation of Yahweh. Their focus is on the redemptive purposes of Yahweh to create a community through which he would impact the nations and ultimately all of creation. We now turn to this broader impact as we consider the creational dimension of these three creeds whose rhythms can be discerned throughout the OT canon and beyond.

God from the land of Egypt" (אָנֹכִי יהוה אֱלֹהֶיךָ מֵאֶרֶץ מִצְרָיִם) in Hosea 12:9; 13:4 as "a self-introduction already long known to Israel" and "Israel's confessional formula."

6

Creation and the Creedal Rhythms

To this point our focus has been on the three creedal traditions whose rhythms can be heard at regular intervals throughout the OT canon. What has clearly dominated these three traditions is their focus on redemption. Each of them assumes that sin is a reality in this world and depicts Yahweh as the God whose historical action, active character, and relational identity reflect his passionate resolve to redeem a particular community on earth, that is, Israel. However, though all the creedal traditions in the OT are dominated by this focus on the redemption of Israel, all of the creeds ultimately make a connection to the rest of creation, showing that the revelation of Yahweh to Israel has global implications. Yahweh's redemptive plans are intended to transform all of creation in and through his people.

Narrative Creed: Confessing the Creational Action of God

As argued in chapter 2, God's redemptive action on behalf of Israel in the exodus and conquest lies at the core of the narrative creed. This is evident in the ubiquity of these two events in examples of the short historical creed throughout the OT. As the historical creed develops throughout Israel's history and canon, other key events are included, such as the patriarchal, wilderness, life-in-the-land, and even exilic traditions. However, the latest examples of the short historical creed include a tradition that is not focused on redemption, but rather on creation.[1] Thus, at the beginning of the Levites' prayer in Neh. 9 we find the following:

> Then the Levites, Jeshua, Kadmiel, Bani, Hashabneiah, Sherebiah, Hodiah, Shebaniah *and* Pethahiah, said,
>> "Arise, bless Yahweh your God forever and ever!
>> O may Your glorious name be blessed
>> And exalted above all blessing and praise!
>> **You are Yahweh** alone
>> You have made the heavens,
>> The heaven of heavens with all their host,
>> The earth and all that is on it,
>> The seas and all that is in them.
>> You give life to all of them
>> And the heavenly host bows down before You.
>> **You are Yahweh** God,
>> Who chose Abram
>> And brought him out from Ur of the Chaldees,
>> And gave him the name Abraham." (Neh. 9:5–7)

After introducing the speakers of the prayer, the prayer begins with an invitation to the congregation to join in praise of Yahweh as found in the psalms tradition.[2] The addressee then shifts from the people to Yahweh, announcing the hope that God's name would be blessed and exalted. The phrase "You are Yahweh" (אַתָּה־הוּא יְהוָה) at the beginning of 9:6 matches exactly the opening phrase of 9:7.

---

1. Brueggemann, *Theology of the Old Testament*, 159–64, expresses an important concern that the creational dimension not be downgraded, as did von Rad early in his career, something Brueggemann traces to the creed hypothesis. Here we show the intimate link between redemption and creation.

2. The phrase בָּרוּךְ יְהוָה regularly occurs within the doxologies at the seams of the books of the Psalter (Pss. 41:14 [41:13 Eng.]; 72:18; 89:53 [89:52 Eng.]; 106:48; 145:21; although see Pss. 103:20–22; 119:12; 124:6; 134:1; 135:19–21; 144:1). The combination of "arise" (קוֹם) with bless (ברך, Piel) appears elsewhere only in 2 Chron. 30:27, there in a description of a blessing of the people by Levitical priests.

While 9:7 begins the rehearsal of the redemptive history of Israel, 9:6 expresses the divine action in creation. The repetition of the phrase "You are Yahweh" forges an important relationship between the two parts of this narrative creed, reminding the speakers and audience that Yahweh the redeemer is the creator of the universe.[3]

The creational acts of Yahweh are identified in the five clauses that follow in Neh. 9:6. The first three focus on the three parts of creation (the heavens, the earth, and the seas), with the first of these divided into two parts: the heavens and the heaven of heavens. This bipartite structure to the heavens suggests a distinction between the heaven as sky that is visible to the human eye and the high heavens, where heavenly beings dwell. Mention of the three major parts of the creational structure is followed in each case by a reference to living creatures that populate these creational structures: for the heavens/ heaven of heavens, "with all their host"; for the earth, "all that is on it"; and for the seas, "all that is in them." These first three lines make clear that all of creation has been made by Yahweh.

The final two lines in 9:6 shift the focus from God's initial creative act to his enduring relationship to this creation. Yahweh not only creates the structure for life and initiates life by making living creatures, an act that is described using the finite verb "made" (עָשִׂיתָ) at the outset of 9:6, but he continues to sustain the life of all creation, an act that is described using the participle "giving life" (מְחַיֶּה) near the end of 9:6. The final statement in the verse ("and the heavenly host bows down before You") shifts the scene to the heavenly throne room of Yahweh, where the heavenly host reveres this creator God, the exemplary response that matches the praise offered by this community on earth (see Neh. 9:3, where the same verb is used).

It is important not to miss one short word the supplicants include between the opening declaration of "You are Yahweh" and the rehearsal of his creational acts. That word is לְבַדֶּךָ, translated as "you alone," which emphasizes the exclusive status of Yahweh and the unique activity of Yahweh as the one who created the universe. Yahweh's creational activity thus sets him apart from others, and

---

3. Rendtorff, *Covenant Formula*, 1, notes this repetition in Neh. 9 and concludes that the election of Abraham "is seen on almost the same level as creation itself."

this suggests a polemic against other gods that might rival Yahweh's status. The creational motif thus brings into view not only the broader context of creation, including other nations and the created order, but also other heavenly beings that might question his exclusivity.

The appearance of the creation tradition at the outset of the narrative creed is an important development in this form of theological expression. While the emphasis of Neh. 9 remains the story of redemption, it is now placed within a broader context, that of creation.

The inclusion of the creation tradition is not limited to Neh. 9 but can be seen in other later texts. Jeremiah 32:17–23 not only rehearses the core redemptive actions of Yahweh in the exodus and conquest (32:20–23) but at the outset depicts Yahweh as creator: "Ah, Lord Yahweh, You have made the heavens and the earth by Your great power and by Your outstretched arm. Nothing is too difficult for You" (32:17). Here a phrase associated with God's redemptive work in the exodus, "by Your great power and outstretched arm" (Deut. 9:29), is employed in reference to creation. Appearing at the outset of the prayer, it highlights the act of creation as foundational for all redemptive activity by Yahweh, especially in light of the fact that "outstretched arm" is repeated in the rehearsal of the exodus tradition later in this prayer (Jer. 32:21). Yahweh's creational activity prompts Jeremiah's statement, "Nothing is too difficult for You," which is a key theological foundation for producing hope in the midst of Judah's present predicament.

The creation tradition is also employed in Ps. 135. Just prior to the rehearsal of the exodus and conquest traditions in 135:8–12, we find this focus on God's creational activity:

> For I know that Yahweh is great
> And that our Lord is above all gods.
> Whatever Yahweh pleases, He does,
> In heaven and in earth, in the seas and in all deeps.
> He causes the vapors to ascend from the ends of the earth;
> Who makes lightnings for the rain,
> Who brings forth the wind from His treasuries. (Ps. 135:5–7)

Reference is made to the various parts of creation (heaven, earth, seas, all deeps) as well as the physical processes through which he cares for this creation (vapors, lightning/rain, wind). Here the focus is on Yahweh as sustainer of the creation. His providential care is evidence not only of his complete freedom to act (whatever Yahweh pleases, he does) but also of his exalted status over all gods. This freedom to act and exalted status based on his creational activity are here foundational for the redemptive activity that follows in 135:8–12. It is also important to the critique against idols in 135:15–18.

Psalm 136 displays a similar strategy related to creation. Immediately prior to the recitation of Israel's redemptive traditions in 136:10–24, the psalmist declares Yahweh's covenant loyalty in relation to his creational activity. The psalmist describes Yahweh's formation of the three parts of creation (the heavens, earth, and waters) before focusing on the "great lights" that were placed into the heavens (sun, moon, and stars) to control the rhythms of day and night. This rehearsal of day/night parallels the constant repetition of "for his steadfast love is enduring." Israel is being reminded that they experience God's enduring love in the perpetual rhythm of day and night set in motion by Yahweh's creational activity. From this initial focus on creation follow Yahweh's great acts of redemption, which have occurred within time created by Yahweh in the beginning.

Psalm 89 rehearses God's redemptive story related to David (89:15–37; cf. 89:1–4), followed by a lament over the present predicament of the royal house (89:38–51). However, this rehearsal begins with a focus on Yahweh as creator, sustainer, and ruler over all creation. This focus on creation points to Yahweh's incomparability (89:6–8), which is thus seen as foundational to the royal claims of the Davidic house and the status of the people of this kingdom.

In the arrangement of the Psalter, it is interesting that Pss. 105 and 106 contain significant rehearsals of the story of redemption, with Ps. 105 reviewing the story without mention of human rebellion and Ps. 106 interweaving God's redemption with the story of human rebellion. In the final arrangement of the Psalter, however, these two psalms are preceded by a third storied rehearsal, Ps. 104, which presents God as creator (see v. 2) and sustainer (see v. 27) of the universe.

These various texts that employ a creational introduction to the narrative creed highlight the various functions creation played within this tradition. Creation is employed for the purpose of praise in Pss.

104; 135; and 136. This praise is closely linked with Yahweh's unique-
ness in comparison to the idols of the nations (Ps. 135). But this creation tradition also plays an important role in cries for help in the OT.
In Neh. 9 and Ps. 106 creation is foundational for the penitential cry,
especially relevant because of the predicament of the people either in
exile (Ps. 106:46–47) or in their own land (Neh. 9:36–37) dominated by
foreign powers. Jeremiah 32 follows a similar approach, engendering
hope for the ultimate restoration of the community of God. Yahweh
as creator exercises authority that transcends any imperial control.

Character Creed: Confessing the Creational Character of God

Chapter 3 showed how God is also revealed and confessed through
the character creed of the OT. What lies at the core of the character
creed is God's redemptive character expressed through participles emphasizing his covenant faithfulness, which entails both forgiveness and
justice. These participles point to a diversity of adjectives and nouns
that range from those associated with his gracious mercy (gracious,
merciful, slow to anger, abundant in covenant faithfulness and truth)
to those associated with his passionate power (jealous, great, mighty,
awesome, holy). The character revealed and confessed is inextricably
linked with the name of Yahweh. At many places throughout the OT,
however, we are given glimpses of God that transcend the redemptive
categories of the character creed. Participles are foundational to the
revelation and confession of the name of Yahweh in the redemptive
character creed tradition. So also participles are used to express the
character of Yahweh as creator and sustainer of the universe. Evidence
for this expansion in the character creed tradition can be discerned in
particular in the prophetic, wisdom, and worship traditions of Israel.

Evidence that the creational has built on the redemptive can be
discerned in references to the name of Yahweh within the prophetic
books. Thus, for instance, the phrase "Yahweh (of hosts) is his name"
(יהוה צְבָאוֹת שְׁמוֹ) is used at several places in connection with the
participle of the verb "redeem" (גאל):

> Our **Redeemer**, Yahweh of hosts is His name,
> The Holy One of Israel. (Isa. 47:4; cf. 48:2)

> You, O Yahweh, are our Father,
> Our **Redeemer** from of old *is Your name*. (Isa. 63:16b)

> Their **Redeemer** is strong, *Yahweh of hosts is His name*;
> He will vigorously plead their case
> So that He may bring rest to the earth,
> But turmoil to the inhabitants of Babylon. (Jer. 50:34)

In other cases the name of Yahweh alone is linked to the participle:

> For I am *Yahweh* your God, who upholds your right hand,
> Who says to you, "Do not fear, I will help you."
> "Do not fear, you worm Jacob, you people of Israel;
> I will help you," declares Yahweh,
> "and your **Redeemer** is the Holy One of Israel." (Isa. 41:13–14)

> Thus says *Yahweh*, the King of Israel
> And his **Redeemer**, *Yahweh* of hosts:
> "I am the first and I am the last,
> And there is no God besides Me." (Isa. 44:6)

> Thus says *Yahweh*, your **Redeemer**, the Holy One of Israel,
> "I am Yahweh your God, who teaches you to profit,
> Who leads you in the way you should go." (Isa. 48:17)

> Thus says *Yahweh*, the **Redeemer** of Israel *and* its Holy One,
> To the despised One,
> To the One abhorred by the nation,
> To the servant of rulers,
> "Kings will see and arise,
> Princes will also bow down,
> Because of Yahweh who is faithful,
> the Holy One of Israel who has chosen you." (Isa. 49:7)

> And all flesh will know that I, *Yahweh*, am your Savior
> And your **Redeemer**, the Mighty One of Jacob. (Isa. 49:26b)

> "In an outburst of anger
> I hid My face from you for a moment,

> But with everlasting steadfast love I will have compassion on
>   you,"
> Says *Yahweh* your **Redeemer**. (Isa. 54:8)

> Then you will know that I, *Yahweh*, am your Savior
> And your **Redeemer**, the Mighty One of Jacob. (Isa. 60:16b)

In one case Yahweh as redeemer is linked to Yahweh as the creator
of Israel:

> Thus says *Yahweh* your **Redeemer**, the Holy One of Israel,
> "For your sake I have sent to Babylon,
> And will bring them all down as fugitives,
> Even the Chaldeans, into the ships in which they rejoice.
> "I am *Yahweh*, your Holy One,
> The **Creator** of Israel, your King." (Isa. 43:14–15)

This connection between redeemer and creator in relation to Israel
takes on a more universal scope in Isa. 44:24 and 54:5.

> Thus says *Yahweh*, your **Redeemer**,
> and the one who formed you from the womb,
> "I, *Yahweh*, am the **maker** of all things,
> **Stretching** out the heavens by Myself
> And **spreading** out the earth all alone." (Isa. 44:24)

> For your husband is your **Maker**,
> Whose name is *Yahweh* of hosts;
> And your **Redeemer** is the Holy One of Israel,
> Who is called the God of all the earth. (Isa. 54:5)

At times, however, the connection to redemption disappears in
these texts as the prophetic voice juxtaposes the name of Yahweh
with participles related to his creational activity:

> I am *Yahweh*, your Holy One,
> The **Creator** of Israel, your King. (Isa. 43:15)

> I am *Yahweh*, and there is no other;
> Besides Me there is no God.

I will gird you, though you have not known Me;
That people may know from the rising to the setting of the
   sun
That there is no one besides Me.
I am *Yahweh*, and there is no other,
The **One forming** light and **creating** darkness,
Causing well-being and **creating** calamity;
I am *Yahweh* who does all these. (Isa. 45:5–7)

For thus says *Yahweh*, **who created** the heavens
(He is the God **who formed** the earth and **made** it,
He **established** it *and* did not create it a waste place,
But **formed** it to be inhabited),
"I am *Yahweh*, and there is none else." (Isa. 45:18)

Similarly, the fuller phrase "Yahweh (of hosts) is His name" appears
in key prophetic texts in connection with the participles of verbs
related to creational activity:

For I am *Yahweh* your God, **who stirs up** the sea and its
   waves roar
(*Yahweh of hosts is His name*). (Isa. 51:15)

The portion of Jacob is not like these;
For the **Maker** of all is He,
And Israel is the tribe of His inheritance;
Yahweh of hosts is His name. (Jer. 10:16; cf. 10:12, 13)

Thus says *Yahweh*,
Who gives the sun for light by day
And the fixed order of the moon and the stars for light by
   night,
Who stirs up the sea so that its waves roar;
Yahweh of hosts is His name. (Jer. 31:35)

Thus says *Yahweh* **who made** *the earth*,
Yahweh **who formed** it to establish it,
Yahweh is His name. (Jer. 33:2)

For behold, **He who forms** mountains and **creates** the wind
And declares to man what are His thoughts,

He who makes dawn into darkness
And treads on the high places of the earth,
Yahweh God of hosts is His name. (Amos 4:13)

He who made the Pleiades and Orion
And changes deep darkness into morning,
Who also darkens day *into* night,
Who calls for the waters of the sea
And pours them out on the surface of the earth,
Yahweh is His name. (Amos 5:8)

This evidence highlights a key development in the revelation (I am Yahweh) and confession (Yahweh is His name) of the character creed, from a focus on Yahweh as redeemer to Yahweh as creator. The creational vocabulary is rich, as participles are dominantly employed to express Yahweh's key role as creator and sustainer of the universe:

- creator (בָּרָא): Eccles. 12:1; Isa. 40:28; 42:5; 43:1, 15; 45:7 (darkness, calamity), 18; Amos 4:13 (wind)
- creator (קָנָה): Gen. 14:19, 22; Deut. 32:6
- maker (עָשָׂה): Job 4:17; 9:9; 31:15; 32:22; 35:10; 40:19; Pss. 95:6; 115:15; 121:2; 124:8; 134:3; 136:5, 7; 146:6; 149:2; Prov. 14:31; 17:5; 22:2; Eccles. 11:5; Isa. 17:7; 27:11; 44:24; 45:7 (well-being), 18; 51:13; 54:5; 66:22; Jer. 10:12; 33:2; 51:15; Hosea 8:14; Amos 4:13 (dawn into darkness); 5:8; Zech. 10:1
- maker (פָּעַל): Job 36:3
- one who formed (יָצַר): Isa. 27:11; 43:1 (Israel); 44:2 (Jacob), 24 (Israel/Jacob); 45:7 (light), 9, 11, 18 (earth); 49:5 (Servant Israel); 54:5; Jer. 10:16 (of all); 33:2 (earth); 51:19 (of all); Amos 4:13 (mountains); Zech. 12:1 (the spirit of humanity within them); Pss. 33:15 (the hearts of them all); 94:9 (eye)
- one who planted (נָטַע) the ear: Ps. 94:9
- one who established (כּוּן): Isa. 45:18; Jer. 10:12; 33:2
- one who laid the foundation (יָסַד) of the earth: Isa. 51:13; Zech. 12:1; cf. Isa. 48:13; 51:16; Pss. 24:2; 78:69; 102:26; 104:5; Job 38:4; Prov. 3:19

- one who stretched out (נטה) the heavens: Job 9:8; Isa. 40:22; 42:5; 44:24; 45:12; 51:13, 16; Jer. 10:12; 51:15; Zech. 12:1
- one who spread out (רקע) the earth: Isa. 42:5; 44:24; Ps. 136:6
- one who treads (דרך) on the high places of the earth: Amos 4:13
- "Yahweh, who stretched out the heavens and laid the foundations of the earth": Isa. 51:13; Zech. 12:1; cf. Isa. 42:5; 44:25; 45:12; 48:13; 51:13; Jer. 10:12; 51:15; Job 9:8
- "maker of heaven and earth": Gen. 14:19, 22 (קנה); Pss. 115:15; 134:3 (עשׂה)
- "maker of all things": Jer. 10:16; 51:19 (יצר); Isa. 44:24; Eccles. 11:5 (עשׂה)

Yahweh's creational activity is consistently traced back to the original formation of the universe, but many of these texts focus on Yahweh's role as sustainer of this universe.

This creational character of Yahweh is especially important to the prophetic polemic against idolatry, showing how Yahweh's responsibility for the creation and sustenance of the universe is what qualifies him as the only God. The creational function, however, is also important within the Wisdom literature of the OT (as the texts above show), as the sages explore the cosmos and its mysteries as well as human culture and its complexities. The appearance of these participles throughout the liturgical tradition of the Psalter highlights the key role of the creational character within Israel's worship.

Relational Creed

Chapter 5 focused on the key tradition of redemptive relational creeds throughout the OT, expressed fundamentally through the relational identity statements: I am God (Father) and you are people (son). These kinds of statements express the identity of two relational partners in reciprocal relationship. These statements are often connected to and are structured throughout the history of Israel through a series of relational agreements identified as "covenants" (בְּרִית): Abraham/ Sarah, Israel at Sinai, the priestly line, the Davidic dynasty. This tradition plays a key role in defining the relationship between God and his redeemed community, Israel. But there is another relational agreement that precedes those already considered, the agreement between God and all creation in Gen. 9. This agreement lies at a key juncture in biblical history, providing structure for the relationship between God and all creation in light of the fall of humanity in Gen. 3, which produced the crisis described in Gen. 6:5–8. Noah, one who "found favor in the eyes of Yahweh," emerges as "a righteous man, blameless in his time" who "walked with God." It is obvious from Gen. 8:21 and the narratives that follow the covenantal agreement (Gen. 9:20–27; 11:1–9) that sin is not eradicated by the flood. The focus then is on the establishment of this relationship after producing a new creation. As with the redemptive covenants, this creational covenant is identified as an "everlasting" covenant (9:16).

While once again Yahweh takes the initiative to establish this agreement, the reciprocity of this covenant is evident in the use of the two pronouns for the two parties in Gen. 9:7 and 9:9: "as for you" (וְאַתֶּם) and "as for me" (וַאֲנִי), each followed by their core responsibilities:

> And God blessed Noah and his sons and said to them, "**Be fruitful and multiply, and fill the earth**. The fear of you and the terror of you will be on every beast of the earth and on every bird of the sky; with everything that creeps on the ground, and all the fish of the sea, into your hand they are given. Every moving thing that is alive shall be food for you; I give all to you, as *I gave* the green plant. Only you shall not eat flesh with its life, *that is,* its blood. Surely I will require your lifeblood; from every beast I will require it. And from *every* human, from every human's sibling I will require the life of a human.

> > Whoever sheds human blood,
> > By human his blood shall be shed,
> > For in the image of God
> > He made humanity.
> > <u>As for you</u>, **be fruitful and multiply;**
> > **Populate the earth abundantly and multiply in it.**"

> Then God spoke to Noah and to his sons with him, saying, "<u>As for me</u>, indeed, I do establish My covenant with you, and with your descendants after you; and with every living creature that is with you, the birds, the cattle, and every beast of the earth with you; of all that

comes out of the ark, even every beast of the earth. I establish My covenant with you; and all flesh **shall never again be cut off by the water of the flood, neither shall there again be a flood to destroy the earth.**" (Gen. 9:1–11)

In both cases the focus of the responsibilities is on the population of the earth, with creation fulfilling its mandate to be fruitful and multiply and God fulfilling his promise to never again destroy the earth.

The reciprocity is also seen in the repeated descriptions of the covenant agreement in Gen. 9:9–17:

- My covenant with you, and with your descendants after you; and with every living creature that is with you, the birds, the cattle, and every beast of the earth with you; of all that comes out of the ark, even every beast of the earth (9:9–10)
- My covenant with you (9:11)
- the covenant which I am making between Me and you and every living creature that is with you, for all successive generations (9:12)
- a covenant between Me and the earth (9:13)
- My covenant, which is between Me and you and every living creature of all flesh (9:15)
- the everlasting covenant between God and every living creature of all flesh that is on the earth (9:16)
- the covenant which I have established between Me and all flesh that is on the earth (9:17)

The various nondivine partners in this agreement reveal the representative character of Noah, who functions on behalf of future human descendants (זַרְעֲכֶם), every living creature (כָּל־נֶפֶשׁ הַחַיָּה), and their descendants (לְדֹרֹת עוֹלָם), as well as the earth (הָאָרֶץ). Earth here may simply refer to the human and nonhuman living creatures referred to throughout 9:9–17. However, Gen. 8:22, with its references to seedtime/harvest, cold/heat, summer/winter, and day/night (cf. Jer. 33:20, 25), refers to the earth in terms of the physical environment.

The Noachic covenant represents a key transition in the relationship between Yahweh and humanity and needs to be understood in terms of both the creation accounts in Gen. 1–3 and the redemptive accounts that begin in earnest in Gen. 12.

The language used in Gen. 7–9 tips us off that the flood narrative depicts a reversal and renewal of creation.[4] The creation story in Gen. 1 structures creation in two phases: out of chaos (תֹהוּ וָבֹהוּ, Gen. 1:2) with the/a "spirit/wind of God" (רוּחַ אֱלֹהִים) hovering over the waters (הַמָּיִם), described as the deep (תְּהוֹם), God creates "form" on days 1–3 (light/darkness, expanse between upper and lower waters, earth/sea/vegetation; 1:3–13), and then fills this form on days 4–6 (sun/moon, water/sky creatures, animals, humans; 1:14–31). The creation of humanity stands apart from the formation of animals on day 6 as God creates male and female, blesses them, and says: "be fruitful and multiply, and fill the earth and subdue it." Genesis 2 focuses attention on the creation of humanity (2:7), depicting Yahweh God forming humanity from the dust of the ground and breathing into the human's nostrils the breath of life (נִשְׁמַת חַיִּים) so that the human became a living being (נֶפֶשׁ חַיָּה).

Genesis 7 describes a reversal of creation. Genesis 7:11 (NIV) describes how "all the springs of the great deep (מַעְיְנֹת תְּהוֹם) burst forth, and the floodgates of the heavens (אֲרֻבֹּת הַשָּׁמַיִם) were opened," an action that reversed the creative activity of day 2 in Gen. 1 that formed the "expanse between upper and lower waters." Genesis 7:19 (NIV) reveals how these intermingled waters "rose greatly on the earth, and all the high mountains under the entire heavens were covered," an action that reversed the creative activity of day 3 in Gen. 1 that resulted in the distinction between "earth" and "sea." These two verses in Gen. 7 thus describe the reversal of the "form" on days 2–3 in Gen. 1, which then results in the eradication of the "fill" connected with these two days on days 5–6 in Gen. 1, described in Gen. 7:22 (NIV) as: "Everything on dry land that had the breath of life in its nostrils died."

Genesis 8 then signals a renewal of creation as God sends a spirit/ wind (רוּחַ) to pass over the earth covered by the waters (הַמָּיִם; 8:1).

---

4. See also Gentry and Wellum, *Kingdom through Covenant*, 161–65; cf. Waltke and Fredricks, *Genesis*, 128–29; Blenkinsopp, *Creation, Un-creation, Re-creation*.

This has an effect on the deep since "the springs of the deep (מַעְיְנֹת תְּהוֹם) and the floodgates of the heavens (אֲרֻבֹּת הַשָּׁמַיִם) were closed, and the rain from the heavens was restrained" (8:2). The repetition of the language of Gen. 1:2 and 7:11 identifies this as a re-creation. Furthermore, the separation of waters below from waters above in 8:2 is thematically identical to the formation of the expanse (רָקִיעַ) on the second day of creation in Gen. 1:6–7, as is the receding of the water from the earth until it was dry (יבשׁ) on the third day of creation in 8:3–14 (see vv. 7, 14) to the separation of the waters from the dry land (יַבָּשָׁה) in 1:9–10. The dove returning with "a freshly picked olive leaf" in 8:11 reflects another allusion to the third day of creation, on which vegetation sprouted forth after the separation of water from land (1:11–12). The dove's failure to return in 8:12 is not only a sign that the earth had dried up but also that re-creation had reached the fifth day of Gen. 1, when God created water and winged animals (1:20–22). The sixth day of creation in Gen. 1, on which land animals and humans were created, is reached in 8:15–19 as Noah, his family, and all the animals on the ark disembark. The command/blessing to "be fruitful and multiply (and fill) the earth" (פְּרוּ וּרְבוּ וּמִלְאוּ אֶת־הָאָרֶץ) in 8:17; 9:1, 7 is identical to God's original mandate to humanity in 1:28. In Gen. 9 this command-blessing is followed by the reference to "the fear of you and the terror of you" falling on the animals of land and sky as evidence of these creatures being "given into your hand" (בְּיֶדְכֶם נִתָּנוּ). This is the language of rulership (e.g., Judg. 1:2), which also follows the command-blessing in Gen. 1:28 ("rule over . . ."). And finally the allusion to rulership in Gen. 9 is followed by the provision of food for humanity, this time expanding the original provision of vegetation in Gen. 1:29–30 to include animals.

Therefore, similarities in language, theme, and structure show that Gen. 7–9 is being presented as a reversal and renewal of creation. The flood narrative is thus pivotal in the story of humanity and acts as a bridge between the original creation in Gen. 1 and the redemptive story of Israel that begins in Gen. 12.

But why is this reversal and renewal of creation necessary? A clue to answer this question can be found in the fact that the word בְּרִית (covenant) appears for the first time in Gen. 9. As we saw in chapter 4, this term appears in the OT when a relationship is formalized between one kinship cluster (family) and another kinship cluster (family). A בְּרִית (covenant) is not necessary within a family unit, that is, a parent does not need a covenant with a child, nor a sibling with another sibling. These are natural, trustworthy relationships. No covenant is necessary in the original creation since Yahweh God is identified as a parent producing children, as the "image/likeness of God" language makes clear (see Gen. 5:1–3).[5] Once the human couple is banished from the garden in Gen. 3, this family status is annulled, and a covenant is now necessary to structure the relationship between humanity and God, and this covenant makes possible a renewal of the kinship relationship.

The Noachic covenant forms an important bridge between creation and redemption, as God reestablishes kinship relationship with humanity and all of creation. By placing the Noachic covenant in canonical position before Israel's redemptive story and its relational agreements (with Abraham/Sarah, Israel at Sinai, priestly, royal), we are reminded that the redemptive agreements with Israel were part of a much larger story of redemption that would impact not just all nations (Gen. 10) but also all creation. The relational agreement with Noah thus is key to understanding humanity's function as vice-regents over all creation and God's desire through a redeemed humanity to see creation realize its full potential.

The Noachic covenant is not only placed as foundational to the redemptive covenants in the Torah but is also highlighted as key to the future vision of the prophets.[6] The many allusions to Gen. 1–9 within Isa. 24[7] and Zeph. 1–2 reveal that the re-creation highlighted

---

5. See now McDowell, *Image of God*; cf. Lima, "צלם and דמות." Key also is the structural flow of Gen. 1, which speaks of animals producing "after their kind" (לְמִינֵהֶם; 1:21, 24–25), followed in one case by the command-blessing (ברך Piel) to "be fruitful and multiply, and fill . . ." (פְּרוּ וּרְבוּ וּמִלְאוּ; 1:22), capped off with the creation of humanity "in our own image/according to our likeness" (בְּצַלְמֵנוּ כִּדְמוּתֵנוּ; 1:26–27), who are then given the command-blessing to "be fruitful and multiply, and fill . . ." (פְּרוּ וּרְבוּ וּמִלְאוּ). The parallel between "after their kind" and "in our own image/according to our likeness" suggests that humanity is portrayed as the offspring of God.

6. See Dumbrell, *Covenant and Creation*, 39–40; Gentry and Wellum, *Kingdom through Covenant*, 172–74.

7. See esp. Childs, *Isaiah*, 179; Seitz, *Isaiah 1–39*, 180; with thanks to Adam Brown.

by these initial texts in Genesis is part of the future eschatological vision of the prophets. This future involves a re-creative judgment much like the Noachic texts. But the prophets also leverage the Noachic covenant in positive ways. Isaiah 54:9–10 bases a hopeful message to God's people on the promises related to the Noachic covenant. Explicit reference is made to Noah and the flood in 54:9 and to the mountains and hills in 54:10 (cf. 55:12). This link to the Noachic agreement with all creation explains why Yahweh is identified as "your Maker" and "the God of all the earth" in 54:5. Allusions are made to creational motifs in 55:10, suggesting a link between the promises of God and the Noachic covenant, especially because of the reference to the regular provision of the natural rhythms that produce harvest (cf. Gen. 8:22). The joyous response of all creation in 55:12–13 ends with a reference to "an everlasting sign which will not be cut off," echoing the language of the Noachic covenant in Gen. 9:16–17 ("everlasting covenant . . . sign"). Jeremiah's future hope for the priestly and royal covenants is intricately linked with the enduring hope of the Noachic covenant (Jer. 33:17–26). Jeremiah 31:31–37 links the future hope for the Sinai covenant with the Noachic covenant, reminding the people of God that God's commitment to them is intricately linked with his commitment to all creation. Psalm 89:36–38 (89:35–37 Eng.; cf. 89:4–6 [89:5–7 Eng.]) intertwines the Davidic and Noachic covenants.

Thus, the Noachic covenant plays many functions within the OT. While it shows the creational and universal implications of the redemptive agreements established with Israel, it also provides hope that those redemptive agreements will endure and reach their fullest potential (Jer. 30–31). At times it is used to comfort (Isa. 54–55) and even to announce judgment in the present (Nah. 1:8) as well as the future (Isa. 24; Zeph. 1–2). It can prompt praise (Ps. 29:10) but also be used in lament (Ps. 89).

The Creational Pulse and the Old Testament Canon

These connections between the various creeds and creation remind us of the overall creational shape of the canon. In what some have called the first great "Primary History," that is, Genesis–2 Kings,[8] Gen. 1–11 sets a context for the story of redemption. By presenting key creational (and re-creational) narratives, this text identifies the need for redemption and sets the more localized and national story of redemption against the larger backdrop of creation. Thus, God's mandate to humanity—to fill the earth and rule it as his vice-regents—is the larger purpose behind God's redemption of humanity.

A similar structure can be discerned in the book of Chronicles, which may be considered the canon's second great Primary History. The Chronicler begins with Adam (1 Chron. 1:1) and ends with Cyrus (2 Chron. 36:23), drawing on material from the first great Primary History (Genesis–2 Kings) and again reminding the readers that the story of Israel and its redemption should not be separated from that of all creation.[9]

This helps us draw Wisdom literature into our OT theology.[10] Many have noted the absence of redemptive history within Wisdom literature and the dominance of creational motifs. But a careful look at Wisdom literature reveals that "the fear of Yahweh" is indeed the beginning and goal of wisdom (Prov. 1:7; 2:5; 9:10; Eccles. 12:13; Job 28:28).[11] If we understand "the fear of Yahweh" as the response demanded of Israel in the wake of the exodus (e.g., Deut. 10:12, 20), then Wisdom literature highlights the opportunity to fully engage the creational mandate and context that precedes redemptive history. The creational context is foundational for redemption, and redemption has as its goal the full realization of creational priorities. Wisdom literature showcases a redeemed community beginning to engage their creational responsibilities and priorities, often using general revelation to gain understanding.

Prophetic literature also sees re-creation (new heavens and earth) as the destination of history (Isa. 24–27; 65:17–25; Zech. 14). The prophets also looked to a re-creation of humanity (Ezek. 37), akin to the Gen. 2 scene of creation, as the Spirit breathes new life into the community of God.

8. Freedman, *Unity.*
9. Boda, *1–2 Chronicles*, 29–30.
10. Boda, "Delight of Wisdom."
11. Waltke, "Book of Proverbs."

The final form of the canon thus matches the later forms of the narrative creed that highlight the important link between redemption and creation. Creation is the context for which redemption is set in motion by Yahweh and is the goal of the redemption realized by Yahweh's great acts. What we see in the OT are three creedal expressions that confess the action, character, and relational passion of God not only for the formation of Israel but also for the renewal of all culture and creation.

For Christians, however, the canon does not end with the close of the OT but extends into the NT. As we turn to the final phase of revelation found in Matthew–Revelation, we will continue to hear the rhythms of the heartbeat so key to OT theology.

7

Taking the Old Testament Pulse in the New Testament

The selective intertextual-canonical approach that we adopted at the beginning of this volume involved identifying core expressions of God that appear throughout the OT canon. It is selective in that it focuses on what is most important in the message of the OT, and this importance is discerned by identifying what is consistent and ubiquitous throughout the canon. Such a selective intertextual-canonical approach is not limited to the OT canon, although my goal has been to allow the heartbeat of the OT to be felt and heard as part of the Christian canon. The OT has a unique contribution to make to the canon as a whole, and we prioritized listening to the text of the OT on its own terms without the pressure of NT perspectives or the interpretations of NT scholars. This is not to disparage the contribution of the NT. Differences between the messages of the two Testaments are important to grasp, considering that revelation and redemption are progressive in nature. Similarly, fresh work on the OT without reference to the NT can provide new perspectives on NT study.

This chapter will show that the theological rhythms clearly and consistently heard throughout the OT can also be discerned in the NT.[1]

The Narrative Rhythm of the New Testament: The Historical Action of God through Christ and the Church

The NT as canonical document has a fascinating opening. Affixed to the beginning of the Gospel of Matthew is a "record of the geneal-ogy of Jesus the Messiah, the son of David, the son of Abraham." The summary statement in Matt. 1:17 makes explicit what can be discerned from the genealogy itself: it reviews the story of Israel from Abraham to David to the exile to Christ.[2] This narratological purpose is evidenced not only in the use of these four key markers in the history of Israel but also by the mention of five women in the genealogy: Tamar (v. 3), Rahab (v. 5), Ruth (v. 5), Bathsheba (v. 6), and Mary (v. 16). Comparing the various narratives in which these characters appear in the OT, Schaberg has argued brilliantly that mention of the first four is designed to set up the final woman and introduce the opening narrative of the Gospel (Matt. 1:18–25).

> Mention of these four women is designed to lead Matthew's reader to expect another, final story of a woman who becomes a social misfit in some way; is wronged or thwarted; who is party to a sexual act that places her in great danger; and whose story has an outcome that repairs the social fabric and ensures the birth of the child who is legitimate or legitimated.[3]

Both the explicit structuring and the implicit connections reveal the role of this opening genealogy to connect the story of Jesus to the grand story of OT redemption. Such connections can be discerned at

---

1. For further details on why and how the OT relates to the NT, see the appendix: "Biblical Theology and the Old Testament." See also Boda, *"Return to Me,"* 19–34; Boda, "Old Testament and Romans."

2. This narratological purpose is made clear by the inclusion of "exile" rather than a person to open the third phase of the genealogy.

3. Schaberg, *Illegitimacy of Jesus*, 38–39. Although I do not agree with all her conclusions, this observation is appropriate and accurate.

the outset of the two other Synoptic Gospels with their allusions to Malachi and Isaiah (Mark 1:1–8, esp. vv. 2–3; Luke 1:5–25, esp. v. 17).[4]

This evidence reveals the important role that the OT story played in NT theology and the prominence of story as a form of revelation in the NT corpus.[5] According to the book of Acts, the proclamation of the gospel in the early days of the church was saturated with the flow of redemptive history from OT to Christ.[6] In the opening sermon in the book of Acts (2:14–36), the apostle Peter tells the story of the redemptive work of God in Christ (2:22–24) by creating a link to the OT story of redemption through the prophet Joel. Joel's prophecy speaks of the wonders of God that would occur among the returned remnant of Israel (see Joel 2:32b). According to Peter, this prophecy has been fulfilled in Acts 2 in the context of a remnant returned from "exile" (see the list of returned Jews in 2:9–11). He is claiming that Pentecost is in continuity with the OT story of redemption, introducing the final phase. This focus on the OT story of revelation and redemption underpins various sermons throughout Acts.

Near the end of his sermon in Acts 3 Peter provides an encapsulation of redemptive history related to prophecy:

> But the things which God announced beforehand by the mouth of all the prophets, that His Christ would suffer, He has thus fulfilled. Therefore repent and return, so that your sins may be wiped away, in order that times of refreshing may come from the presence of Yahweh; and that He may send Jesus, the Christ appointed for you, whom

4. Other studies have revealed the many explicit and implicit ways that the NT presents Jesus Christ in continuity with the OT story. See the appendix below: "Biblical Theology and the Old Testament."

5. See the helpful review of recent research on what Hood and Emerson call "Summaries of Israel's Story" within Hebrew Bible, Second Temple Judaism, and NT texts; see Hood and Emerson, "Summaries of Israel's Story"; cf. Bauckham, "Reading Scripture"; Brown, "Future of Biblical Theology." Ooi (*Scripture and Its Readers*) identifies Neh. 9, Ezek. 20, and Acts 7 as "Readings of Israel's Story."

6. In Acts 2:11 (NIV) the crowd of God-fearing Jews in Jerusalem on the day of Pentecost states: "we hear them declaring the wonders of God in our own tongues." The wonders of God are the mighty deeds of God (Deut. 11:2), which is the focus of the narrative creed. Peter then stands up and traces the story of God's redemptive acts, as is the custom in the sermons in Acts. On Luke 24 as setting the agenda for these sermons in Acts, see Hays, "Reading Scripture," 230.

heaven must receive until *the* period of restoration of all things about which God spoke by the mouth of His holy prophets from ancient time. Moses said, "THE LORD GOD WILL RAISE UP FOR YOU A PROPHET LIKE ME FROM YOUR BRETHREN; TO HIM YOU SHALL GIVE HEED to every-thing He says to you. And it will be that every soul that does not heed that prophet shall be utterly destroyed from among the people." And likewise, all the prophets who have spoken, from Samuel and *his* successors onward, also announced these days. It is you who are the sons of the prophets and of the covenant which God made with your fathers, saying to Abraham, "AND IN YOUR SEED ALL THE FAMILIES OF THE EARTH SHALL BE BLESSED." For you first, God raised up His Servant and sent Him to bless you by turning every one *of you* from your wicked ways. (Acts 3:18–26)

Notice the flow of the redemptive action of God through "the mouth of His holy prophets from ancient time" (v. 21), beginning with Moses (vv. 22–23), then on to Samuel, his successors (v. 24), and to the present audience, who are "the sons of the prophets" (v. 25) for whom God raised up "His servant" Jesus to prompt repentance (v. 26). Peter's recitation of God's redemptive acts through revelation ends with the present audience as the final outcome of the history (vv. 25–26).

In Acts 7 the martyr Stephen begins his rehearsal of God's redemp-tive acts with Abraham (vv. 2–8a), then proceeds to Isaac (v. 8b); Jacob and his sons, including especially Joseph (vv. 8c–16); the exodus experience, including especially Moses (vv. 17–36a); the wilderness, including the golden calf and tabernacle (vv. 36b–44); the conquest, including especially Joshua (v. 45); the building of the temple, includ-ing especially David and Solomon (vv. 46–50); and finally the rebel-lious generation that resisted the prophets in the land (vv. 51–53). Stephen ends by connecting the present generation as exemplifying this final generation (v. 51).

Paul also recites the redemptive actions of God as he declares the gospel in Acts 13, beginning with the exodus (v. 17), then the wilder-ness (v. 18), the conquest (v. 19), life in the land—including the periods of Samuel, Saul, David—and ending with Jesus (vv. 20–23). The redemptive story continues into the ministry of John (vv. 24–25) and reaches its fulfillment in Jesus's death, resurrection, and proclamation of the gospel (vv. 26–32). Again the depiction of this redemptive action ends with the present generation being confronted by the gospel claims about Jesus Christ (vv. 33–41).

Each of these examples reveals how the redemptive action of God in the OT flows into the redemptive actions of God in and through Jesus Christ.[7]

At times, however, the OT phase of the redemptive story is left out, focusing on the final phase of the events associated with Jesus Christ. An example of this more focused creedal form (death, resurrection, proclamation) can be found in Luke 24:45–48, a description of one of the last encounters between Jesus and his disciples:[8]

> Then He opened their minds to understand the Scriptures, and He said to them, "Thus it is written, that the Christ would suffer and rise again from the dead the third day, and that repentance for forgiveness of sins would be proclaimed in His name to all the nations, beginning from Jerusalem. You are witnesses of these things."

Here we see a focus on Christ's death, his resurrection, and the proclamation of his name to all nations. The very next verse, 24:49, alludes to two other key events that still lie in the future: ascension and spirit-outpouring: "And behold, I am sending forth the promise of My Father upon you; but you are to stay in the city until you are clothed with power from on high." These two future events are then included in the first summary of the redemptive story after the day of Pentecost, in Peter's sermon in Acts 2:22–24, 32–33, which includes life, death, resurrection, ascension, and spirit-outpouring.

> People of Israel, listen to these words: Jesus the Nazarene, a man attested to you by God with miracles and wonders and signs which God performed through Him in your midst, just as you yourselves know—this *Man*, delivered over by the predetermined plan and fore-knowledge of God, you nailed to a cross by the hands of godless men

---

7. Further examples could be culled from Rom. 9–11, esp. 9:7–33, which traces a theological theme (God's elective grace) from Abraham through Isaac, Jacob, Esau, Moses, Hosea, to Isaiah; also see Heb. 11:1–12:2, which traces a theological theme (faith) from creation to Jesus.

8. Ascension and spirit-outpouring still lie in the future, as Luke 24:48–49 indicates.

and put *Him* to death. But God raised Him up again, putting an end
to the agony of death, since it was impossible for Him to be held in
its power. . . . This Jesus God raised up again, to which we are all
witnesses. Therefore having been exalted to the right hand of God,
and having received from the Father the promise of the Holy Spirit,
He has poured forth this which you both see and hear.

Similar encapsulations of the narrative creed can be culled from the
following passages:

death, resurrection

Let it be known to all of you and to all the people of Israel, that by
the name of Jesus Christ the Nazarene, whom you crucified, whom
God raised from the dead—by this *name* this man stands here before
you in good health. (Acts 4:10)

prior glory, life, death, resurrection/ascension

Have this attitude in yourselves which was also in Christ Jesus, who,
although He existed in the form of God, did not regard equality with
God a thing to be grasped, but emptied Himself, taking the form of
a bond-servant, *and* being made in the likeness of humanity. Being
found in appearance as a man, He humbled Himself by becoming
obedient to the point of death, even death on a cross. For this reason
also, God highly exalted Him, and bestowed on Him the name which
is above every name, so that at the name of Jesus EVERY KNEE WILL
BOW, of those who are in heaven and on earth and under the earth,
and that every tongue will confess that Jesus Christ is Lord, to the
glory of God the Father. (Phil. 2:5–11)

death/burial, resurrection, proclamation

Now I make known to you, brothers and sisters, the gospel which I
preached to you, which also you received, in which also you stand, by
which also you are saved, if you hold fast the word which I preached
to you, unless you believed in vain. For I delivered to you as of first
importance what I also received, that Christ died for our sins according to the Scriptures, and that He was buried, and that He was raised
on the third day according to the Scriptures, and that He appeared to
Cephas, then to the twelve. After that He appeared to more than five
hundred brothers and sisters at one time, most of whom remain until
now, but some have fallen asleep; then He appeared to James, then to

all the apostles; and last of all, as to one untimely born, He appeared to me also. For I am the least of the apostles, and not fit to be called an apostle, because I persecuted the church of God. But by the grace of God I am what I am, and His grace toward me did not prove vain; but I labored even more than all of them, yet not I, but the grace of God with me. Whether then *it was* I or they, so we preach and so you believed. (1 Cor. 15:1–11)

life, resurrection, ascension, proclamation
By common confession, great is the mystery of godliness:

> He who was revealed in the flesh,
> Was vindicated in the Spirit,
> Seen by angels,
> Proclaimed among the nations,
> Believed on in the world,
> Taken up in glory. (1 Tim. 3:16)

In these texts we can sense one key rhythm of the heartbeat first discerned in the OT, expressed through the narrative creed that highlights the redemptive actions of God, which culminates in and through the actions and message of Jesus Christ and the community that bears his name. It should not be missed that the recitation of the redemptive actions of God does not end with Christ's resurrection but rather continues with spirit-outpouring on the community and proclamation of the gospel. In this we see how the redemptive acts of God continue through the proclamation of Christ's community. This matches the canonical shape of the three Synoptic Gospels, all of which begin by noting how the story of Jesus continues the story of Israel and all of which end with a call to Jesus's disciples to proclaim the kingdom in word and deed to the nations (Matt. 28:18–20; Mark 16:14–20; Luke 24:47). For the Gospel of Luke this understanding of the gospel necessitated a second volume that, following on the first volume "about all that Jesus began to do and teach" (Gospel of Luke, Acts 1:1), traces what can only be understood as what "Jesus continued to do and teach" (book of Acts) as the Spirit of Christ fills his disciples to proclaim the gospel to the nations (Acts 1:8).

The Character Rhythm of the New Testament: The Active Character of God in Christ and the Church

The characteristics of God revealed and confessed in the character creed of the OT can be traced throughout the NT.[9] There is a slight challenge in tracking instances with accuracy because of the shift in language from Hebrew to Greek, but beginning with evidence from the OG translation of the OT, several passages highlight the importance of this tradition for NT writers.[10] A comparison of the Hebrew and Greek traditions of Exod. 34:6–7 is a helpful starting point.

Author Trans.	Hebrew	Old Greek	NETS
Yahweh, Yahweh, God	יְהוָה יְהוָה אֵל	Κύριος ὁ θεὸς	The Lord, God is*
compassionate	רַחוּם	οἰκτίρμων	compassionate
and gracious	וְחַנּוּן	καὶ ἐλεήμων,	and merciful
slow to anger	אֶרֶךְ אַפַּיִם	μακρόθυμος	patient
abundant in steadfast love	וְרַב־חֶסֶד	καὶ πολυέλεος	and very merciful
and truth	וֶאֱמֶת	καὶ ἀληθινὸς	and truthful
keeping steadfast love to thousands	נֹצֵר חֶסֶד לָאֲלָפִים	καὶ δικαιοσύνην διατηρῶν καὶ ποιῶν ἔλεος εἰς χιλιάδας,	and preserving righteousness and doing mercy for thousands
forgiving iniquity, and rebellion, and sin	נֹשֵׂא עָוֹן וָפֶשַׁע וְחַטָּאָה	ἀφαιρῶν ἀνομίας καὶ ἀδικίας καὶ ἁμαρτίας,	taking away acts of lawlessness and of injustice and sins,
yet he will by no means leave [the sin/sinner] unpunished	וְנַקֵּה לֹא יְנַקֶּה	καὶ οὐ καθαριεῖ τὸν ἔνοχον	and he will not acquit the guilty person
visiting the punishment for iniquity of parents on the children and on the children of children to the third and fourth generations.	פֹּקֵד עֲוֹן אָבוֹת עַל־ בָּנִים וְעַל־ בְּנֵי בָנִים עַל־שִׁלֵּשִׁים וְעַל־רִבֵּעִים	ἐπάγων ἀνομίας πατέρων ἐπὶ τέκνα καὶ ἐπὶ τέκνα τέκνων ἐπὶ τρίτην καὶ τετάρτην γενεάν.	bringing lawless acts of fathers upon children and upon children of children, upon the third and fourth generation.

*Departing from NETS, following Göttingen.

9. See Spieckermann, "God's Steadfast Love," 305–27; Joosten, "חסד, 'Benevolence,' and Ελεος, 'Pity'"; Knowles, Unfolding Mystery.

10. Understanding that the NT writers were not confined to the translation options evidenced in the OG.

In the OG of Exod. 34:6, God's compassion (רַחוּם) is identified as "merciful" (οἰκτιρμός).[11] This term is connected with God in 2 Cor. 1:3 ("Father of mercies"), Rom. 12:1 ("the mercies of God"), and Luke 6:36 ("be merciful, just as your Father is merciful"). In drawing on the story of Job, James 5:11 highlights "that Yahweh is full of compassion (πολύσπλαγχνός) and *is* merciful (οἰκτίρμων)." The use of "full of compassion" (πολύσπλαγχνός) may reflect "abundant in steadfast love" (רַב־חֶסֶד) in the character creed of Exod. 34:6.[12] This would then mean that a characteristic from the first doublet of characteristics (compassionate and gracious, רַחוּם וְחַנּוּן) is fused with a characteristic from the second doublet of characteristics (abundant in steadfast love and truth, רַב־חֶסֶד וֶאֱמֶת).

Hebrews 2:17 links two characteristics to Christ, the "merciful (ἐλεήμων) and faithful (πιστός) high priest." In this case the writer may have in mind the other characteristics of the two doublets, since merciful (ἐλεήμων) is used to translate חַנּוּן (gracious) in the OG of Exod. 34:6, and there are times in the OG tradition when πιστός (faithful, trustworthy) is used to translate truth (אֱמֶת, Prov. 14:25).[13] In the OG πιστός is dominantly a translation of הַנֶּאֱמָן (faithful [see below]), the key term linked to Yahweh in the grace character creed of Deut. 7:9. It may be then that Heb. 2:17 has in mind the two major grace character creed traditions in the Pentateuch.

In the OG of Exodus the phrase רַב־חֶסֶד (abundant in steadfast love) in Exod. 34:6 is translated as πολυέλεος (very merciful), and the word חֶסֶד (steadfast love) in 34:7 is translated as ἔλεος (mercy). While πολυέλεος (very merciful) does not appear in the NT, ἔλεος (mercy) is common. The phrase "full of mercy" (μεστὴ ἐλέους) in James 3:17,

---

11. See the citation of Exod. 33:19 in Rom. 9:15.

12. Similarly, Knowles, *Unfolding Mystery*, 113–14. In Exod. 34:6 OG רַב־חֶסֶד (great in steadfast love) is translated as πολυέλεος (very merciful). The Greek word πολύσπλαγχνός is not used in the OG of the OT, but the word σπλαγχνός (compassion) is used in Prov. 12:10 to translate רַחֲמִים (compassionate), a cognate of רַחוּם (compassionate). Thus it is possible that πολύσπλαγχνός (full of compassion) in James 5:11 also refers to the cognate רַחוּם (compassionate) from Exod. 34:6, although the prefix πολύ- (full of) is conspicuous.

13. Even though in Exod. 34:6 ἀληθινός (truthful) is used to translate truth (אֱמֶת). It should be noted, however, that in the OG the cognate πίστις (faith) is used to translate אֱמֶת in Prov. 3:3; 14:22; 15:27; Jer. 39:41 (32:41 Heb.); 35:9 (28:9 Heb.); 40:6 (33:6 Heb.).

used to describe the wisdom that comes from above (that is, from God), is reminiscent of "abundant in steadfast love" (רַב־חֶסֶד), as is "rich in mercy" (πλούσιος . . . ἐν ἐλέει), which describes God in Eph. 2:4. Hebrews 4:16 refers to the mercy and grace (ἔλεος καὶ χάριν) that one finds at God's throne. The second word here, grace (χάρις), is used dominantly to translate the Hebrew word חֵן (grace), a cognate of חַנּוּן (gracious) of Exod. 34:6. Hebrews 4:16, therefore, may be another example of an allusion to the character creed by referring to one characteristic from each of the two doublets in Exod. 34:6.

The word אֱמֶת (truth) in Exod. 34:6 is translated as ἀληθινός (truthful) in the OG. In the NT this Greek word is regularly associated with God and Christ especially in the Johannine tradition (John 7:28; 17:3; 1 John 5:20; Rev. 3:7; 6:10; 15:3; 16:7; 19:2, 11; 22:6; cf. 1 Thess. 1:9). Ἀληθινός (truthful) appears with holy (ἅγιος) in Rev. 3:7; 6:10, with righteous (δίκαιος) in Rev. 15:3; 16:7; 19:2, and with faithful (πιστός) in Rev. 19:11; 22:6. Δίκαιος (righteous) is nearly always a translation for cognates of the verb צדק (to be righteous; צַדִּיק 182×, צֶדֶק 22×, צדק 15×, צְדָקָה 6×) but in Isa. 57:1 is used for both צַדִּיק (righteous) and חֶסֶד (steadfast love).[14] Possibly, then, Rev. 15:3; 16:7; 19:2 allude to Exod. 34:6. Πιστός (faithful) is nearly always the translation for the attribute of God in Deut. 7:9–10 (faithful, הַנֶּאֱמָן), suggesting an interlinking again between the two grace character creed traditions in Exod. 34:6–7 and Deut. 7:9–10.

In the OG the phrase slow to anger (אֶרֶךְ אַפַּיִם) is translated as μακρόθυμος (patient), a word that does not appear in the NT.[15] Cognate terms that are used include the verb μακροθυμέω (to be patient) and the noun μακροθυμία (patience), both used in 2 Pet. 3 in relation to Yahweh's patience in order that none should perish (vv. 9, 15, 20). Matthew 18:26 uses the verb μακροθυμέω (to be patient) in reference to the lord in the parable (a figure for God, see 18:35), as does Rom. 2:4.

The word הַנֶּאֱמָן (faithful) in Deut. 7:9 is translated as πιστός (faithful, cf. Isa. 49:7), which is typical in the OG translation of the OT. The word πιστός (faithful) is linked to Jesus or God at several

14. Data from *Lexham Analytical Lexicon to the Septuagint*.
15. See Acts 26:3 for the adverb μακροθύμως. The Christian virtue of being "slow to anger" (βραδὺς εἰς ὀργήν) is reminiscent of the Hebrew phrase used in Exod. 34:7 (אֶרֶךְ אַפַּיִם).

points in the NT. As noted above, Heb. 2:17 identifies Jesus as "a merciful (ἐλεήμων) and faithful (πιστός) high priest," possibly bringing together the second word of the Exod. 34 character creed with the key attribute of Deut. 7:9–10. As noted above, the book of Revelation employs πιστός (faithful) multiple times alongside ἀληθινός (truthful/true; Rev. 3:14; 19:11; 21:5; 22:6), thus bringing together the attribute of Deut. 7:9–10 (הַנֶּאֱמָן, faithful) with the final attribute in Exod. 34:6 (אֱמֶת, truthful). These passages in Revelation relate to Jesus Christ or his words. God is referred to as faithful (πιστός) elsewhere in the NT: 1 Cor. 1:9; 10:13; 2 Cor. 1:18; 1 Thess. 5:24; Heb. 10:23; 11:11; 1 Pet. 4:19; 1 John 1:9.

We noted in chapter 3 the importance of the descriptor "holy/holiness" (קָדוֹשׁ, cf. קֹדֶשׁ) for understanding Yahweh in the OT. In the OG this is typically translated as ἅγιος (holy), a characteristic that is linked to God (Luke 1:49; 1 Pet. 1:16) and more specifically to the Father (John 17:11; Rev. 4:8; 6:10; cf. Matt. 6:9//Luke 11:2, where ἁγιάζω [to be holy] is connected with the Father's name), the Son (John 6:69; Rev. 3:7), and the Spirit (e.g., Matt. 28:19).

Yahweh's jealousy/zeal (קַנָּא) in Exod. 20:5; 34:14; Deut. 4:24; 5:9; 6:15 is translated with the noun ζηλωτής (jealous) in the OG. While this noun is not connected with God in the NT, Paul uses the cognate verb παραζηλόω in 1 Cor. 10:22 to express the danger of provoking Yahweh to jealousy. So also Paul speaks of being "jealous for you with a godly jealousy" (ζηλῶ γὰρ ὑμᾶς θεοῦ ζήλῳ) in 2 Cor. 11:2, pointing to this jealousy rooted in the character of God.

The threefold attributes (great, mighty, awesome) seen in the later prayer traditions of Nehemiah, Jeremiah, and Daniel (גָּדוֹל = μέγας, גִּבּוֹר = κραταιός, נוֹרָא = φοβερός; Neh. 1:5; 9:32; Jer. 32:18; Dan. 9:4) can also be traced into the NT. Christ Jesus is identified as "our great (μέγας) God and Savior" in Titus 2:13. Peter calls his audience to humble themselves under "the mighty (κραταιός) hand of God" in 1 Pet. 5:6. And Hebrews regularly speaks of φοβερός (fear) as the condition created in humans in the presence of God (10:27, 31; 12:21).

Whether all of these passages can be linked to the specific influence of the character creed is not the main point. Rather, they highlight the fact that the same characteristics of God that play such an important role in the OT are also identified with God in the NT.

The Relational Rhythm of the New Testament: The Relational Identity of God in Christ and the Church

The name "New Testament" is a constant reminder that the relational creed and the covenantal agreements associated with it are foundational to the theology of the NT. The relational creed is expressed in several places in the NT:

> This is My beloved Son, in whom I am well-pleased. (Matt. 3:17 echoing Ps. 2:7; cf. Isa. 42:1; Jer. 31:20 [38:20 OG])

> This is My beloved Son, in whom I am well-pleased. (Matt. 17:5//Mark 9:7; Luke 9:35; echoing Ps. 2:7; cf. Isa. 42:1; Jer. 31:20 [38:20 OG])

> YOU ARE MY SON; TODAY I HAVE BEGOTTEN YOU. (Acts 13:33 citing Ps. 2:7)[16]

> As He says also in Hosea,
> "I WILL CALL THOSE WHO WERE NOT MY PEOPLE, 'MY PEOPLE,'
> AND HER WHO WAS NOT BELOVED, 'BELOVED.'"
> "AND IT SHALL BE THAT IN THE PLACE WHERE IT WAS SAID TO THEM,
> 'YOU ARE NOT MY PEOPLE,' THERE THEY SHALL BE CALLED SONS OF THE
> LIVING GOD." (Rom. 9:25–26 citing Hosea 2:23; 1:10)

> AND I WILL BE THEIR GOD, AND THEY SHALL BE MY PEOPLE. (2 Cor. 6:16 citing Exod. 29:45; Ezek. 37:27)

> And I will be a father to you, And you shall be sons and daughters to Me. (2 Cor. 6:18 echoing 2 Sam. 7:14//1 Chron. 17:13)

> AND I WILL BE THEIR GOD, AND THEY SHALL BE MY PEOPLE. (Heb. 8:10 citing Jer. 31:33)

> For you once were NOT A PEOPLE, but now you are THE PEOPLE OF GOD; you HAD NOT RECEIVED MERCY, but now you HAVE RECEIVED MERCY. (1 Pet. 2:10 citing Hosea 1:10; 2:23)

> And they shall be His people, and God Himself will be among them. (Rev. 21:3 citing Exod. 29:45; Ezek. 37:27)

16. OT quotations appearing in the NT are set in capital letters in the NASB.

These passages containing the relational creed allude to two key OT relational agreements: the Sinai covenant (Rom. 9:25–26; 2 Cor. 6:16; Heb. 8:10; 1 Pet. 2:10; Rev. 21:3) and the Davidic covenant (Matt. 3:17; 17:5; Mark 9:7; Luke 9:35; Acts 13:33; 2 Cor. 6:18).

The new Sinai covenant motif can be discerned in the Passion account of the Gospel of Luke as Jesus takes the cup and declares: "This cup which is poured out for you is the new covenant in My blood" (Luke 22:20). This is echoed in 1 Cor. 11:25 as Paul instructs the Corinthian church as to proper conduct related to the Eucharist. The connection between covenant and blood points us to Exod. 24:8, where Moses confirms the Sinai covenant with the people by sprinkling blood on the people and declaring: "Behold the blood of the covenant, which Yahweh has made with you in accordance with all these words."[17] But, of course, the use of "new covenant" suggests that the Sinai covenant tradition in Exodus is being viewed through the lens of the future covenantal hope of Jeremiah (e.g., Jer. 31:31). A similar trend can be discerned in 2 Cor. 3:6, which uses the terminology of "new covenant" reminiscent of Jeremiah as well as motifs drawn from the Torah, in particular the renewal of the Sinai covenant in Exod. 34. Allusions to the Sinai covenant fill the book of Hebrews, with explicit citations from Jeremiah (Heb. 8:8–12; cf. Jer. 31:31–34) as well as the Torah (Heb. 9:20; cf. Exod. 24:7). The Sinai covenant is also in view in the use of the relational tradition from Hosea in Rom. 9:25–26 and 1 Pet. 2:10 (Hosea 1:10; 2:23), as well as the priestly tradition that links together God's presence and relationship from Exod. 29:45 and Ezek. 37:27, which can be discerned in 2 Cor. 6:16 and Rev. 21:3. It is clear throughout the NT, as it is in Jeremiah, that the covenant envisioned represents a new phase in redemptive relationship between Yahweh and his people, even though there are points of continuity between old and new covenants.

Passages in the NT that contain echoes of the relational creed at times refer to the Davidic covenant. References to Jesus as Yahweh's "son" in the Gospels (Matt. 3:17; 17:5; Mark 9:7; Luke 9:35) most likely reflect connections that were drawn in the early church between

---

17. Also note Zech. 9:11, which speaks of "the blood of *My* covenant with you" in reference to freedom from exile/bondage.

Jesus and the Davidic king as expressed in Ps. 2:7 (Acts 13:33). But one should not miss that this same relational agreement is extended to the community that followed Jesus, as evidenced in 2 Cor. 6:18. Although Jesus and his community are treated as fulfilling the Davidic covenant, there is a sense in which this fulfillment extends beyond the original expectations of that earlier relational agreement, with Jesus combining in his person both the human royal ruling from Zion and also the divine king (Ps. 2; Rom. 1:1–4). The NT, thus, envisions not only a new Sinai covenant but also a new Davidic covenant.

And this "new" dimension to the relational agreement should also be extended to the other major relational agreements found in the OT, including the priestly covenant with Aaron, which the book of Hebrews sees Jesus fulfilling and transcending in his priestly role (Heb. 5:6, 10; 6:20; 7:11, 17) and sacrificial act in the heavenly tabernacle (Heb. 9:11–14; cf. 8:1–2; 9:24). His priestly status clearly transcends that of the first priestly covenant with Aaron (e.g., Heb. 7:11). As with the Davidic covenant, so also the priestly covenant extends to the entire community that bears Christ's name: Heb. 13:15; 1 Pet. 2:5; cf. 1 Pet. 2:9; Rev. 1:6.

Similarly, the relational agreement between Yahweh and Abraham/ Sarah is taken up in the NT and connected with both Jesus (Luke 1:54–55, 72–73; Gal. 3:16–17; cf. Matt. 1:1) and the Christian community (Gal. 3:29). Here again there is "newness" in these connections to the relational agreement between Yahweh and Abraham/Sarah, or at least an increase in level of fulfillment that was never realized in the OT, especially in terms of the particularity of the seed promised to Abraham/Sarah (seed that would bring salvation through faith) and the universality of the seed in the blessing of all nations (Gal. 3:29; cf. 3:8–9).

Creation and Creed in the New Testament

As with the OT, our three creedal rhythms as found in the NT are dominated by the goal of creating a redeemed community. The creational dimension not only is evident but is treated as the goal of the redemption.

First of all, Jesus is clearly identified as the one who created and sustains the universe (see 1 Cor. 8:6; Heb. 1:2). John 1 presents Jesus as the "Word," a subtle allusion to the depiction of creation in Gen. 1, in which God speaks the world into existence. Furthermore, the opening words of John 1, "in the beginning," are designed to bring to mind the opening words of Gen. 1. This link is made explicit in 1:3 as John writes: "All things came into being through him, and apart from him nothing came into being that has come into being" (cf. 1:10). Paul identifies Jesus not only as the creator but also as the sustainer of the universe, the one in whom "all things hold together" (Col. 1:16–17). The Gospel of John ends with another allusion to the creation accounts in Genesis, this time to the creation of humanity in Gen. 2. In one of Jesus's appearances to his disciples after his resurrection, we are told that Jesus "breathed on them and said to them, 'Receive the Holy Spirit'" (20:22). This echoes Yahweh's act of creation in Gen. 2:7, in which, after forming the human from the dust of the ground, Yahweh "breathed into his nostrils the breath of life; and the human became a living being." This clearly links the redemptive work of Christ to creation, showing that his redemption is designed to produce a new humanity. Similarly, the apostle Paul refers to those who are "in Christ" as "a new creation" (2 Cor. 5:17).

Second, alongside references to Jesus as creator we find Jesus identified as the new humanity. This is evident in Paul's articulation of Jesus Christ as the second Adam (Rom. 5; 1 Cor. 15:22, 45) but also of Jesus Christ as made in "the image of God" (2 Cor. 4:4; Col. 1:15). Jesus thus fuses together both creator and creature and through this ushers in a redemption that transforms the creation.

Third, as creator and firstborn of the new creation, Jesus renews in his people the image of God (Col. 3:10) as he makes them also "a new creation" (2 Cor. 5:17). Romans 8 reveals that through Christ people are "conformed to the image of His Son, so that He would be the firstborn among many siblings" (Rom. 8:29). And as Christians receive the life associated with the Spirit of God, Christians as children of God signal to all the cosmos that the new creation has begun in and through Christ (8:19–25). In this we see how redemption in Christ has significant implications for the entire cosmos.

It is not surprising, then, that as we come to the end of the Bible we find a picture of re-creation, through motifs drawn from the garden, depicting a new heaven and new earth, a new Eden in Rev. 21–22. These are reminders of the destination of the gospel, that is, transformation of all creation as well as transformation of all humanity to their proper place as vice-regents over creation.

Conclusion

This evidence from the NT reveals crucial intersections between OT and NT theology. The theological emphases on Yahweh as redeemer and creator with their rhythms in the narrative, character, and relational creeds are not only echoed in the NT but continued and brought to a climax in and through Jesus and his community. It is the impact of this theology on the faith and life of this community to which we turn in the final chapter.

8

Taking the Old Testament Pulse in the Christian Life

To this point in our examination of the heartbeat of OT theology we have described the theological rhythms that reflect the core revelation and confession of God in the OT. We have also described how these rhythms can be discerned within the NT. In light of the dominance of these theological expressions in the OT and their clear continuation and further development in the NT, we now consider the impact of this truth on church, culture, and creation today.[1]

1. I am carefully trying to avoid the language of description versus prescription, that is, the hermeneutical approach that drives a wedge between "what the text meant" and "what the text means." Of course, I have been sensitive to the historical distance between the ancient text and our contemporary context. But I have also not treated these texts in merely anthropocentric and atheological ways. As I lay out in the appendix below, there are some key presuppositions about the nature of the Scriptures that I think are essential to my approach to Biblical Theology. In particular, the authoritative and relevant, as well as cohesive and accumulative, character of the Scriptures underlies this entire project. See further the helpful reminder of the theological character of the Scriptures and its impact on our hermeneutic in Green, *Practicing Theological Interpretation*.

Considering the impact of OT theology on our contemporary context has not been welcomed by all. On the one side are those who see the OT as the dark backdrop against which we can see the brilliance of the NT, a view that can be traced throughout all ages of church history. The OT, however, was clearly Christian Scripture for the early church, as evidenced by its ubiquitous use in the NT and the writings of the church for the past two millennia.

On the other side are those who do not embrace the OT or any Scripture as authoritative for their lives. These people treat with suspicion those who embrace a religious view of Scripture, convinced that such a view will lead to a coloring of one's interpretation, partly because the text will be seen as containing a certain inherent quality (inspired) and therefore certain types of analysis will be deemed inappropriate and partly because the possibilities of the text will not be explored because they will be deemed irrelevant to the believing community. The ultimate context of these ancient texts, however, is a canonical context that demands a certain reading strategy. Although within the canon one finds a plethora of genres (law, narrative, poetry, prophecy, wisdom, apocalyptic), each demanding sensitivity to their literary difference, these various literary types have been gathered into a canonical collection. This demands sensitivity to the impact of their new context on the reading strategy because of the ultimate generic context of authoritative Scripture, which captures the imagination, demands obedience, and shapes the values of the receiving community.

With this in mind we seek now to ascertain how these streams of OT theology address the believing community today, and in particular I will focus on my own evangelical faith tradition. I hope that the heartbeat we have felt throughout the OT and the NT will also be felt in our lives and the communities, cultures, and creation that constitute our context of life.

The Narrative Rhythm of the Christian Life

The redemptive story can be discerned in the earliest formulations of faith by the church. For instance, the Apostles' Creed encapsulates Christian faith in the following words:

I believe in God, the Father Almighty,
the Maker of heaven and earth,
and in Jesus Christ, His only Son, our Lord:
Who was conceived by the Holy Ghost,
born of the virgin Mary,
suffered under Pontius Pilate,
was crucified, dead, and buried;
He descended into hell.
The third day He arose again from the dead;
He ascended into heaven,
and sitteth on the right hand of God the Father Almighty;
from thence He shall come to judge the quick and the dead.
I believe in the Holy Ghost;
the holy catholic church;
the communion of saints;
the forgiveness of sins;
the resurrection of the body;
and the life everlasting.

The redemptive story of Jesus Christ dominates this early creed, not surprising in light of the importance of the redemptive acts of God in both the OT and the NT. This redemptive story is also important to the later Nicene Creed, although there is a progressive lessening of its dominance as time progresses, as the Athanasian Creed shows.

Certainly the redemptive story has captured the imagination of Protestantism in general from its roots in the Reformation, especially in its battle against medieval soteriology, and later in Protestant evangelicalism, especially in its battle against liberal depictions of Jesus as social justice prophet. The early Protestant rhetoric was clear: salvation through faith in Christ's death and resurrection, not through works. The later evangelical rhetoric was just as clear: Jesus came as atoning sacrifice for personal salvation, not as mere moral teacher for social transformation. However, living today in the wake of these two Protestant reactions, the evangelical church has jeopardized their appreciation of the redemptive story.

Losing the Story

Heirs of the Protestant Reformation's reaction to medieval liturgical abuses, the evangelical church has abandoned the important weekly liturgical rhythm of rehearsing the mighty acts of God in Christ through the Lord's Supper. Filling this void has been a greater focus on the proclamation of the written Word, an important and necessary aspect in the Reformation. However, there is no need to juxtapose these two important components of communal celebration. Marva Dawn has highlighted the importance of the liturgy of the Mass in contemporary Catholic communal life in her book *Reaching Out without Dumbing Down: A Theology of Worship for the Turn-of-the-Century Culture*. She writes:

> Catholic campus chaplain Michael Hunt has surveyed student participants for many years and asserts that, when asked why they attend mass, they almost unanimously respond, "God." Since Catholics don't "publish sermon topics or emphasize guest speakers" and "the music is often very routine," there is "little ambiguity about the point of the mass. It is God."[2]

And we should add: ". . . and God's redemptive actions." The power of the weekly celebration of the Lord's Supper is that it keeps the redemptive work of God in Christ front and center in the believing community.

Similar to the loss of this weekly rhythm has been the loss of the yearly rhythm of the Christian year within the evangelical tradition.[3] The Christian year was designed to rehearse the redemptive story throughout every year of the life of the Christian community. The church took their lead from the ancient Israelite festal schedule, during which redemptive history was rehearsed. It is significant that Passover was intertwined with the Passion of Christ in the Gospel texts, as the Christ event now fulfills the key role of the exodus event in the new covenant, and the cup and bread of the old covenant Passover redemption are now the new cup and bread of the new covenant Passion redemption. Such calendars are helpful rhythms reminding the community of the grand story of redemption.

---

2. Dawn, *Reaching Out without Dumbing Down*, 94.

3. On one level, we do have a "liturgical year" within North American evangelicalism, but it is an odd amalgamation of the "sacred" and the "secular": Valentine's Day, Easter, Mother's Day, Memorial Day (USA), Father's Day, National Day (i.e., Canada Day or US Independence Day), Thanksgiving, Remembrance Day (Canada), and Christmas.

Another legacy of the Protestant reaction to medieval abuses is the individualistic tone of evangelical theology. In response to the church's focus on salvation through the church, its services, and its structures, the Reformers emphasized the doctrine of election and predestination. Through this they showed that God is not restricted to the abusive structures of the church but rather works immediately on the hearts and minds of the elect. This theological "end run" around the medieval ecclesiastical structure was an important part of the Reformation and appropriate criticism of a church that needed renewal. However, its lasting legacy in the Protestant tradition in general and the evangelical stream in particular is a dominant individualism in matters spiritual.

The narrative creed in OT theology reminds us that salvation is defined in communal rather than individual terms. God saves and transforms a community in order to bring transformation and salvation to the entire cosmos. This is intimated from the outset in God's promises to Abraham, promises that spoke of the creation of an entire nation through whom the nations of the earth would be blessed. These same promises are communicated to the church in the NT, and through this new humanity God will transform the cultures of our world.

While the first two issues arose from the general Protestant reaction to the medieval church, this third issue has arisen from the particular evangelical reaction to mainline Protestant liberalism. Liberalism's attack against the veracity of the Bible on historical grounds led to evangelical defense of the Bible's historicity. This apologetic agenda is not entirely inappropriate, for often the liberal agenda was only masking antisupernatural assumptions. However, in defending the "historical" context lying behind the ancient text, evangelicals lost their appreciation and at times even the content of the story itself. This was foreshadowed by the late nineteenth-century Canadian Presbyterian William Caven as he called for a balance in theological education:

> All topics of the nature of Introduction must be regarded as subsidiary to the unfolding of the contents of Scripture—to its faithful interpretation. . . . It must therefore be important that the theological teacher

should handle Introduction in due subordination to the study of the actual contents of the Word of God.[4]

In the years following Caven's statement, the evangelical church would lose its emphasis on these "actual contents" in their defense of the text and in doing so de-emphasize the glorious redemptive story so essential to the message of OT and NT theology.

The final threat to evangelical appreciation of the redemptive story is the propensity of Western culture toward pragmatism. From homiletics professors to seminar leaders, the conventional wisdom in the evangelical church is that great preaching is *relevant* preaching. It is preaching that connects with people in *practical* ways. While ethical formation is certainly an important part of evangelical proclamation,[5] evangelical preachers find it difficult to meet together *merely* to celebrate and rehearse the story of redemption. Preachers in the evangelical tradition need to be released from the pressure of relevance to proclaim and celebrate the transforming story of redemption.

These trends in evangelical worship and proclamation are not easily reversed, but unless addressed the redemptive story so central to biblical revelation is in danger of extinction.

Power of Story

The narrative creed reminds us that God's great acts of salvation in the past are *foundational for our faith*. Christian faith is intertwined with historical reality. God has intervened in human history and worked salvation for his people. This was essential to faith for OT believers as well as those believers who have experienced the fullness of this redemptive history in Christ. Paul makes this clear in 1 Cor. 15:14, 17, where he points to a key event in the NT narrative creed (resurrection) as essential for Christian faith: "if Christ has not been raised, then our preaching is vain, your faith also is vain . . . if Christ has not been raised, your faith is worthless; you are still in your sins." This is what motivated Luke to write his Gospel: "so

4. Caven, *Christ's Teaching*, 262.
5. See my vision for redemptive-historical and redemptive-ethical interpretation and proclamation of the OT in Boda, *Haggai, Zechariah*, 63–65.

that you may know the exact truth about the things you have been taught" (Luke 1:4). And it is why 1 John emphasizes the historical reality of Christ's life in its introduction:

> What was from the beginning, what we have heard, what we have seen with our eyes, what we have looked at and touched with our hands, concerning the Word of Life—and the life was manifested, and we have seen and testify and proclaim to you the eternal life which was with the Father and was manifested to us—what we have seen and heard we proclaim to you also, so that you too may have fellowship with us; and indeed our fellowship is with the Father, and with his Son Jesus Christ. (1 John 1:1–3)

As believers we place our faith in a God who has entered into our broken world personally and provided concrete salvation, not in a God who is distant and abstract (deism) or impersonal and intrinsic (pantheism). He is the transcendent One who immanently enters our world to rescue us and offer us life. The narrative of God's past action on our behalf prompts our response of worship to the One who has saved us.

The narrative creed also reminds us that God's great acts of salvation in the past are *foundational for our faithfulness*. The narrative creed was regularly used to motivate God's people to remain committed to God's agenda on earth as they recited not only God's disciplinary actions from the past but also his covenant loyalty to his people. The declaration "I am Yahweh your God, who brought you out of the land of Egypt, out of the house of slavery" served as the foundation for the call to the core ethic of the OT: the Decalogue (Exod. 20:2//Deut. 5:6). The narrative creed so key to biblical revelation and confession motivates us to live faithfully as participants within this grand historical drama.

The narrative creed is not, however, oriented merely toward the past but also *toward the future*. The story in both the OT and the NT remains open ended.[6] Each recitation does not view the past as the

---

6. Goldingay makes the important point that the OT story does not really end with closure: it remains open ended, which explains why it is appropriate for the church to trace the continuation of the story; cf. Goldingay, *Israel's Gospel*, 33. Of

end of redemptive history but the foundation for a story that extends into the future, offering hope that the trajectory that has begun will continue into eternity. This future trajectory can be seen in the way the various canonical sections end, especially the Torah, Former Prophets, and Latter Prophets. The same can be said for the NT witness, which ends with Revelation and the hope for a transformed heavens and earth. We are thus a people oriented toward the future even as we recite the past. And this future orientation prompts a level of hope that is virtually unknown in a world that sees no future.

And so also we *place ourselves in our present* into this redemptive story. Christ made this clear in Luke 24:47–49 as he included the proclamation of the gospel in the narrative creed, reminding the disciples that their work would continue redemptive history: every kingdom expansion in word or deed through the Holy Spirit's power was part of this redemptive history, and the disciples were invited to place their own lives in the present into the story of God. This brings significance to the everyday lives of those who follow Christ: their lives matter because they are part of an epic story that began millennia ago and is heading toward the climax of human history.

In our proclamation of the gospel we have the opportunity to *embed others within this story*. The book of Acts shows us the consistent reflex of the early church not only to orient their audiences to God's redemptive story but also to show how that story intersects with their own lives and destinies. This has great potential within a postfoundational cultural context. OT theology reminds us that deep within the structure of biblical revelation is a story to be rehearsed rather than an argument to be debated. For a world skeptical of propositional truth, the story in OT theology offers an ancient means to communicate the gospel in twenty-first-century culture. This is why it is so important to rehearse this story without shame before a watching world. This rehearsal should celebrate the ways in which this ancient story of redemption has intersected and transformed the stories of communities and individuals in our world today.

---

course, as Goldingay notes, this is true also of the NT: "The biblical story comprises a beginning and a development but no end."

Finally, the narrative creed prompts us to *reflect on our own salvation history*, which is, as we saw above, a continuation of the salvation history that began in the OT. A key rhythm in our walk with God should be deep and careful reflection on God's particular acts of salvation within our lives. By this I am referring not only to written, spoken, or prayed reflections on an individual life but also to reflection on the life of a family or community of faith. These kinds of rehearsals of faith are by nature intergenerational, taking a long view of the salvation acts of God throughout generations. Such reflections need not be candy-coated, focusing only on the positive acts of salvation. They should be as brutally honest as the expressions of the narrative creed we find in the OT and the NT, especially when it comes to the human component in the story. Sometimes the narrative creed presents an exclusively positive depiction of human participation in the story, and this focuses attention on God's grace and provides a vision of what is possible to experience relationally with God. But more often than not we see honest rehearsal of human failure, which shows that sin is not to be hidden or ignored but rather voiced so that we can move forward in our own particular experience of salvation history.

The Character Rhythm of the Christian Life

Creedal expressions within Protestantism have been dominated by careful articulations of the character of God.[7] Drawing from the early church creeds, these Protestant creeds focused initial attention on the nature of God as triune. The Reformation's deep concern with soteriology and ecclesiology is reflected in their creeds (e.g., Augsburg Confession, Belgic Confession, Westminster Confession of Faith). Early Fundamentalist creeds were especially concerned with the nature of Scripture, but creeds focused on the nature of God, soteriology, and ecclesiology were also set forth. The nature of God has thus always been key to the theological tradition of Protestantism, even if the focus was more abstract than what we have seen in the character creed tradition in the OT and the NT. The character

7. See the wise introduction to the Christian creeds and their enduring relevance in Demarest, "Contemporary Relevance."

rhythm in the OT redemptive-theological beat reminds the church of its role in preserving not only the revelation of God's actions but also the revelation of his character.[8]

Losing the Character

We are in danger of losing such theological reflection due to several pressures within and on the church. The power of story, which makes the narrative creed so attractive within our present postfoundational culture, may be the greatest threat to the character creed. In a culture that has rejected the rationalism and abstraction that dominated the modern era, theology expressed in terms of God's attributes no longer has the impact or attraction it once did.

If pragmatism threatens the narrative stream of theological expression, it crushes the character stream. From the perspective of a worldview looking for practical advice, recitation of the character of God appears irrelevant and certainly unhelpful for living life.

One key threat to the character creed arises from our postmodern secular condition, that is, that we live within a cultural context that has largely abandoned conceptions of God as a being who personally interacts with us. Yes, there is an increase in spirituality, but this is a spirituality with humanity at its center, an opportunity to find inner peace through tapping into a divine principle that appears to be little more than the human spirit. A God with transcendent personality is no longer considered part of postmodern secular daily experience. Ironically, the same may be said for many conservative evangelicals who, fearful of charismatic excesses, adopt a virtually deistic approach to the Christian life, defending a God who worked miraculously in the biblical past but no longer works that way in the present. This condition is also a reality for many who have been catechized as children within the Christian faith, memorizing statements about the divine nature but never coming to personal and living relationship with God. We have seen how important regular encounters with the person of God are to the development of the character creed, a development that moves the character creed from mere revelation to actual appropriation in confession. As we experience God in particular acts

---

8. Note esp. Cole, "Exodus 34."

in everyday life, we begin to perceive a pattern of divine behavior that ultimately leads to recognition and identification of his key attributes. But if God is no longer a transcendent personality actively interacting with our daily lives, it is difficult to embrace the character creed and its claims.

Not only is the mode by which God's redemptive character is communicated under threat in the present era, but certain elements of that character are deemed not only irrelevant but actually immoral. The depiction of a God who judges, punishes, and disciplines has largely been rejected as evidence of an earlier phase of human development. The rise of a militant and violent Islam has only complicated matters. And certain streams of Christian fundamentalism, with their judgmental mode of challenging cultural shifts, have not always been helpful. In the process, a significant dimension of the character creed has been deemed unworthy of postmodern sensibilities and explained away through either developmental approaches to the biblical canon (that was the OT, but now we have the NT) or abandonment of the biblical vision of God entirely. The disciplinary character of the biblical God, however, cannot be so easily dismissed, not only because it is a consistent emphasis in both OT and NT (it is not that God was angry in the OT era and then one day woke up happy) but more so because this disciplinary dimension has the potential to provide hope.

Power of Character

A little book by Sinclair Ferguson titled *A Heart for God* significantly influenced my choice of seminary for my MDiv.[9] This book, akin to A. W. Tozer's classic *Knowledge of the Holy*,[10] presented the attributes of God according to traditional Christian systematic theology but with a view to their relevance to the Christian life. Sinclair emphasized what he called "personal knowledge" of God: for him, reflection on God's character was always connected with a relationship. Such an approach to the character of God is inescapable in the character creed tradition we have highlighted in the OT and

9. Ferguson, *Heart for God.*
10. Tozer, *Knowledge of the Holy.*

the NT. God is revealed and confessed as one defined by relationship with humanity.

The character creed tradition in OT theology has great potential to capture the imagination of the present generation, especially if one is able to express this character creed tradition in terms of its expression in the Bible. We have discovered how this tradition brings considerable attention to the more abstract ontological characteristics of God, expressed through nouns and adjectives. But we have been careful to note that the functional characteristics of God, expressed through nonperfective verbs (e.g., participles), bind this tradition together. These verbal expressions focus attention on the concrete (yet typical) acts of God in relationship to humanity. Even what are called "abstract ontological characteristics of God" in the character creed are qualities that are dominantly relational, that is, expressed in a way that is not abstracted from human encounter. Therefore, we hear of God's merciful compassion or jealous passion, qualities that assume relationship. The old gospel song that says "I praise you, not for what you've done, but for who you are" would make little sense to the people of God in antiquity, since what God has done—whether his particular actions in the history of redemption or the typical actions in the experience of Israel that prompted the character creed tradition—is always in focus in OT theology.

The character creed tradition also reminds us that we are called to reflect on God's mercy as well as his discipline. Some Christian traditions are more focused on the one or the other, but both are essential in the characterization of God in both OT and NT. The present generation more than any other needs to experience God as a divine parent in whom they will find security through his tender mercy as well as his measured discipline. Both of these aspects of God are expressions of his love, as the NT so clearly teaches (compare Rom. 5:5, 8; 8:37–39 with Heb. 12:5–6; Rev. 3:19). Crying "Abba, Father" means that we are open to all aspects of God's parenting and trust him implicitly with our development as his children. As with any human parent, the early phases of development demand experiencing and understanding tender mercy. These early phases lay a foundation for later phases when discipline and correction are sorely needed. In this way, a Christian needs to fully grasp the tender mercy of God in the early phase of their Christian walk, but there will come a time when measured discipline is necessary, and this discipline will only make sense to those secure in God's parental mercy.

The character creed tradition also alerts us to watch for God's regular activity in our lives that has shaped and will shape us theologically. As we trace—through either personal reflection and journaling or public testimony and praise—God's working in our lives, we are developing theologically, identifying those typical activities of God that point to his character and characteristic behavior. This is both an individual and a communal exercise. Sharing one's interactions with God with one another is thus more than just a bonding experience; it is a theologically enriching experience because it develops one another, as well as the community as a whole, theologically. When we hear weekly that God has healed someone in our church, we eventually come to the realization that God is "healer," and we actually go about expecting it in our lives.

Our present generation needs to experience God on a consistent basis and will not relate to this God based merely on past testimony, even if in storied form. The character creed, with its participial descriptions of God's typical actions, has the potential to lead this generation to embrace this kind of God. It is not the one-off testimony but the consistent encounter with God day in and day out that has the potential to break through to a generation hardened by religious claims.

And honest descriptions of God are also key. As I noted above, the character creed speaks of God's tender mercy and measured justice. We may be tempted to accentuate the former and avoid the latter, but this is a mistake. While there is a desperate need for people to experience God's tender mercy, they do not need to be protected from God's measured discipline. For a generation that has not known tough love, the latter actually provides the security of One who cares about their safety and is willing to tell them when there is a threat to their existence. And to a community that values fairness and has seen and experienced injustice, it grants a God who cares deeply about justice and will not allow those who have abused the vulnerable to remain unaccountable.

The diversity of expression we have found in the character creed, ranging from God's mercy to God's holiness, and the diversity of contexts in which it occurs, ranging from those needing mercy to those needing warning, reminds us that God's character is always appropriate to its context. By appropriate I mean appropriate according to God's design for any given moment. We also must be careful not to place God in our proverbial box, realizing that he does not always act in the way we had hoped or expected (so Jonah).

The Relational Rhythm of the Christian Life

Covenant has played a significant role within the Reformed tradition of the Reformation (esp. by John Calvin, the later Westminster divines, and Jonathan Edwards), with the focus on covenants presumed to have taken place within the Trinity (covenant of redemption) prior to creation and then between God and humanity in the garden of Eden (covenant of works, covenant of grace). This final covenant in particular was considered foundational for the covenants we have identified in the canon. Of course, this focus on covenant relationship was also important to other streams in the Reformation. The law/grace dichotomy in Lutheranism emphasizes the contrast between the old (Sinai) and new covenants, with the former structured according to law and the latter according to grace. In modern evangelicalism the debate between covenantal versus dispensational theologians was largely focused on a common interest in the biblical covenants and their relationship to one another. This evidence reminds Protestants that covenant relationship has always been key to the articulation of faith.

Losing the Relationship

There is a danger, however, of losing sight of the importance of covenant relationship in the present age. Reformed descriptions of covenant relationship are not as strongly linked to the biblical expression of the covenants, emphasizing covenants that are not explicitly mentioned in the biblical witness, which appear to be speculative and abstract. At the same time, Lutheran covenantal dichotomy is not sustainable, since grace is certainly a key principle in the OT (as we have seen in the character creed), and law is an enduring principle in the NT (the law of Christ).

There are also broader trends within culture (both Christian and secular) that threaten the importance of covenant relationships. We are witness to a general rejection of accountability in relationships today. Whether in the prevalence of common-law marriage, the lack of submission to leaders, or the absence of commitment to church or denomination, we have become a generation that wants relationship without strings attached. Thus, the kind of relational agreements we find in the Bible are foreign to most in modern society.

Power of Relationship

While accountability is under attack today, relationship is not. Front and center in the relational creed is the opportunity for a relationship with God. While story has its danger of being relegated to past irrelevance, and character has its danger of being relegated to abstract irrelevance, relationship provides an opportunity for people to engage God intimately, to capture a vision for encounter with their Creator.

The relational creed is consistently expressed in family terms as God invites humanity into a kin relationship, whether understood as parent/child or husband/wife. Paul's prayer in Eph. 3:14 (NIV) expresses this so nicely when he begins, "I kneel before the Father, from whom every family in heaven and on earth derives its name." God's parental relationship extends to all families, and he invites us to recognize and join his family and the identity that comes from the life of that eternal clan. Of course, this is challenging within our postindustrial culture, with so little family cohesion and such great family dysfunction. People are no longer embedded in their families of origin and often live at significant distances from one another. On the one hand, we may then think that avoiding a familial framework would be the most seeker sensitive. But on the other hand, if humanity is wired for family, then a familial framework is the best way to reach out to the God-shaped craving within their hearts. The relational creed is perfectly suited then for the needs of the present generation since it describes God in passionate pursuit of relationship with his people and even identifying himself in terms of relationship ("I am your God," "I am your Father") even as he extends relational identity to all those who will respond ("you are my people," "you are my sons and daughters").

But with relationship comes accountability, and by placing relationship as the core value, as it is in the relational creed, accountability is given a context and makes sense. Accountability expresses the greater security of this relationship, and such security produces an environment conducive to greater intimacy. God's initiative toward humanity sends the message that God pursues us passionately. And the reciprocity of this relationship allays any fears that this is a one-sided relationship of duty to a distant God. He makes commitments alongside our own.

This relationship is not merely individualistic. There is a communal character to the relational creeds, especially those established with Abraham/Sarah and with Israel at Sinai. When we think of relationships we think of a single individual with another single individual, but these relational creeds seek to establish connections with whole communities. This means that relational identity is found with God in community, which only increases the relational quality of this understanding and experience of God. There is also an intergenerational character to the relational creeds. They envision relationships not merely with one particular generation but with multiple generations. Modern society often thinks in terms of an individual living in a particular era, but this is quite foreign to the biblical worldview, where God makes a covenant with a generation not yet born (Deut. 5:3), where we are surrounded by a cloud of witnesses (Heb. 11–12), and where Levi encounters Melchizedek (Heb. 7:9–10). Our relational identity is thus with a God who spans the generations, and we experience connectedness with the saints in all ages.

Creation, the Creeds, and the Christian Life

Our consideration of the revelation and confession of God in the OT and the NT has demonstrated that redemption of God's people has a broader goal: the transformation of all creation. And thus the revelation and confession of God as creator is essential to both OT and NT theology. This creational focus is evident in the early Apostles'

Creed, cited above, which begins with the confession "I believe in God, the Father Almighty, the Maker of heaven and earth" before reciting the redemptive acts of God in Jesus Christ. This emphasis on God as creator is expanded in the later Nicene Creed to include all members of the Trinity:

> I believe in one God, the Father Almighty, Maker of heaven and earth, and of all things visible and invisible.
>
> And in one Lord Jesus Christ, the only-begotten Son of God, begotten of the Father before all worlds; God of God, Light of Light, very God of very God; begotten, not made, being of one substance with the Father, by whom all things were made . . .
>
> And I believe in the Holy Ghost, the Lord and Giver of Life . . .

Christian theology has always emphasized God as creator and sustainer of the universe, distinct from yet personally active within creation. As the seraphim cried in their praise of Yahweh in Isa. 6: "Holy, holy, holy, is Yahweh of hosts. The whole earth is full of His glory" (6:3).

Losing the Creational Dimension

We live in a world with many needs and one in which many have not heard and been touched by the gospel, so it is not surprising that the church focuses its attention on communicating in word and deed the redemptive actions, character, and relational identity of God. However, we run the danger of treating redemption as an end in itself, and especially of making the church the exclusive context for the redeemed to function.

We also live in a world that has great interest in the natural environment. For some this interest is motivated by a secular concern for nature and the ecological crisis caused by human technology.[11] This secular concern may look beyond the lifetime of those involved, but the concern is for future generations of humanity. For others

---

11. Note, e.g., Suzuki and Taylor, *Big Picture Reflections*; Jackson, *Consulting the Genius of the Place*; with thanks to Alexander Breitkopf.

this interest in the natural environment has a spiritual dimension, often understood within the framework of pantheistic religion or indigenous spiritualities.[12] These secular and spiritual trends within broader culture, which are responses based on the image of God within all humanity, have certainly alerted society to the present crisis. However, their approaches to the issue have eliminated the personal, transcendent, interactive God of biblical revelation and faith.

Power of the Creational Dimension

The creational dimension in Biblical Theology reminds us that redemption is a means to another end, that is, to restore humanity to their place as image bearers of God who enjoy relationship with God and all creation. This means that the gospel ultimately has cultural and creational implications.[13] The church should not be fleeing from creation and culture but rather engaging it, transforming it, and leading the way as image bearers of God. As restored image bearers, we are enabled to enjoy God's creation and explore human culture as no one else on earth.

Often, Christians focus on redemptive purposes and activities because the majority of the Bible is about redemption. But we need to distinguish between majority of text and ultimate purpose. That is, while redemption is essential for the realization of creational transformation, it is creational transformation that is the main purpose. The Great Commission of Matt. 28 serves the creational mandate of Gen. 1:26–28. The spread of the gospel has as its destiny the transformation of the cosmos—all creation—and church leaders need to work out the implications of this for their ministries. The redeemed are not in the church only to staff Great Commission efforts, but leaders are there to equip their people to fulfill the creational mandate to be transformative influencers within culture

12. Livingstone, *PaGaian Cosmology*; Taylor, *Dark Green Religion*; Sponsel, *Spiritual Ecology*; Vaughan-Lee, *Spiritual Ecology*.

13. See esp. Wolters, *Creation Regained*. See also the seminal article by White, "Historical Roots"; Bouma-Prediger, *For the Beauty of the Earth*; Deane-Drummond, *Eco-Theology*; Swoboda, *Tongues and Trees*. The papal encyclical *Laudato Si'*, produced by Pope Francis, provides a helpful Christian response to creation care.

and creation since, according to Rom. 8, the creation, both physical and social, groans for the revelation of the children of God, who have been redeemed.

What does it mean to engage God as a God who created and sustains creation and is seeking to redeem creation? Worshiping God, whose very attributes are seen in creation (Rom. 1), means living a life of wonder in creation: stopping as a child to look and take in and feel our place in creation and through this experience the wonder of God our creator and sustainer. If general revelation is truly from God, then we need to be prompted to worship in creation, and we can actually lead people to encounter God in new ways that will lead to covenant relationship with this God through encounters with creation. It means that we look to him in dependence: returning to that dependence that those who care for the land have. It means that we take seriously the fact that the death and resurrection of Christ are indeed creational acts: death was introduced in the garden, and that death is placed on Christ, and his resurrection is proof that the death principle is defeated. These redemptive-historical acts have creational implications for us: we begin to live in a new reality as new creations. The firstfruit of this new creation reality is healing, so we can look to God to delight us with this because of the cross and resurrection. There is an opportunity to live as the redeemed "already" even as we look to the "not yet." And we have the opportunity to point people to the creator God and the impact of our worship of the creator and sustainer God on our everyday interactions with creation.

Part of creation is, of course, humanity in all of its diversity. Thus, first and foremost we encounter God in human creativity and culture. God's touch is mediated to us through culture because of the image that he has placed within humanity. Thus, we can appreciate the echoes of God's character in artwork, music, architecture, literature, and the diverse expressions of culture across the world. Of course, one cannot deny the fallenness of humanity, and one must realize that not all expressions nor all aspects of particular expressions fully reflect the glory of the God in whose image humanity has been made. But there are opportunities to worship God in the midst of our human cultures as we see God at work through even those who have not yet entrusted their lives into the hands of their creator and redeemer. In their role as vice-regents of God on earth redeemed humans have the opportunity to reflect God's cultural care and discipline. Christians have the opportunity to showcase the best of cultural expressions and advances—from art to science, from business to entertainment, from education to government. At times this will involve building Christian institutions of excellence like King David and Solomon, but at others it will entail involvement within non-Christian institutions much more like Joseph, Daniel, Esther, Ezra, and Nehemiah. This engagement in cultural activities beyond the church walls is not subsidiary work, but rather a reflection of the heart of the God who creates and sustains the universe.

Conclusion

And so we come to the end of our journey of discovery of the heartbeat of OT theology. At the outset I made clear that my focus was on God, who is the main topic of "theology" and the fear of whom is the foundation from which we can speak of theology and the goal of all our theological reflection. It is this God of the Scriptures who continues to interact with humanity and all creation who is our only hope and so our only object of trust and worship.

In his classic *The Supremacy of God in Preaching*, John Piper calls contemporary preachers to theocentric preaching:

> My burden is to plead for the supremacy of God in preaching—that the dominant note of preaching be the freedom of God's sovereign grace, the unifying theme be the zeal that God has for his own glory, the grand object of preaching be the infinite and inexhaustible being of God, and the pervasive atmosphere of preaching be the holiness of God. Then when preaching takes up the ordinary things of life—family, job, leisure, friendships; or the crises of our day—AIDS, divorce, addictions, depression, abuses, poverty, hunger, and, worst of all, unreached peoples of the world, these matters are not only taken up. They are taken all the way up to God.[14]

14. Piper, *Supremacy*, 20.

Piper reminds us of what Packer said about hearing the great British preacher D. Martyn Lloyd-Jones during 1948 and 1949. Lloyd-Jones brought Packer "more of a sense of God than any other";[15] furthermore,

> Is this what people take away from worship nowadays—a sense of God, a note of sovereign grace, a theme of panoramic glory, the grand object of God's infinite being? Do they enter for one hour in the week . . . into an atmosphere of the holiness of God which leaves its aroma upon their lives all week long?[16]

This is my hope as you near the conclusion of this exploration of the heartbeat of OT theology and as these insights shape your reading of the Scriptures as well as your relationship with the Triune God. My hope is that you will have encountered and will continue to experience a sense of God as you feel the rhythms of God's actions, character, and relational identity in Scripture and life.

But we are not quite finished with this exploration. Let me conclude this volume with an invitation to respond to this God we have encountered in the OT and to whom the NT witnesses.

15. Ibid., 21.
16. Ibid., 22.

9

Postscript

Calling for Response

FACE TO FACE (EXOD. 33:7–11)

About February each year, the final unbroken New Year's resolution begins to unravel before our very eyes. With the ball in Times Square plummeting toward the ground we whispered that pledge to finally read through the entire Bible in the coming year. But that was then, and that promise of under two months ago seems now years away. The first phase was fine: Genesis, with its great stories of the heroes of the faith. By February we've now polished off the first half of Exodus ahead of schedule. But as we round the corner into the second half of Exodus, we're knee deep in golden pomegranates, almond blossoms, coverings of porpoise skins, and a few cherubim for good measure.

A sermon on the occasion of the Hayward Lectureship, Manning Memorial Chapel, Acadia Divinity College, Acadia University, Wednesday, October 23, 2013.

And with the greatly feared Leviticus but a mirage in the distance, let alone Malachi and Revelation, our steps are faltering and with them our final New Year's resolution.

For many the book of Exodus is, as its name indicates, a book about the exciting rescue of Israel from slavery in Egypt, but that is really only the first fifteen chapters. The bulk of the book is focused on how this rescuing God established covenant relationship with his rescued people and did so at that mountain named Horeb, that is, Sinai.

The majority of the book is focused on how the great and awesome God, that One who inspired such fear in Israel's heart as thunder cracked, lightning flashed, and dark clouds swirled about, would descend from the heights of Mount Sinai into the center of the camp, how the holy creator God of Exod. 19–20 would tabernacle himself among the created people in the tented community below. Here is what happens in the closing moments of the book:

> Then the cloud covered the tent of meeting, and the glory of the Lord filled the tabernacle. Moses was not able to enter the tent of meeting because the cloud had settled on it, and the glory of the Lord filled the tabernacle. (40:34–35)

Those tabernacle details that threaten our New Year's resolution highlight the precautions needed to enable the holy creator to live among his people, not just for his own sake, but more importantly for the sake of those people.

The necessity of these precautions is made clear at the very center of the tabernacle instruction, for just as Moses has received the final instructions for building the tabernacle and is about to commence its construction, the people offend their holy creator in unspeakable ways. They make for themselves a golden calf and break the foundational commandments of the Decalogue. Exodus 33:7–11 is plucked from the center of this dramatic core. As the destiny of the people and the future of their relationship with God are threatened, we are reminded of Moses's regular practice as they camped in the wilderness.

For a moment the narrator of Exodus suspends action. In the midst of all the confusion that swirls about the scene of the golden calf incident come these five short verses. They are kind of a "by the way," but we'll soon see how this "by the way" is what made all the difference between life and death. The eternal balance of an entire community of faith hung on this "Oh, by the way . . ."

A Separated and Intimate Place (Exod. 33:7, 11)

Verse 7 relays Moses's regular practice:

> Moses used to take the tent and pitch it
>   outside the camp, a good distance from the camp,
>   and he called it the tent of meeting.
>   And everyone who sought the Lord
>   would go out to the tent of meeting
>   which was outside the camp

This "tent of meeting" was a separated place, a spot outside the camp, a good distance away. It was separate most likely to preserve its holy status, a place where Yahweh could come down from the mountain above, near the community with which he had made covenant relationship. A distance away because of the danger of contamination by a potentially common and unclean community, due to their sin or finite status. But it was also an intimate place, a tent of "meeting" or "assembly," a place of connection between God and humanity (see also Exod. 29:42–43). And there people could seek Yahweh. What was true for the whole community in verse 7 was particularly true for Moses, who along with Joshua, his aide, was the only one allowed inside the tent of meeting. Verse 11 focuses again on the intimacy of this tent of meeting:

> Thus the LORD used to speak with Moses face to face, just as a person speaks to their friend. When Moses returned to the camp, his servant Joshua, the son of Nun, a young man, would not depart from the tent.

This tent of meeting was a place that verse 7 says was for "seeking the Lord." It was a place to speak to God, to communicate to him one's deepest longings and questions, inquiring after his will. Moses pitched the tent so that he could speak to the Lord. But this tent was also pitched so that the Lord could speak to Moses, as verse 11 notes: "the LORD used to speak with Moses." This was a place of intimacy, a place where a human being talked with the almighty creator of the universe and could listen to this same mighty king's words to him, as if conversing with a friend: as verse 11 says: פָּנִים אֶל־פָּנִים—face to face. This tent was a separated place of intimacy.

A Public Place (Exod. 33:8–10)

While separate and intimate, the tent of meeting was not a private place (vv. 8–10); it was very much on display before the entire people.

> And it came about, whenever Moses went out to the tent, that all the people would arise and stand, each at the entrance of their tent, and gaze after Moses until he entered the tent. Whenever Moses entered the tent, the pillar of cloud would descend and stand at the entrance of the tent; and the LORD would speak with Moses. When all the people saw the pillar of cloud standing at the entrance of the tent, all the people would arise and worship, each at the entrance of their tent.

> *People* would arise, stand at the entrance of their tents and gaze at **Moses** entering the tent (v. 8).

> *Yahweh* would descend, stand at the entrance of the tent and speak with **Moses** (v. 9).

> As *people* saw *Yahweh* at the entrance of the tent, they would arise and worship at the entrance of their tent (v. 10).

Here we see triangulation: Moses entering the tent, Yahweh standing at the entrance of the tent, the people standing at the entrance to their tents. This reveals that what happened in this separated tent of intimacy had everything to do with the people who stood at the entrance to their tents.

Thus, right in the middle of this entire section of Exod. 32–34, those chapters that describe Israel's abandonment of their God in their worship of the golden calf, when all hope of God "tabernacling" among his people seems to be lost because of the golden calf incident and even the very choice of Israel as God's people is called in question, in the midst of this tragic story when all seems to be lost, we find this recollection of God's pattern with Moses prior to the building of the tabernacle, the practice of God descending and meeting with Moses for now outside the camp.

Here we see Moses experiencing God's presence before the people. The nation knew him as one who experienced the presence of God, and this prompted them to worship God. And little did they know how indebted they were to this one who had cultivated a friendship with God. It is most fascinating that at their time of deepest need, it was not their penitence or remorse that saved them before this holy God; it was the intercessory plea of their mediator, Moses.

Invitations to This Separated, Intimate, and Public Place

First, we need to hear this text in light of the coming of Christ, the Son who surpasses this servant (Heb. 3:5–6), the one through whom we have access to God directly and whose intercession on our behalf saves us from punishment.

As I freeze the frame of this drama, I cannot help but identify where I want to be: I want to be in the tent of meeting, not standing at a distance watching and gazing but inside the tent of meeting, at least like Joshua, but who am I? For those standing on the outside of that tent in Exod. 33, there was no chance of the kind of friendship that Moses enjoyed except through Jesus, the one sent by God the Father, who not only entered into the very presence of God (Heb. 9) but who also, according to Heb. 4, invites us all to approach the same throne of grace with confidence so that we may receive mercy and find grace to help us in our time of need. By his death, resurrection, and ascension, Jesus has opened the way for all to leave their tents at a distance and to enter the tent of meeting, to be able to speak to God and listen to his voice in intimate friendship through a new connection created by the indwelling Spirit.

When I was a child growing up in Regina, Saskatchewan, my father worked at a seminary as a dean. The president who had hired him lived six houses away at what was known as the "president's house." In our minds it was as grand as the prime minister's house in Ottawa, but in reality it was merely a 1950s bungalow. This was the nicest house on campus. It even had a garage next door. But few adults on campus knew what the faculty kids knew. At the top of this garage was a loft. Built into the rafters of the president's garage was a secret lodging, a place for kids to escape the life of the college. It was there that three neighborhood boys began a secret club: the sons of two faculty members and their mutual friend from school who lived down the street. This secret club was an expression of their friendship: a place where they could say anything they wanted, where no one else could listen. Shortly after the beginning of this club, my brother Matt informed me of the "new club" and invited me along for the next meeting. I can remember the exciting walk down to their club loft, up the ladder, and finally into the "tent of meeting." What a rush . . . what power. I was on top of the world! But then began the whispering, and I watched as the three were caught up in intense conversation in the opposite corner of the loft from me. Moments later an upset brother Matt announced he was leaving. Any club that couldn't include little brother Mark was no club for him. And his two friends were livid and would not give in. First Matt and then I climbed down the ladder and marched home. The loft represented a place of intimacy, a place where conversation between friends could occur face to face, and yet it became a place of exclusivity, a place that could not allow for the little brother. Exodus 33 does reveal a level of exclusivity to this place of encounter between God and his people. Through Jesus the tent of meeting is opened up wide for access by humanity. This is the wondrous message of the gospel.

Through Exod. 33 God calls you through faith in Christ into intimate relationship with him, into a place of vulnerability where you express yourself to God and hear his word to you. Thus, the scene in Exod. 33 is a scene of intimacy, of friendship between God and humans, and forces us to take seriously what Christ has done for us. Through him we are able to enter into the presence of a holy God with no questions asked or whispers in the corner. This mediator, Jesus Christ, ushers us into God's presence, and we are accepted without reservation.

While this text points us to the glorious opportunity of the gospel, it also provides insight for us into an enduring role for leaders within God's kingdom, those whose leadership must be typified by the experience of the presence of God, one that will prompt others to seek God and bring blessing on an entire community of faith.

For pastors, the pressure today is to be those who "do," whether one is known as a great preacher or a sensitive counselor. But what if as pastors and leaders we were known as those who experience the manifest presence of God? I remember when, as a youth pastor in my early twenties, I would stumble into the church office midmorning after a late night out with teens at various activities. Passing through the main church door into the church office to retrieve my mail or any phone messages, I remember a few times seeing the curtains of a key mentor in my life slightly open and peering inside his pastoral office. I remember the sight of him with hands clasped and Bible open, communing with God, and I remember pausing for a moment and feeling a slight sense of jealousy. I think this was a holy jealousy, a jealousy to pursue God in deeper ways and to experience his manifest presence in my life as I commune with him. I can see that in the gaze of the people toward the tent of meeting, and that is what I still long for each day of my life.

For professors, the pressure today is to be those who "know," that she or he is known as the world's expert on this or that topic or text or method. But at midcareer I am being challenged in this area. As Sinclair Ferguson stressed in theology class so many years ago, I must constantly ask the question, "Do I have a *personal* knowledge of God?" This question expresses the desire that as professor I may be known as one who experiences the manifest presence of God in my life.

As the millennium approached in late 1999, John Piper addressed the annual meeting of the Evangelical Theological Society on the topic "Preparing a New Generation of Pastors and Missionaries for the New Millennium." I will never forget his address, identified by him as a sermon since he was a preacher at heart. During the speech, Piper spoke to a typical issue in any seminary class on hermeneutics, that is, the inevitable moment in the semester when someone wiser and older than the professor would ask the question that was on many people's hearts: "What is the role of prayer in biblical interpretation?" And Piper noted that the professor would reply that this was the foundation of all that is taught at the seminary. But then Piper paused and defined "foundation" for us: that basement of a house that is largely a place for storing tools and junk and after the door is closed, forgotten. And then he said: "God doesn't like being taken for granted," a reminder that struck close to our hearts if we were honest that evening. A few years later my now late colleague Clark Pinnock placed a note in my mailbox with the following reflection:

> *A thought for the day from Clark:*
>   *The cloud of unknowing states that by love can God be gotten and holden, but by thought and understanding, never. Even when the understanding fails, love keeps us close to the flame of the Spirit.*

This word from Clark, someone vastly different theologically from John Piper, was an important reminder of the importance of intimacy with God for those in our generation who reflect theologically.

My prayer today is that we will all long for the kind of intimacy with God showcased at that ancient tent of meeting and realize its importance to those with whom and before whom we walk.

Appendix

Biblical Theology and the Old Testament

Biblical Theology is an essential discipline for releasing the Bible's theological treasures for the contemporary church, academy, and culture. By placing the message of individual biblical passages into the broader context of the message of the Bible as a whole, the biblical witness has greater potential to speak to the theological issues of the day. Christian biblical-theological analysis is by nature trinitarian, not because it finds within the OT a fully developed trinitarian theology, but rather because it takes seriously the inseparable link between the OT and the NT. The presupposition that makes the message of the OT relevant for Christians is that the trinitarian God of the NT is the same creator and redeemer revealed in the OT. And Christian interpretation of the OT revelation not only begins with this trinitarian foundation but also takes into account that Jesus Christ represents the climax of the redemptive and revelatory activity of

---

This appendix is a revised version of an article originally published in *Hearing the Old Testament: Listening for God's Address*, ed. Craig Bartholomew and David Beldman, 122–53 (Grand Rapids: Eerdmans, 2012) and is used by permission of the Wm. B. Eerdmans Publishing Company. I have included it in this volume because it provides my theological hermeneutic for the biblical-theological reflection represented in this book as well as guidance for how to responsibly interpret the Scriptures with sensitivity to Biblical Theology.

this trinitarian God and that the Holy Spirit is responsible to form a covenant community with the potential to transform all of creation. A Christian Biblical Theology will thus place the message of the OT within these broader redemptive and revelatory realities.

Definition

Biblical Theology is a theological discipline that reflects on the theological witness of the Bible in its own idiom with attention to both its unity and diversity.[1] In partnership with sound exegetical theology, understood as disciplined reading of the individual pericopae and books of the Bible that seeks after their theological messages to their historical audiences, Biblical Theology discerns macrolevel connections within the biblical witness without ignoring disconnections between these various texts and books. The emphasis in Biblical Theology is on the messages of whole books, canonical sections, entire Testaments, and the Bible as a collection and the connections between individual texts and these larger literary-canonical units. By ascertaining "inner points of coherence and development,"[2] it seeks for a "comprehensive presentation of the theological character of the biblical literature."[3]

History of Biblical Theology

Biblical Theology as an Academic Discipline

The origin of Biblical Theology as an academic discipline is often traced to Johann Philipp Gabler's late eighteenth-century inaugural lecture whose title in English (delivered originally in Latin) is "Address

1. See esp. Bartholomew, who defines Biblical Theology as "the attempt to grasp the Scripture in its totality according to its own, rather than imposed, categories" ("Biblical Theology and Biblical Interpretation," 1). Also Goldsworthy: "Biblical theology as a discipline presupposes that the Bible, notwithstanding its great diversity, has some kind of perceptible unity" ("Relationship," 81); cf. Hasel, *Basic Issues*, 112; Barr, *Concept*, 7.
2. Hafemann, "Biblical Theology," 16.
3. Miller, "Theology from Below," 3.

about the Correct Distinction of Biblical and Dogmatic Theology and the Right Definition of their Goals."[4] As the title suggests, Gabler's concern was to delineate two theological disciplines within the academy. Such "correct distinction" was needed, according to Gabler, so that the Bible could be understood as a document with a message rooted in history before it was used for constructing normative and abstract theology for the church. Gabler, however, was not innovative in expressing this concern to distinguish between the theology of the Bible and that of the church.[5] In the century before Gabler's appearance, pietistic leaders such as Spener had already outlined an agenda to distinguish between biblical and dogmatic theology in order to stimulate a biblically based godliness within the church by avoiding the theological controversies of their day. Interestingly, in the period before Gabler, scholars such as Semler had called for a similar distinction but for a different reason, that is, in order that rationalist scholars might be freed from the constraints of creed in order to investigate Scripture. Unlike these earlier movements, however, Gabler saw an enduring role for systematic theology but argued that Biblical Theology served as a foundation for dogmatics.

These two interpretive streams that gave rise to the delineation of Biblical Theology as an academic discipline separate from systematic theology can be discerned throughout the centuries after Gabler's address.[6] Some, rejecting the divine origins of the Scriptures, used this freedom from systematic theology to investigate the message of the Bible as history of religion, while others, embracing the Bible's divine origins, used this freedom to highlight the theological content of the Bible using its own idiom and categories. Most produced works that represented a combination of these two streams, but at times the discipline would be dominated by one or the other hermeneutical agenda. The late nineteenth and early twentieth centuries were dominated by the agenda of history of religion. However, the second half of the twentieth century witnessed a resurgence of Biblical Theology as a discipline with a variety of approaches represented among the

4. Sandys-Wunsch and Eldredge, "J. P. Gabler."
5. See further Helmer, "Biblical Theology."
6. On this history, see Hasel, *Basic Issues*; Helmer, "Biblical Theology"; Martens, "Old Testament Theology."

many books produced in this period. In general one can see how the reigning hermeneutical approach of a particular decade influenced the various approaches to Biblical Theology, ranging from traditio-historical, to literary, to ideological approaches.

In general the history of the academic discipline of Biblical Theology has been driven by an agenda to bring greater focus to the meaning of the biblical texts within their original context, without regard to the alignment of that meaning with creedal expressions of the Christian faith associated with systematic theology. On the positive side, this agenda has provided theological space for the biblical texts in general and the OT in particular to speak in their own idiom without concern to force the meaning of these texts into one's own or community's confessional theological grid. There is great opportunity for the biblical text to reassert its authority within ecclesial communities if this discipline takes this as its ultimate goal. On the negative side, however, this agenda has often led to an abandonment of the theological enterprise, resisting any contribution to creedal development and ethical formation. Furthermore, distinguishing Biblical Theology from systematics has led to an abandonment of creedal direction for understanding the character of the texts in view and often an embrace of an atheological and at times antitheological hermeneutic for reading Scripture. It is essential at this present juncture in history to bring Biblical Theology back into conversation with systematic theology.[7] These two disciplines should be practiced in dialogue, each functioning as foundational for the other. Biblical Theology needs some measure of systematic theology to function,[8] but systematic theology must be based on and constantly challenged by Biblical Theology.[9]

---

7. Christine Helmer speaks of Biblical Theology as "a bridge-building discipline" that "is wonderfully poised to address both the historical and the theological dimensions of biblical texts"; Helmer, "Introduction," 7. See further Ollenburger, ed., *So Wide a Sea*; Carson, "Systematic Theology and Biblical Theology"; Vanhoozer, "Exegesis and Hermeneutics"; Green and Turner, *Between Two Horizons*; Bartholomew et al., eds., *Out of Egypt*, esp. the essays by Hart (341–51) and Reno (385–408); Welker and Schweitzer, eds., *Reconsidering the Boundaries*.

8. See Goldsworthy, "'Thus Says the Lord.'"

9. See esp. the interaction between Warfield and Vos, noted in Lints, "Two Theologies or One?"

Biblical Theology as a Scriptural Impulse

While the origin of the academic discipline of Biblical Theology is often traced to the eighteenth century, it is important to note that the ecclesial practice of Biblical Theology is evident in the church from its inception, inherited from its Jewish forebears.[10] One discovers within the OT itself various reflective summaries and rehearsals of what lay at the core of Israelite theology. Of note in this regard are the theological rehearsals of the core of Yahweh's character of mercy and justice revealed in Exod. 34:6–7 (Num. 14:18; Joel 2:13; Jon. 4:2; Nah. 1:2–3; Pss. 86:5, 15; 103:8; 111:4; 112:4; 145:8; Neh. 1:5; 9:17, 19, 27, 28, 31; cf. Exod. 20:5–6; Deut. 5:9–10; 7:9–10; Jer. 32:18),[11] the theological depictions of the story of Yahweh's acts of mercy and justice reflected in what von Rad called the "*kleine geschichtliche Credo*" ("short historical creed," Deut. 6:20–24; 26:5–9; Josh. 24:2b–13; 1 Sam. 12; Pss. 78; 105; 106; 135; 136; Neh. 9; Jer. 32; Ezek. 20),[12] and the theological declarations of Yahweh's relational identity with Israel and humanity in the covenantal tradition of the Bible (Gen. 9:9–17; 17:7–8; Exod. 6:7; Lev. 11:45; 22:33; 25:38; 26:12; Num. 15:41; Deut. 29:12 [29:13 Eng.]; 2 Sam. 7:14; Jer. 31:33).[13]

A good portion of Deuteronomy is presented as a rehearsal of the core narrative and legal traditions found in Exodus–Numbers. Zechariah 1:3 and 7:7–10 offer what is explicitly called a summary of the "earlier prophets," that is, "Return to Me, that I may return to you." The book of Chronicles represents a re-presentation of the earlier inscripturated traditions in Genesis–2 Kings in both its genealogies and its narratives. Besides such summaries and large-scale re-presentations there is significant evidence of innerbiblical allusion and exegesis within individual verses and passages, especially in later books in the OT.

---

10. For evidence of this ecclesial practice in the postapostolic era, see Bartholomew, "Listening for God's Address."

11. See Scharbert, "Formgeschichte und Exegese"; Dentan, "Literary Affinities"; Trible, *God and the Rhetoric of Sexuality*, 1–5; Fishbane, *Biblical Interpretation*, 335–50; Clark, *Hesed*, 247–52.

12. See von Rad, *Gesammelte Studien*, 9–86; von Rad, *Problem of the Hexateuch*, 1–78; von Rad, *Old Testament Theology*; cf. G. Wright, *God Who Acts*, 11, 13.

13. See Williamson, *Sealed with an Oath*; Hahn, *Kinship by Covenant*; Gentry and Wellum, *Kingdom through Covenant*.

This impulse toward theological reflection and summary, re-presentation, and innerbiblical allusion can be discerned as well within the NT. The theological rehearsal of Yahweh's character can be discerned at several points (e.g., John 1:14–18; 1 John 1:9; Rev. 19:11–12). So also the practice of theologically rehearsing the story of Yahweh's acts of mercy before and through Jesus continues in the NT witness (e.g., Acts 2:14–36; 3:12–26; 7:2–53; 13:16–41; Heb. 11–12; cf. Luke 24:45–47; Phil. 2:6–11; 1 Cor. 15:1–11; 1 Tim. 3:16). In the Gospels Jesus provides a theological summary of what he calls the Law and the Prophets (Matt. 7:12; 22:37–40), a reference to the Hebrew Scriptures. After Jesus's resurrection, Luke tells us that Jesus was concerned to trace the revelation of himself throughout the OT canon (Luke 24:27, 44). The witness of the early church found in the epistles follows this practice of Christ. This witness consists largely of theological reflection on key broader themes (for example, the theme of sin in Rom. 3:9–20 or that of faith in Heb. 11) and ubiquitous in-nerbiblical citation and allusion to earlier OT passages.[14]

What we see then in the foundational canonical witness of the church is a consistent impulse toward summary, re-presentation, and innerbiblical allusion,[15] which represents reflection on the theology of the Bible in whole or in part, and this is what we can identify as Biblical Theology.

Hermeneutical Agenda for Biblical Theology

Since the impulse for Biblical Theology can be discerned in both the OT and the NT, it is helpful to look more carefully at the hermeneutical framework that underlies this impulse in the biblical witness. For Christian Biblical Theology that means giving attention to NT texts that describe the character of revelation and express a more

14. See Beale and Carson, *Commentary*.

15. See further the thoughtful voicing by Möller ("Nature and Genre," 55) on the typical concern of biblical scholars that theological abstraction is by nature "alien to the biblical material" and even "inherently distorting and unsuitable." He is wise to challenge the second concern by noting that academic discourse itself is by nature "second-level discourse." My review here questions the first concern that somehow denies the biblical tradition the ability to engage in theological abstraction.

global agenda for reading the biblical witness. It will be seen that NT reflection on the character of this revelation is not foreign to the OT but rather an echo of the OT's witness to its own character. These characteristics of OT Scripture must impact the discipline of Biblical Theology.[16]

Character of Old Testament Revelation

COMMUNICATIVE

First, the NT clearly teaches the communicative character of OT revelation, claiming that in the OT God has successfully communicated himself to humanity, not only through the oral proclamations of his servants (e.g., Heb. 1:1–3; 2 Pet. 1:21) but also through the scriptural witness formed from such proclamations (e.g., Acts 1:16). This echoes the witness of the OT itself, which consistently portrays a God seeking to communicate with humanity, whether that is directly or through the agency of created figures (e.g., Exod. 20:1–18). That this communication was successful is obvious in the rehearsal of these words within the biblical text itself.

This communicative character of revelation makes possible a Biblical Theology rather than merely a history of religion. The Scriptures represent God's successful communication of his character and ways. Such a claim also runs counter to the prevailing notions of a post-foundational age in which the efficacy of all communication is called into question. But attempts to thwart the communicative efficacy of the biblical witness run against the grain of the text. This claim that God speaks successfully through Scripture encourages us to approach Scripture to hear God's address. It is not merely the record of human attempts at religion, but a theological witness of divine origin.

INCARNATIONAL

Second, the NT teaches the incarnational character of revelation, that is, that divine revelation is communicated through created means.[17]

16. For a superb review of the key hermeneutical issues related to developing biblical-theological method, see Sailhamer, *Introduction to Old Testament Theology.*
17. See, e.g., Goldsworthy, "Relationship," 82–83; Enns, *Inspiration and Incarnation*; Sparks, *God's Word in Human Words.* Some have expressed concerns over

This is seen in the foundational oral proclamations of the prophets, through whom God spoke "at many times and in various ways" (Heb. 1:1). This revelation was delivered at times through a fully human personality embedded within a particular era of history, as Acts 1:16 reminds us: "long ago through the mouth of David." Although "moved by the Holy Spirit," it was still "people" who "spoke from God" (2 Pet. 1:20–21). Even when communicated directly from God's mouth, this revelation was delivered by necessity through human language that is historically conditioned. That this is foundational for the character of Scripture is made clear in 2 Tim. 3:15–16, which reveals that the "human writings" (Scripture) are "God-breathed" and "holy." Such a view of revelation is not unique to the NT. The Torah and Latter Prophets in particular emphasize how divine words are delivered in human language and most often through human figures. Although contained in a physical book in human language, the people in Ezra's day respond to this book with reverence akin to that reserved for God himself (Neh. 8).

The incarnational nature of revelation reminds us that, although divine in origin and character, OT revelation is simultaneously fully human in its communicative form. This revelation is not presented in timeless form but rather is particularized to unique historical situations in languages and forms understandable to that audience. The divine dimension infuses unity and timelessness into this theological witness, and yet the human dimension simultaneously infuses it with diversity and time-boundedness. Attention then must be given to both of these dimensions, since they are inextricably linked. This will mean attention to the historical and literary aspects of texts without losing sight of their theological and spiritual aspects.

---

utilizing incarnation as a model for Scripture, especially because debates over incarnation were not originally focused on Scripture but rather on the nature of Christ, and links to incarnation can easily lead to bibliolatry (see a superb review in Chapman, "Reclaiming Inspiration"). However, one cannot deny a close relationship between revelation and incarnation in the NT witness (see Heb. 1:1–3), and, as is argued here, one cannot deny the simultaneous divine-human character of the Scriptures. The link to incarnation is not necessarily the first step toward bibliolatry any more than links between the relational character of the Trinity and the character of the church or the image of God in humanity are necessary steps toward deification of the church or humans.

One of the greatest challenges in the modern development of the discipline of Biblical Theology has been the tension between whether the discipline is concerned with reflection on the shape of the theology of the OT or delineation of the history of the religion depicted in the OT text. The former is typically considered a category more closely associated with the belief that the OT is a record of divine revelation, while the latter is associated with the assumption that the OT is a record of human religion.[18]

That these two categories need not be juxtaposed is seen in the explicit assertions in the NT that divine revelation is communicated through human means, that is, through human personalities (e.g., 2 Pet. 1:10; Heb. 1:1–3) and human language (e.g., 2 Tim. 3:14–17). While all forms of revelation found within the biblical canon are communicated through an inseparable and mysterious combination of divine origin and human agency, the expression of some forms is dominated more by the divine side of this combination with explicit claims of divine origin, while the expression of others is dominated more by the human side with explicit claims of human origin.[19] For instance, the Psalms in the main constitute human speech to God, although at times one does hear God's direct voice. And yet early on this was considered a normative text (some would suggest Ps. 1 makes this clear),[20] that is, these human speeches were considered as revelatory and normative, prompted by God to shape faith and reveal God. Furthermore, prophecy in the main constitutes divine speech to humanity, although it is clear that this divine speech is being delivered through human characters who speak about Yahweh and even challenge this God at times. However, all such text is recognized as normative. For those reflecting on the character of these various forms of revelation, there is no difference in authority. All forms are considered Scripture, authoritative for the development of Christian doctrine.

18. See such juxtaposition in VanGemeren, *Interpreting the Prophetic Word*, 19–27; also Waltke and Yu, *Old Testament Theology*, 30, 64–65, although I understand that much depends on the definition of "religion" (cf. 1 Tim. 5:4; James 1:26–27).

19. On this, see further Goldingay, *Theological Diversity*.

20. See McCann and McCann, *Theological Introduction*; cf. Childs, *Introduction*, 513–14.

In this way one can truly speak of the OT as simultaneously a depiction of the faith of Israel and the revelation of God. It is both religion (if understood as a record of human interaction with God) and revelation (a record of divine interaction with humanity). At all times revelation takes the form of human religious interaction, whether that is in the prophets' records of their revelatory experiences or the psalmists' rehearsals of the cry of their souls. The biblical witness, and so by extension Biblical Theology, has both anthropological and theological dimensions that are inseparable, and in that way it is incarnational.

INSCRIPTURATED

Third, the NT teaches the inscripturated character of revelation, that while the oral proclamations of those ancient servants who delivered God's word to generations long past are considered divine revelation, such revelation is now preserved in the inscripturated witness. Even 2 Pet. 1:20–21, which focuses on how men and women moved by the Holy Spirit spoke orally within their generation, identifies such proclamations as "prophecy *of Scripture*," that is, prioritizing its inscripturated form (cf. Rom. 16:26). According to 2 Tim. 3:15–16, this inscripturated form is "God-breathed" and "holy," and according to Rom. 15:4, it is authoritative to instruct. For this reason we find throughout the NT nearly monotonous employment of the phrase "it is written" and the term "Scripture(s)" to introduce uses of the OT as authoritative witness for theological reflection. This fixation with the text is reflected in Christ's statement that "not one jot or tittle" would disappear from the Law (Matt. 5:18). At times Scripture takes on a life of its own as it functions as an active subject that Paul tells us foresaw God's future actions (e.g., Gal. 3:8).

Such focus on the inscripturated character of OT revelation is not restricted to the NT. It is evident throughout the Torah (Exod. 31:18; 34:28–29; 40:20; Lev. 26:46; 27:34; Num. 36:13; Deut. 31:9). The Former Prophets emphasize the "book of the law" both at the outset in Joshua's commission (Josh. 1:8) and near its close in the renewal under Josiah in 2 Kings 22. The Latter Prophets allude to the written character of their prophetic witness at several points:

Isa. 8:1–2, 16; Jer. 36:1–32; 51:59–64; Ezek. 2:9–3:3; 43:10–11; Nah. 1:1. The Writings witness to this at several points, especially Psalms (Pss. 1; 19; 119) and Neh. 8–9, which highlight the Torah as authoritative inscripturated tradition, and Dan. 9:2, which highlights the importance of the Prophets as authoritative inscripturated tradition (cf. Dan. 7:1).

The inscripturated nature of revelation reminds the biblical theologian that the source of biblical-theological reflection is first and foremost the biblical text in its canonical form.[21] It is not the experiences or traditions that underlie the biblical text but rather the biblical text itself that is the defined corpus in view.[22]

A biblical-theological reading of the OT means primarily a reading of the text within its broader canonical witness. It seeks to discern how an individual text or biblical book contributes to and participates within the Bible's broader theological witness. One may understand this broader witness in various ways, but for it to be truly a *biblical-theological* reading it must focus on the witness of the canonical text, that final literary form of books that now constitute an authoritative collection.[23] This then lays bare a key presupposition for biblical-theological study of the OT: the form of the text in view as well as the context for reading this text is identified as canonical within a community of faith. Christian communities have identified the form and extent of this text in a variety of ways, but this is the text in view in Biblical Theology.

This means that precanonical forms or collections of the text are not the primary context in view in Biblical Theology, although they may provide insights into understanding that final form. For instance, an understanding of the theology of the Deuteronomic or Priestly traditions, often seen as underlying the Torah or Former Prophets, may be helpful for delineating the meaning of particular words or concepts, but ultimately Biblical Theology is focused on the meaning of the text in its present form. Thus, while some may

21. See Childs, *Old Testament Theology*, 6.
22. See further Hafemann, "Biblical Theology," 20.
23. On the implications of the canonical shape of the biblical text for Biblical Theology, see Dempster, "Canon and Old Testament Interpretation"; as well as Bartholomew et al., eds., *Canon and Biblical Interpretation*; and Boda, *Severe Mercy*.

use the identification of tradition streams within a text as a point of departure for insights into those traditions, the direction is reversed in Biblical Theology: insights from those tradition streams may be helpful for interpreting the text in its present shape. So also non-canonical forms or collections of the text are not the primary focus in a biblical-theological reading of the text. In the end the theology in view is that articulated by texts within the canon under consideration. This, however, does not render noncanonical texts irrelevant for the interpretation of the text in its present shape. For those embracing what is often called the Protestant canon (excluding the Apocrypha), the broader ancient Near Eastern, Mediterranean, and Second Temple Jewish literary traditions may provide insights into the meaning of the biblical text, but the interpretation of the biblical text drives the agenda of Biblical Theology.

Authoritative

Fourth, the NT teaches the authoritative character of this written revelation. The inscripturated revelation is normative for the believer and not to be resisted. It is for this reason that Timothy was to give close attention to the Scriptures (2 Tim. 3:14–17), that Paul could declare that he believes all that agrees with the Law and is written in the Prophets (Acts 24:14), and that Jesus prohibited the breaking of the Law's demands (Matt. 5:17–20). That the OT was treated as normative for the early church is seen in the constant appeals to the OT for the establishment of foundational doctrine (e.g., Rom. 3:9–18).

This focus on the authoritative character of written revelation is seen also in the OT itself. Passages such as 2 Kings 22 reveal how the book of the Torah was considered authoritative, prompting a penitential response and adherence to its demands communicated in written form. It is the book of the law that brackets the book of Joshua and is connected with the demand for obedience to Yahweh (Josh. 1:8; 24:25–26). It is the book of the law raised high in Neh. 8 that prompts the submissive and penitential responses of the people and the reading of the book of the law that precedes the penitential response of the community in Neh. 9 (see vv. 3–4).

The authoritative nature of revelation reminds biblical theologians that the agenda of Biblical Theology is not merely descriptive, simply describing what the Bible states, but is also prescriptive, responding to the Scriptures as a normative voice that speaks to interpreters and makes demands on them even as they articulate its claims. The Bible "draws its readers into transformative discourse" and challenges their "willingness . . . to inhabit Scripture's own story."[24] As a result, Biblical Theology "aims at Christian formation rather than historical reconstruction."[25] Biblical Theology is not just a foundation for systematic theology or ethics but functions as a key component of these two normative disciplines. Furthermore, those engaged in Biblical Theology are, because of the authoritative character of the canon they study, involved in these other theological exercises.

Cumulative and Progressive

Fifth, the NT teaches the cumulative and progressive character of revelation.[26] After highlighting the revelation of God through the prophets "long ago," Heb. 1:1–3 is careful to note that "in these last days" revelation has now come "in His Son." Second Peter 1:19–21 speaks of "the prophetic message *made* more sure." Revelation must not be treated as all on the same level but rather as what accumulates and progresses in significance as history unfolds. Such a view of revelation is evident in the OT witness itself as Yahweh transcends his self-revelation to the patriarchs of Israel in Genesis by revealing himself in heightened ways through the exodus and Sinai accounts (Exod. 6:2–8; cf. 34:6–7).

The cumulative and progressive character of revelation helps the biblical theologian arrange and prioritize the variety and diversity of the biblical witness. It helps the biblical theologian deal with the diversity within the biblical witness not only in the historico-cultural particularity of the witness (see above, incarnational nature) but also in its historico-theological particularity. This highlights the

24. Green, "Scripture and Theology," 42.
25. Wall, "Canonical Context," 175.
26. The word "cumulative" reminds us that in the NT witness the progressive character of later phases of the biblical witness did not eliminate the enduring role of earlier phases of this witness, with thanks to Martens, "Reaching," 93–95.

need for sensitivity to the accumulation and progression of God's redemptive and revelatory acts throughout history. Redemption was not fully accomplished, nor was revelation fully disclosed, in a single moment in history. Rather, there was a progressive accomplishment of redemption and a progressive unfolding of revelation in history, and this explains some of the diversity within the Bible's theological witness.

The Cohesion of the Biblical Witness: Innerbiblical Use of Scripture

This hermeneutical agenda for Biblical Theology that arises from the self-witness of Scripture explains the ubiquitous interconnections between the various parts of the canon. The OT canon itself displays inner cohesion through the regular use of quotations, allusions, and echoes of earlier OT passages. This trend, which is observable in the OT, only increases in the NT.[27] It is important to take a closer look at this phenomenon of innerbiblical connectivity by examining how NT writers used the OT and how OT writers used other parts of the OT.[28] The biblical witness itself lays the foundation hermeneutically for Christian biblical theologians to follow as they seek to read the OT as Christian Scripture.[29]

If one were to speak of the various connections between the OT and the NT using the image of roads built between two distant locations, one could think of the different levels in the construction of a road, the different routes each road may take to its destination, and

27. See further Boda, *Haggai, Zechariah*, 48–65; Boda, *After God's Own Heart*. For an application of these insights and methodology to the book of Romans, see Boda, "Old Testament and Romans."

28. The realization that NT approaches to appropriating the OT can also be discerned in the OT itself calls into question the dismissal of these NT approaches by Goldingay, *Israel's Gospel*, 25–27.

29. In his earlier work, Childs proposed doing Biblical Theology based on the NT use of the OT but later abandoned this. Compare Childs, *Biblical Theology in Crisis*, with Childs, *Biblical Theology of the Old and New Testaments*, 76. The present chapter advocates a recovery of Childs's original project, although carefully nuanced to include a greater variety of ways that the biblical witness is interlinked (see the sections titled "Levels" and "Routes") and without restriction to the explicit links made in the biblical witness (see the section titled "Conclusion" below).

the place at which each road intersects on its way to the NT and the life of the church.

Levels

First, using the imagery of the building of roads (connections) between the OT and the NT, instances of the NT use of the OT can be discerned at several levels in the structure of the road. Some connections are obvious on the road's surface, painted in the pavement (explicit), while others are hidden below the surface in the road's deeper substructure (implicit). The most explicit cases are those that overtly claim connection with an OT expectation, event, or figure (e.g., Heb. 12:15–17: Esau) or where there is a formal citation of an OT passage in the NT (e.g., Acts 2:16–21: Joel 3:1–5 [2:28–31 Eng.]). The most implicit are those that assume a foundational OT theological theme (e.g., James 3: the tongue) or narrative structure (Matt. 11:5: Elisha tradition). Between these two extremes lies a range of levels of connection through allusions employing common vocabulary and imagery.[30] These various levels are not restricted to the NT use of the OT but are also displayed in the reuse of the OT within the OT itself.[31] One can find everything from overt connections (e.g., Hosea 11:1–4) and formal citations (e.g., Lev. 23:42 in Neh. 8:14) to implicit development of themes (e.g., Deuteronomic themes in Joshua–2 Kings) and narrative structures (e.g., Exod. 25–40 in 2 Chron. 1–10),[32] and all levels in between.

Routes

Second, because the NT speakers and writers connect their message to the OT does not mean that each part of the OT is related in an identical way to the NT. Some elements in the OT are related

30. One needs to be sensitive to the diversity of ways biblical texts reference other biblical texts, since, for example, as Kaiser notes, "the book of Revelation, which probably contains more Old Testament imagery and phrases than any other New Testament writing . . . does not contain a single formal quotation from the Old Testament!"; Kaiser, *Uses*, 3.

31. See Fishbane, *Biblical Interpretation*.

32. See Boda, "Legitimizing the Temple."

nearly directly to the NT, while others are transformed significantly. Returning to the analogy of roads connecting two locations, these ways of relating the message of the OT to the NT could be described as the variety of routes through which Christ and his early followers connected the witness of the OT with that of the NT.[33] Some of these routes are very direct and close (continuity), while others are very indirect and distant (discontinuity).

The Old Testament Initiates What the New Testament Continues

The closest and most direct route between the OT and the NT is the one in which *the OT initiates what the NT continues*. This route represents the greatest continuity between the Testaments. In Matt. 22:36–40 Jesus cites Deut. 6:5 and Lev. 19:18 and identifies them as the two greatest commandments on which hang the Law and the Prophets, that is, loving the Lord your God with all your heart, soul, and mind and loving your neighbor as yourself. Paul follows Christ in citing Lev. 19:18 in Rom. 13:8–10 as the foundation for Christian ethics. For Jesus and Paul these OT commandments had enduring relevance for the Christian community. Admittedly, there remains some element of discontinuity, since the fulfillment of this is possible only through the work of Christ and the Spirit (see below), but here the content of the law is identical, even though the process by which it is fulfilled has shifted (precisely as indicated in Jer. 31:31–34; Ezek. 36:26–27; cf. 2 Cor. 3:1–18; Heb. 8:7–12). Paul follows this route in Rom. 12:20 as he draws on Deut. 32:35 and Prov. 25:21, 22 to teach the church how to treat one's enemy. So also 1 Pet. 2:9–10 applies titles connected to Israel of old (Exod. 19:5–6; Hosea 1:8–9) to the church in order to teach believers how to walk within an often hostile world. At times the NT draws from the OT examples both positive (James 5:11, 17–18 = Job, Elijah) and negative (1 Cor. 10:6–14 = Israel in the wilderness) in order to encourage positive and discourage negative behavior. The emphasis in all these instances is on continuity.

33. On such a multiplex approach see Hasel, *Basic Issues*, 183; Baker, *Two Testaments*; cf. overview in Perrin, "Dialogic Conceptions." I am unconvinced by Dunn ("Problem," 182) that these are "superimposed paradigms."

This route between OT and NT can also be discerned in the OT itself. For example, one can see how legislation initiated in the Torah is carried on throughout the OT witness, whether it is shaping the renewal under Josiah (see close connections between Deuteronomy and 2 Kings 22–23) or the restoration in Ezra–Nehemiah (see references to the Torah in Ezra 3:2; 6:18; 7:6; Neh. 1:7, 8; 8:1, 14; 9:14; 10:29; 13:1).[34]

The Old Testament Falls Short of the New Testament That Surpasses It

The longest and most indirect route between the OT and the NT is the one in which *the OT falls short of the NT that surpasses it.* This route represents the greatest discontinuity between the Testaments. Passages that reflect this route include Gal. 3:23–25, which speaks of the function of the law to lead us to Christ, or Rom. 10:5, which cites Lev. 18:5 in order to describe a righteousness that comes through the law rather than through faith.[35] The NT makes much of the new covenant promises of Jeremiah, which spoke of the divine work of writing the law on the hearts of believers. The difference between old and new covenants was not the content of ethics but rather the mode by which this ethic would be realized. This route may also be discerned in Christ's statements in Matt. 5:21–22, where he first cites Exod. 20:13 ("Do not murder") and then challenges his followers not to disregard this law but to understand its spirit and eschew even anger and hatred toward one's brother or sister. This helps us understand Christ's statement that he did not come to abolish the law but to fulfill it (Matt. 5:17–20). The NT treatment of the ceremonial law (food, festal) is related to this category (e.g., Matt. 15:11; Mark 7:19; Acts 10:9–15; Rom. 14; Col. 2:16–17), but even so it is important to note that this was legitimate revelation that was operative for a time and thus does have theological significance as a revelatory witness as understood within its own phase of redemptive history (see Matt. 23:23; Luke 11:37–42).

34. On this phenomenon in the OT, see Fishbane, *Biblical Interpretation,* 91–277.
35. Of course, for Paul this did not eliminate the law as a source for the gospel, as the very next verses in Rom. 10:6–8 reveal, citing Deut. 30:14. Also, Paul did not eliminate the law as a key source for Christian ethics, as is obvious from passages such as Rom. 13:8–10; cf. Dunn, "Problem," 182.

The OT itself also reflects this route between OT and NT. The failure of the Sinai covenant and the prophetic agenda of repentance due to hardness of human hearts opens the way for the promise of a new covenantal approach (Jer. 31:30–33).[36] The failure of nondynastic leadership in the book of Judges leads to the rise of royal leadership (Judges–Samuel).[37]

The Old Testament Promises What Is Fulfilled in the New Testament

Within these two extremes of routes between the OT and the NT are a variety of routes with relatively similar directness and length, representing a balance between continuity and discontinuity. Some passages reveal that *the OT promises someone or something that is fulfilled in the NT*. This is one of the most common approaches taken by Christian interpreters. Thus, the OT promised a messianic royal figure, and that figure is identified as Jesus the Christ (e.g., Matt. 1:1; Rom. 1:2–3). The OT promised a new covenant, and Christ establishes this covenant through his redemptive acts (e.g., Luke 22:20; 1 Cor. 11:25; 2 Cor. 3:6; Heb. 8:8, 13; 9:15; 12:24). The OT promised a restoration community that would return from the nations and receive of the Spirit, and this community is identified with those Jewish festal pilgrims at Pentecost in Acts 2.

These promises of old are not always treated as fulfilled in a single figure. Thus, while the Abrahamic hope of seed (Gen. 12:7; 13:15; 24:7) is fulfilled in Israel (Exodus, Joshua) in the OT, Paul links it ultimately to the appearance of Jesus functioning as Israel in Gal. 3:16, and in Gal. 3:29 he links this hope to all those who "belong to Christ." The Davidic hope (2 Sam. 7:14) is considered fulfilled in Solomon (1 Kings 8:19) in the OT and in the NT in Jesus Christ (Heb. 1:5), and yet in 2 Cor. 6:18 the apostle Paul considers this Davidic hope fulfilled in the Christian community as a whole. The hope of an ultimate prophet (Deut. 34) is fulfilled in Christ (Acts 3:21–26), and yet the community that bears his name is identified as a prophetic community (Acts 2:17–21). While the Servant of Yahweh figure in

36. Cf. Boda, *Severe Mercy*.
37. Cf. Boda, "Judges," 14–16, 36–40.

Isaiah (Isa. 40–66) is linked to exilic Israel (e.g., Isa. 41:8–10; 42:18–19; 44:1–5), Jesus is identified as the fulfillment of this figure whose suffering would bring salvation for Israel (e.g., Matt. 8:17; Luke 22:37) and light to the gentiles (e.g., Luke 2:32), and yet the early church linked their own suffering to that of this Suffering Servant (1 Pet. 2:21–25) and considered the role of bringing light to the gentiles their own (Acts 13:46–48).

This route between OT and NT is seen in the OT itself, as already noted in relation to the hoped-for descendant(s) of Abraham and David above, as well as in Jeremiah's promised royal *Zemah* figure (traditionally, Branch, Jer. 23:5–7; 33:14–18), which is fulfilled in Zerubbabel (Zech. 3; 6:9–15).[38]

The Old Testament Is Re-actualized in the New Testament in Order to Complete It

Other passages reveal that *the OT is re-actualized in the NT in order to complete it*. Falling under this category is that approach referred to as "typology," which "seeks to discover a correspondence between people and events of the past and of the future or present."[39] Typological connections may exist between persons (Adam), institutions (sacrifices), offices (priesthood), events (exodus), actions (lifting up the bronze serpent), and things (tabernacle).[40] Thus, for example, the Gospel of John creates a close link between Jesus Christ and the tabernacle/temple in the OT. John 1:14 speaks of the Word "tabernacling" among humanity, and Jesus links his own body to the "temple" (John 2:19–22). This reveals that through the incarnation the manifest presence of God that filled the tabernacle/temple of old once again was made manifest on earth. Later in the Gospel of John the lifting up of Christ on the cross is connected to the lifting up of the bronze serpent in the wilderness in order to save the rebellious nation from death (John 3:14–15). Here the focus is not only on the action of lifting up but also on the common call to faith in Yahweh's provision for salvation.

38. Boda, "Oil, Crowns and Thrones."
39. Dockery, "Typological Exegesis," 166. Possibly the term "trajectory" is better than typology, cf. Motyer, "Two Testaments," 159.
40. See Weir, "Analogous Fulfillment," 68.

It is important to distinguish between typological exegesis and allegory. The key difference is that in typology the significance of the elements in the OT person, institution, office, event, action, or thing is derived from the function of those elements within their original context and phase of redemptive history.[41] Thus, typological exegesis does not justify linking anything red within a passage to the blood of Christ, or any wood within a passage to the cross of Christ. However, if that red or wood element functions similarly to the blood or cross of Christ, it may be legitimate in typological exegesis.

In typology the OT is being relived in the NT. There are instances where the mission of figures in the OT is brought to completion by the mission of NT figures. This explains the connection between Jesus and Israel using Hosea 11 in Matt. 2:13–15. Hosea 11 does not promise a future figure but rather traces God's past work for Israel. For the Gospel writer, Jesus's journey during his infancy into and out of Egypt represents a reliving of the experience of Israel. In contrast to Israel, however, Jesus would fully realize all of Yahweh's hopes for Israel. This category may make sense of many passages in the NT that identify in Christ a fulfillment of a hope that appears to have been fulfilled already in the OT. For instance, while the Immanuel prophecy in Isa. 7–8 appears to be linked to an event in Isaiah's own generation, the Gospel of Matthew links this prophecy to the birth of Jesus. One may understand this as a reliving of an OT hope to bring it to a new level.[42] It is also important not to collapse all of the significance of what are often seen as types into one typological connection nor to restrict a type to its function only as a type. This means that while the tabernacle is clearly seen as a type of Christ, it

41. Clowney (*Preaching and Biblical Theology*, 88) wisely identifies two key steps in typological analysis. The first step is "to relate the text to its immediate theological horizon," the second, "to relate the event of the text, by way of its proper interpretation in its own period, to the whole structure of redemptive history; and in that way to us upon whom the ends of the earth have come." Furthermore, he stresses "that this second step is valid and fruitful only when it does come second. All manner of arbitrariness and irresponsibility enter in when we seek to make a direct and practical reference to ourselves without considering the passage in its own biblical and theological setting." See the superb diagram in Clowney, "Preaching Christ," 179–80.

42. See Watts ("Emmanuel," 113), who, in dealing with Isa. 7:14 in Matt. 1:23, writes: "'fulfillment' seems best understood in paradigmatic terms: as Yahweh had acted in the past, so he would act again."

also has theological significance beyond the specific connections to Jesus. Thus the sacrificial system is a type of Christ (Heb. 9:11–15) but also has theological significance in its function within its own phase of redemptive history, let alone for worship within the NT era (see Heb. 13:15–16).

This route between OT and NT can be seen in the OT,[43] for instance, as the exodus motif reappears in texts in Isaiah and Ezra 1[44] and as the tabernacle-building account of Exod. 25–40 functions in relationship to the temple account in Chronicles.[45] It is also seen in the reliving of the Saul traditions from Samuel in the book of Esther as Mordecai redeems Saul's family line and shows how this preserves the exilic community[46] or the reliving of the Moab/ Judah traditions in the book of Ruth as Ruth and Boaz redeem their two family lines and show how they preserve and contribute to the royal line.[47]

The Old Testament Participates in the New Testament by Progressing the Redemptive Story

Another closely related route is seen in those instances where *the OT participates in the NT by progressing the redemptive story.*[48] Several passages in the NT remind the Christian community that their experience is inextricably linked with OT figures. First Peter 1:10–12 declares that their actions in the past "served" the NT community, and Heb. 11:39–40 indicates that only together with us are they made "perfect." Hebrews 12 presents Christ as author and perfecter of faith to whom Christians must look as the host of OT saints watch from heaven, expectant that the Christian community will bring to completion all the hopes of that community of old. This means that

43. On typology (figural representation) in the OT, see Fishbane, *Biblical Interpretation*, 350–79; Baker, *Two Testaments*, 181; Wells, "Figural Representation."

44. For Isaiah, see Watts, *Isaiah's New Exodus*; and for Ezra, see Throntveit, *Ezra–Nehemiah*, 15–18.

45. See Dillard, *2 Chronicles*, 303–18.

46. Horowitz, *Reckless Rites*, 69; Nihan, "Saul among the Prophets," 114n15.

47. Fisch, "Ruth."

48. For a recent articulation of the redemptive story as Biblical Theology, see Bartholomew and Goheen, "Story and Biblical Theology"; Bartholomew and Goheen, *Drama*.

as Christians read the redemptive story in the OT, they are reading their own story, and they are offered a vision for the kind of activity that is essential to bring the kingdom of God into reality in this world. This makes sense of the use of Job and Elijah as exemplars of perseverance and prayer in James 5:11, 17–18. This is also true for negative examples such as Paul's warning using the disobedience of Israel in the wilderness in 1 Cor. 10:1–13.

This route between OT and NT can also be discerned in the OT, for example, in the rehearsal of the Torah narrative traditions in Pss. 78; 104–106; 135–136, which shows how these earlier texts progress or regress the redemptive story in which the psalmists participate.

IMPLICATIONS

These various routes for connecting the biblical witness reflect varying degrees of continuity and discontinuity and yet all contribute to the understanding that the Scriptures are interconnected. These routes provide well-worn interpretive paths for Christian interpreters to traverse as they continue to reflect on the endless connections between passages and sections of the canonical witness, whether that is between OT and NT or various parts of the OT.[49]

Intersection

While there is diversity in terms of the level (explicit to implicit) at which connections between canonical sections are made and diversity in the route (continuity to discontinuity) used for such connections, third, there is unity in a single intersection through which these various roads must pass. While one should resist the temptation to collapse all Biblical Theology into a single "center" and should instead remain open to the multiplex character of the theological expression of the biblical witness,[50] certain core theological values function as an intersection through which all thematic connections on their various routes run as they move between canonical witnesses.

49. See Martens ("Reaching," 90–93) for his wise observations on this issue.
50. On the problem of identifying a limited center or creating simplistic and rigid systems when expressing Biblical Theology, see Hasel, *Basic Issues*, 139–71; Möller, "Nature and Genre," 56–59.

As the revelatory character of the Bible is both divine and human, so also is the revelatory content of this intersection.

Focus on Creator and Redeemer

First of all, the OT and the NT alike make clear that the Scriptures are focused on the revelation of the one true God, revealed as Yahweh in the OT and then as the Triune God in the NT. Interpretation of these Scriptures must then be theocentric in focus.[51] Ultimately the biblical witness points to God, his character, and his ways in this world as both creator and redeemer.

Second, the NT makes clear that the Scriptures have as their goal the redemption of all creation through the Son, Jesus the Christ (2 Tim. 3:14–17; Luke 24). Interpretation of these Scriptures must then be christotelic in character; what has been revealed is by definition part of a larger story that has the revelation of and redemption through the Son as its goal. As William Caven once wrote, "They were wont to say in Europe that every road led to Rome; and so we may affirm that every line of Scripture truth leads to Christ."[52] And Willem VanGemeren states, "Christian students of the OT must pass by the cross of Jesus Christ on their return to the OT, and as such they can never lose their identity as a Christian" since "the center of the Bible is the incarnate and glorified Christ, by whom all things will be renewed."[53] To read the OT (and the NT) as if Jesus did not show up at the turn of the ages and change the course of history would not be Christian.

Third, the NT makes clear that the realization of this christotelic redemption of all creation, witness of which is articulated throughout the canon, is only possible through the agency of the Holy Spirit (Rom. 8; Eph. 3:14–21). Interpretation of these Scriptures must then be pneumamorphic in character, that is, the realization of the redemption and its associated ethic is by definition only possible through the active work of the Holy Spirit within individual, community, culture,

---

51. See Hasel (*Basic Issues*, 168–73) for God as the center of OT theology and Christ as the center of NT theology.

52. Caven, *Christ's Teaching*.

53. VanGemeren, *Progress*, 21, 27.

and creation.[54] To read the OT as if the Spirit were not active would not be Christian. For Christians the ethical demands of the OT are rendered not irrelevant but rather achievable through the indwelling Spirit, who writes the law on the heart.[55]

These christotelic and pneumamorphic values do not mean that one finds Jesus or the Spirit "behind every bush" in the OT, somehow symbolically placed in every passage, for example, through an element with the color red (for Christ's blood) or a bird (for the Spirit's descent). But it does mean that since Jesus inaugurates the age that brings redemption and revelation to its climax, any OT redemptive act or revelatory insight will contribute toward and/or receive greater clarity in and through Jesus Christ and the Holy Spirit. After Christian interpreters have discerned the theological significance of an OT passage and/or an OT theological theme, they must reflect on the significance of the Christ event for this passage and/or theme.

These christotelic and pneumamorphic values also do not require that one avoid reflection on the unique aspects of biblical revelation prior to the arrival of Christ and the Spirit in the NT.[56] This is an essential element in biblical-theological reflection that takes seriously the diversity in Scripture.[57] But the Christian interpreter does understand that the ultimate significance of what has been called the "untamed witness of the OT"[58] is only realized in Christ and through the Spirit in the new age inaugurated by the gospel witness.

54. These christotelic and pneumamorphic aspects can be discerned in Romans and Ephesians. The ethical demands presented in the latter sections of these books (Rom. 12–15; Eph. 4–6) are clearly predicated on what is developed in the earlier sections of these books (see esp. the transitional verses in Rom. 12:1 and Eph. 4:1). These earlier sections are focused on the impact of the redemptive work of Christ, and yet both end with focused attention on the role of the Spirit as the one who empowers the people of God (see Rom. 8 and Eph. 3:14–21).

55. On the role of the Spirit in interpretation, see Boda, "Word and Spirit."

56. In this I am trying to take seriously the later concern of Childs (*Biblical Theology of the Old and New Testaments*, 76) that the discrete witness of the OT has an enduring role and should not be reduced to NT use of the OT.

57. See Wall ("Canonical Context," 180) for a creative approach to diversity within the canon in which the tensions between traditions "commends these same controversies to its current readers."

58. Brueggemann, *Theology of the Old Testament*, 107.

At the center of this intersection that provides cohesion to the biblical witness as a whole is the assumption that all Scripture witnesses to one God who has revealed himself and enacted a plan of salvation in progressive ways throughout history.

FOCUS ON CREATED AND REDEEMED

This central intersection, however, also focuses on what God has created and redeemed. The biblical drama begins with the description of the origins of all creation through the actions of Yahweh God. From the outset of redemptive history it is clear that God is forming a community through whom he will bring redemption into the world. That community emerges from a single family identified with the descendants of Abraham who are called by the name Israel in the OT and by the name of the Son of Israel, Jesus Christ, in the NT.[59] God enters into relationship with this community through a series of interrelated covenants that reach their climax in the new covenant enacted in and through Jesus Christ. God desires to transform all of culture and the cosmos through this covenant community redeemed by the redemptive act of Jesus the Christ and the agency of the Holy Spirit.[60] To read the OT without these broader redemptive goals in mind would not be Christian.

At this intersection that brings cohesion to the biblical witness as a whole is the assumption that all Scripture describes one story of redemption that moves from creation (Gen. 1–2) to new creation (Rev. 21–22) and is enacted through an enduring, single redemptive community. This means that the interpretation of the Scriptures provides resources for living in fellowship within this redemptive community but also for transforming the broader creational context in which this redemptive community lives. Biblical Theology thus offers

59. On the relationship between the church and Israel, see Boda, *Haggai, Zechariah*, 51–57. There is a legitimate discipline called Jewish Hebrew Bible Theology and opportunity for enrichment in dialogue between this discipline and Christian Biblical Theology, even though the latter is by necessity different due to variation in canonical shape, worshiping communities, and theological convictions.

60. The transformation of this community, culture, and creation involves what Hahn has identified as the "clear liturgical *trajectory* and *teleology*" ("Canon, Cult and Covenant," 225, emphasis original). See also the missional matrix of Biblical Theology espoused by C. Wright, "Mission as a Matrix"; cf. C. Wright, *Mission of God*.

perspectives for realms such as politics, education, law, environment, immigration, and economics.[61]

IMPLICATIONS

This central intersection that brings cohesion to the biblical witness should inform Christians desirous to hear the OT. Keeping in mind the convictions that God is the focus of the OT, that Christ is the goal of the redemptive drama depicted throughout the OT, and that the Spirit is the one who makes possible adherence to the demands of the OT, one should listen to the theological witness of individual pericopae of Scripture in order to determine how the particular passage relates to the broader canonical development of a redeemed community and transformed culture and cosmos. It is important to remember that the OT endures as a scriptural witness that makes demands on our lives as it did on the early church. That early church lived after Christ's death, resurrection, ascension, and giving of the Spirit, and yet the NT makes clear that the OT not only testified to the coming of Christ and the Spirit but also continued to inform the church theologically and to make demands on it ethically.

Conclusion

This consideration of innerbiblical connections within Scripture highlights some of the key methods by which biblical writers linked the various parts of the canon. This clearly authorizes biblical-theological reflection and shapes Christian approaches to such reflection. It sensitizes the Christian interpreter to the diverse levels (explicit to implicit) at which connections are made, the diverse routes (continuity to discontinuity) through which connections are made, but the singular intersection (divine and human) through which all connections must pass.

This evidence provides examples that should inspire the Christian interpreter. One does not need to have a citation of the OT in

---

61. See, e.g., O'Donovan, *Desire of the Nations*, on politics; Richter, "Biblical Theology of Creation Care," on environment; and Carroll R., *Christians at the Border*, on immigration.

the NT for that OT passage to have legitimacy as Scripture.[62] Nor does one have to limit one's reading of the OT to only the nuance given to the reading in a NT citation of a particular OT Scripture. The OT is truly Christian Scripture and continues its role now in a new age inaugurated by the work of Christ and empowered by the work of the Spirit.

Hearing the Old Testament with Sensitivity to Biblical Theology

How then does one hear the OT with sensitivity to its biblical-theological character and context? This awareness should shape our reading of the OT, whether that reading is focused on individual pericopae or broader canonical sections.

Disciplined Exegesis

First of all, this demands disciplined exegesis of individual texts within their historical and literary contexts in order to discern wisely their core theological themes. As Heb. 1:1–3 makes clear, OT revelation has been communicated at various times through diverse means, and thus its theological witness cannot be divorced from the historical setting in which and literary forms through which this revelation has come. However, the focus of such exegesis should remain on the theological witness of the text, that is, what the text revealed at particular historical moments and through particular literary forms has to say about God, his character, and his ways in relation to his people and all of creation.

Biblical-Theological Reflection

But, second, this particular theological witness needs to be placed within the broader trajectory of the theological witness of the canon as a whole. Important in this is to avoid suppressing the unique witness of particular passages and books while bringing this witness into dialogue with other voices within the canon. A dual focus is

---

62. Seitz, *Word without End*, 213–28.

necessary as one seeks to connect the particular text to the broader canonical witness. Attention should be given to both continuity and discontinuity. Continuity refers to the ways the theological witness of the particular passage echoes the theological witness of other passages within the canon, while discontinuity refers to the ways the theological witness of particular passages contrasts with the theological witness of other passages. In most cases one discerns points of continuity and discontinuity simultaneously.

One should begin by attending to continuity, reflecting on other passages in Scripture (both OT and NT) that develop the theme(s) of a particular passage. Past approaches to Biblical Theology often focused too much on word studies for investigating theological themes in the biblical corpus. While words are very important for biblical-theological analysis, it is important that one neither equate a single word or few words with a biblical-theological theme nor consider these words apart from their broader linguistic context in terms of the language as a whole as well as the passages in which they appear.[63] While words may be helpful for identifying passages relevant to a biblical-theological analysis, so also are collocations and images.[64] Thus, for instance, while one may investigate the theme of repentance in the Psalms by searching for passages that employ the term שׁוּב (return), the contrastive image of the two ways in Ps. 1 subtly encourages repentance without employing explicit vocabulary. The key is to focus on passages that develop a particular theme in both positive and negative ways.

Focus then should shift to discontinuity, reflecting on how these passages contrast with the witness of others and on how other passages have themes that contrast with that of a particular passage. This entails being sensitive to the sociohistorical, redemptive-historical, and revelatory-historical context of individual passages. As incarnational, the biblical witness is embedded within history, which means in the particular sociohistorical moment of a people who lived in

63. On earlier excesses, see Barr, *Semantics*; Barr, "Semantics and Biblical Theology." See further my approach to the theme of repentance in the OT and the NT in Boda, *"Return to Me,"* 24–32.
64. For an excellent example of OT theological analysis with attention to images, see Goldingay, *Israel's Faith*.

vastly different places. For instance, references to servant-master in different parts of the OT and the NT may not signify an identical social relation, and so one must remain sensitive to this dynamic. The Bible bears witness to a God who has acted in a variety of ways throughout redemptive history as he has unfolded the mystery that has reached its climax in Jesus Christ. Thus, how God acts at a certain phase of redemptive history may not be relevant to how he acts at a later phase. For example, the sacrificial system laid out in Lev. 1–7 was relevant for the covenant community after Sinai but not so for the patriarchs described in the book of Genesis, the Israelites living in exile, or Christians after Christ's death. The Bible also bears witness to a God who has revealed himself in progressive ways throughout history.[65] Thus, as the biblical witness unfolds, readers are given more and more details about the character of this God and the constitution of the spiritual and physical world he has created. For example, while the NT offers much insight into the afterlife, such is not the case in the OT. This is a feature of progressive revelation.

Example

How does this practically impact our reading of a text?[66] A close look at the rhetorical flow of 1 Sam. 16 reveals that the anointing of David by Samuel prompted a transfer of the Spirit of God from Saul (16:14a) to David (16:13) and a simultaneous divine commissioning of an injurious spirit to torment Saul (16:14b).[67] The association of the Spirit with royal anointing is not surprising in light of the earlier account of Saul's rise to power in 1 Sam. 10, where Saul was endued with power by the Spirit of the Lord (10:6), which would enable him to carry out the great feat (1 Sam. 11), which in turn would qualify

---

65. Sensitivity to the impact of the canonical shape to this revelatory history should also be taken into account; see further Dempster, "Canon and Old Testament Interpretation"; and Boda, *Severe Mercy*.

66. See further Boda, *After God's Own Heart*; Boda, *Haggai, Zechariah*.

67. Howard, "Transfer of Power": "The transfer in the immediate context is related to the empowerment by YHWH's Spirit, but it is symbolic of the transfer of political power as well" (477). Later also: "It is not that the Spirit could not have maintained a special presence with both but rather that this appears to be the pattern of his activity in the Old Testament. Particularly in this section of 1 Samuel the presence of YHWH's Spirit symbolizes, among other things, his favor on his chosen king" (480).

him publicly as royal leader (cf. 1 Sam. 17).[68] A biblical-theological perspective provides an important caution for Christian readers well aware of the role of the Spirit of God according to NT and Christian systematic theology.[69] Focusing on continuity rather than discontinuity, one may be tempted to see here a text relevant to the role of the Spirit within NT soteriology, a role that is articulated first in the OT by the prophet Ezekiel, who presaged the enlivening Spirit who would transform the inner motivations of the community of God to obey Yahweh. While one cannot deny a relationship between 1 Sam. 16 and NT soteriology, attention to the role of the Spirit within the textual and theological context of 1 Sam. 16 helps nuance this considerably.

The role of the Spirit here is related to the execution of covenantal leadership for the people of God. The dominant feature of OT pneumatology is that the Spirit of God appears to be restricted to covenantal leaders, whether leader (Deut. 34:9), elder (Num. 11:25), judge (Judg. 3:10), king (1 Sam. 10:6), or prophet (Zech. 7:12), but does not appear to indwell the community as a whole (Num. 11:29). The significance of the promises of the new age (last days) according to Joel 3:1–5 (2:28–32 Eng.) is that the Spirit would indwell the entire covenant community, something that had implications for the gifting of the NT community (1 Cor. 12–14) but also for the NT community's union with Christ (Rom. 8:9), regeneration (John 3:5), and transformation (Rom. 8:1–17). It is interesting that the move of the Spirit from Moses to the seventy elders in Num. 11 presages the ultimate move of the Spirit from the covenant head Jesus to the church as a whole. As Jesus teaches in John 14:17, the Spirit who "abides with you" (that is, in Christ, who had received the Spirit at his baptism) will soon be "in you" (cf. John 20:22). It is Jesus who asks of the Father and grants this community the Spirit who takes up residence within them.

This reality, however, is not yet true in the phase of redemptive history depicted in 1 Sam. 16. What is not in view here is the Spirit's

68. Dumbrell, *Covenant and Creation*, 140.
69. See the superb treatment of OT pneumatology in C. Wright, *Knowing the Holy Spirit*, esp. 87–120; cf. Montague, *Holy Spirit*; Wood, *Holy Spirit*; Fee, *God's Empowering Presence*, 905–10; Hildebrandt, *Old Testament Theology of the Spirit of God*; Gosling, "Unresolved Problem." Also note the sensitivity to OT theology of the Spirit in the systematic theology of Grenz, *Theology*, 361–65.

role in regeneration. This passage is concerned not with the fate of Saul in terms of salvation but rather with his fate in terms of his role within salvation history. The Spirit's role in this era is focused on empowerment for covenantal service, in particular on dynamic endowment for royal leadership within the nation.[70] This role of the Spirit relates, first and foremost, to the function of Jesus Christ as the covenantal leader whose ministry was marked by the power of the Holy Spirit in word and deed.[71] But this same Spirit also continued and continues to endow leaders of the covenant community, whether they serve within the church or more broadly within society. First Samuel 16 reminds redeemed leaders of the necessity of the Spirit's endowment as they seek to transform all of creation.

Conclusion

Biblical Theology is an important resource for the broader theological and religious discourse of the church and society today. However, there is a risk that this resource will not be fully appreciated or utilized if greater attention is not given today to dialogue among the various theological disciplines. With the increasing specialization of the academic world, OT theology has largely been written with attention to discussions within the discipline of OT and Hebrew studies. What is needed today are daring attempts to move outside these disciplinary walls and write and reflect on OT theology within the broader canon (Biblical Theology), the broader Christian theological tradition (historical, systematic theology), and the broader contemporary context (ethics, pastoral theology, worldview studies, political theology, etc.).[72] This interdisciplinary sensitivity is practiced regularly by those involved in church ministry and, interestingly, by those in broader cultural institutions. Such an approach demands hospitality, a willingness to dialogue in community across theological disciplines and life experiences, and also courage to venture outside

70. On the "royal" or "princely Spirit" see Eaton, *Kingship and the Psalms*, 71, 157; cf. Ps. 51:12. Most likely this role of the Spirit is related to dynasty.

71. See esp. the emphasis on this Spirit endowment in Luke 3–4; cf. Boda, "Word and Spirit."

72. See further, Boda, "Theological Commentary."

one's expertise. In this way, then, OT exegetical and biblical theology has the potential to impact the church's preaching and worship as well as its reflection on creational activities ranging from politics to education to law. It is through such reflection that the redeemed community has the potential to realize fully its role as transformative agents within creation.

Biblical Theology is an essential discipline that enables Christians to hear the OT. While highlighting the unique voice of the OT, it provides the theological perspective and interpretive discipline for reading OT texts within their ultimate theological context, that of the canon as a whole, the community gathered around it, and the culture and creation longing for the redemptive work of the creator revealed within these Scriptures.

Works Cited

Alexander, T. Desmond, and Brian S. Rosner, eds. *New Dictionary of Biblical Theology*. Leicester, UK: Inter-Varsity; Downers Grove, IL: InterVarsity, 2000.

Baab, Otto Justice. *The Theology of the Old Testament*. New York: Abingdon-Cokesbury, 1949.

Baker, David L. *Two Testaments, One Bible: A Study of the Theological Relationship between the Old and New Testaments*. Rev. ed. Leicester, UK: Apollos, 1991.

Baltzer, Klaus. *The Covenant Formulary in Old Testament, Jewish and Early Christian Writings*. Oxford: Blackwell, 1971.

Barr, James. *The Concept of Biblical Theology: An Old Testament Perspective*. Minneapolis: Fortress, 1999.

———. "Semantics and Biblical Theology: A Contribution to the Discussion." Pages 11–19 in *Congress Volume: Uppsala 1971*. Edited by Henrik Samuel Nyberg. Leiden: Brill, 1972.

———. *The Semantics of Biblical Language*. Oxford: Oxford University Press, 1961.

Barth, Christoph. *God with Us: A Theological Introduction to the Old Testament*. Edited by Geoffrey William Bromiley. Grand Rapids: Eerdmans, 1991.

Bartholomew, Craig G. "Biblical Theology and Biblical Interpretation: Introduction." Pages 1–19 in *Out of Egypt: Biblical Theology and Biblical Interpretation*. Edited by Craig Bartholomew, Mary Healy, Karl Möller, and Robin Parry. Scripture and Hermeneutics Series 5. Grand Rapids: Zondervan, 2004.

——. "Covenant and Creation: Covenant Overload or Covenantal Deconstruction." *Calvin Theological Journal* 30 (1995): 11–33.

——. "Listening for God's Address: A *Mere* Trinitarian Hermeneutic for the Old Testament." Pages 3–19 in *Hearing the Old Testament: Listening for God's Address*. Edited by Craig Bartholomew and David Beldman. Grand Rapids: Eerdmans, 2012.

Bartholomew, Craig G., and Michael W. Goheen. *The Drama of Scripture: Finding Our Place in the Biblical Story*. Grand Rapids: Baker Academic, 2004.

——. "Story and Biblical Theology." Pages 144–71 in *Out of Egypt: Biblical Theology and Biblical Interpretation*. Edited by Craig Bartholomew, Mary Healy, Karl Möller, and Robin Parry. Scripture and Hermeneutics Series 5. Grand Rapids: Zondervan, 2004.

Bartholomew, Craig G., Scott Hahn, Robin Parry, Christopher Seitz, and Al Wolters, eds. *Canon and Biblical Interpretation*. Scripture and Hermeneutics Series 7. Grand Rapids: Zondervan, 2006.

Bartholomew, Craig, Mary Healy, Karl Möller, and Robin Parry, eds. *Out of Egypt: Biblical Theology and Biblical Interpretation*. Scripture and Hermeneutics Series 5. Grand Rapids: Zondervan, 2004.

Barton, John. "Covenant in Old Testament Theology." Pages 23–38 in *Covenant as Context: Essays in Honour of E. W. Nicholson*. Edited by A. D. H. Mayes and Robert B. Salters. Oxford: Oxford University Press, 2003.

Bauckham, Richard. "Reading Scripture as a Coherent Story." Pages 38–53 in *The Art of Reading Scripture*. Edited by Ellen F. Davis and Richard B. Hays. Grand Rapids: Eerdmans, 2003.

Beale, G. K., and D. A. Carson. *Commentary on the New Testament Use of the Old Testament*. Grand Rapids: Baker Academic; Nottingham, UK: Apollos, 2007.

Blenkinsopp, Joseph. *Creation, Un-creation, Re-creation: A Discursive Commentary on Genesis 1–11*. London: T&T Clark, 2011.

Boda, Mark J. *After God's Own Heart: The Gospel according to David*. Phillipsburg, NJ: P&R, 2007.

——. "Biblical Theology and the Old Testament." Pages 122–53 in *Hearing the Old Testament: Listening for God's Address*. Edited by Craig Bartholomew and David Beldman. Grand Rapids: Eerdmans, 2012.

———. *1–2 Chronicles*. Cornerstone Biblical Commentary 5a. Carol Stream, IL: Tyndale House, 2010.

———. "The Delight of Wisdom." *Themelios* 29 (2004): 4–11.

———. *Haggai, Zechariah*. NIVAC. Grand Rapids: Zondervan, 2004.

———. "Judges." Pages 1043–288 in *Numbers–Ruth*. Edited by Tremper Longman III and David E. Garland. Revised Expositor's Bible Commentary 2. Grand Rapids: Zondervan, 2012.

———. "Legitimizing the Temple: The Chronicler's Temple Building Account." Pages 303–18 in *From the Foundations to the Crenellations: Essays on Temple Building in the Ancient Near East and Hebrew Bible*. Edited by Mark J. Boda and Jamie R. Novotny. AOAT 366. Münster: Ugarit-Verlag, 2010.

———. "Oil, Crowns and Thrones: Prophet, Priest and King in Zechariah 1:7–6:15." Pages 379–404 in *Perspectives on Hebrew Scriptures*. Edited by Ehud ben Zvi. Piscataway, NJ: Gorgias, 2006.

———. "The Old Testament and Romans: Interpreting the Scriptures Which Instruct and Encourage." In *Romans*. Edited by Stanley E. Porter. McMaster New Testament Series. Eugene, OR: Wipf & Stock, forthcoming.

———. "Penitential Innovations in the Book of the Twelve." Pages 291–308 in *On Stone and Scroll: A Festschrift for Graham Davies*. Edited by Brian A. Mastin, Katharine J. Dell, and James K. Aitken. BZAW 420. Berlin: de Gruyter, 2011.

———. *Praying the Tradition: The Origin and Use of Tradition in Nehemiah 9*. BZAW 277. Berlin: de Gruyter, 1999.

———. "Reenvisioning the Relationship: Covenant in Chronicles." Pages 375–92 in *Covenant in the Persian Period: From Genesis to Chronicles*. Edited by Richard J. Bautch and Gary N. Knoppers. Winona Lake, IN: Eisenbrauns, 2015.

———. *"Return to Me": A Biblical Theology of Repentance*. NSBT. Leicester, UK: Apollos, 2015.

———. *A Severe Mercy: Sin and Its Remedy in the Old Testament*. Siphrut: Literature and Theology of the Hebrew Scriptures 1. Winona Lake, IN: Eisenbrauns, 2009.

———. "Theological Commentary: A Review and Reflective Essay." *McMaster Journal of Theology and Ministry* 11 (2010): 139–50.

———. "Word and Spirit, Scribe and Prophet in Old Testament Hermeneutics." Pages 25–45 in *Spirit and Scripture: Examining a Pneumatic*

Hermeneutic. Edited by Kevin L. Spawn and Archie T. Wright. London: T&T Clark, 2011.

Boda, Mark J., and Mary L. Conway. *Judges: A Discourse Analysis of the Hebrew Bible*. Zondervan Exegetical Commentary on the Old Testament. Grand Rapids: Zondervan, forthcoming.

Bosman, Jan P. "The Paradoxical Presence of Exodus 34:6–7 in the Book of the Twelve." *Scriptura* 87 (2004): 233–43.

Bouma-Prediger, Steven. *For the Beauty of the Earth: A Christian Vision for Creation Care*. 2nd ed. Engaging Culture. Grand Rapids: Baker Academic, 2010.

Brown, Jeannine K. "Is the Future of Biblical Theology Story-Shaped?" *HBT* 37 (2015): 13–31.

Brueggemann, Walter. "Futures in Old Testament Theology: Dialogic Engagement." *HBT* 37 (2015): 32–49.

———. *Theology of the Old Testament: Testimony, Dispute, Advocacy*. Minneapolis: Fortress, 1997.

Busenitz, Irvin A. "Introduction to the Biblical Covenants: The Noahic Covenant and the Priestly Covenant." *MSJ* 10, no. 2 (1999): 173–89.

Carmichael, Calum. "A New View of the Origin of the Deuteronomic Credo." *VT* 19 (1969): 273–89.

Carroll R., M. Daniel. *Christians at the Border: Immigration, the Church, and the Bible*. 2nd ed. Grand Rapids: Brazos, 2013.

Carson, D. A. *Exegetical Fallacies*. 2nd ed. Grand Rapids: Baker, 1996.

———. "Systematic Theology and Biblical Theology." Pages 89–104 in *New Dictionary of Biblical Theology*. Edited by T. Desmond Alexander and Brian S. Rosner. Leicester, UK: Inter-Varsity; Downers Grove, IL: Inter-Varsity, 2000.

Caven, William. *Christ's Teaching concerning the Last Things and Other Papers*. Toronto: Westminster, 1908.

Chapman, Stephen B. *The Law and the Prophets: A Study in Old Testament Canon Formation*. FAT 27. Tübingen: Mohr Siebeck, 2000.

———. "Reclaiming Inspiration for the Bible." Pages 167–206 in *Canon and Biblical Interpretation*. Edited by Craig G. Bartholomew, Scott Hahn, Robin Parry, Christopher Seitz, and Al Wolters. Scripture and Hermeneutics Series 7. Grand Rapids: Zondervan, 2006.

Childs, Brevard S. *Biblical Theology in Crisis*. Philadelphia: Westminster, 1970.

————. *Biblical Theology of the Old and New Testaments: Theological Reflection on the Christian Bible*. Minneapolis: Fortress, 1993.

————. *The Book of Exodus: A Critical, Theological Commentary*. OTL. Philadelphia: Westminster, 1974.

————. *Introduction to the Old Testament as Scripture*. Philadelphia: Fortress, 1979.

————. *Isaiah*. OTL. Louisville: Westminster John Knox, 2001.

————. *Old Testament Theology in a Canonical Context*. Philadelphia: Fortress, 1985.

Clark, Gordon R. *The Word Hesed in the Hebrew Bible*. JSOTSup 157. Sheffield: JSOT Press, 1993.

Clements, R. E. *Prophecy and Covenant*. Studies in Biblical Theology 43. Naperville, IL: Allenson, 1965.

Clowney, Edmund P. *Preaching and Biblical Theology*. Phillipsburg, NJ: Presbyterian & Reformed, 1961.

————. "Preaching Christ from All the Scriptures." Pages 163–91 in *The Preacher and Preaching*. Edited by Samuel T. Logan. Phillipsburg, NJ: Presbyterian & Reformed, 1986.

Cody, Aelred. "'Little Historical Creed' or 'Little Historical Anamnesis'?" *CBQ* 68 (2006): 1–10.

Cole, Graham A. "Exodus 34, the Middoth and the Doctrine of God: The Importance of Biblical Theology to Evangelical Systematic Theology." *SBJT* 12, no. 3 (2008): 24–36.

Cross, Frank Moore. "Kinship and Covenant in Ancient Israel." Pages 3–21 in *From Epic to Canon: History and Literature in Ancient Israel*. Baltimore: Johns Hopkins University Press, 1998.

Crüsemann, Frank. *Studien zur Formgeschichte von Hymnus und Danklied in Israel*. WMANT 32. Neukirchen-Vluyn: Neukirchener Verlag, 1969.

Davies, John A. *A Royal Priesthood: Literary and Intertextual Perspectives on an Image of Israel in Exodus 19.6*. JSOTSup 395. London: T&T Clark, 2004.

Dawn, Marva. *Reaching Out without Dumbing Down: A Theology of Worship for the Turn-of-the-Century Culture*. Grand Rapids: Eerdmans, 1995.

Deane-Drummond, Celia. *Eco-Theology*. Winona, MN: Anselm Academic, 2008.

Demarest, Bruce A. "The Contemporary Relevance of Christendom's Creeds." *Themelios* 7 (1982): 9–17.

Dempster, Stephen G. "Canon and Old Testament Interpretation." Pages 154–79 in *Hearing the Old Testament: Listening for God's Address*. Edited by Craig Bartholomew and David Beldman. Grand Rapids: Eerdmans, 2012.

———. *Dominion and Dynasty: A Biblical Theology of the Hebrew Bible*. Leicester, UK: Apollos; Downers Grove, IL: InterVarsity, 2003.

Dentan, R. C. "The Literary Affinities of Exodus XXXIV 6f." *VT* 13 (1963): 34–51.

Dillard, Raymond B. *2 Chronicles*. Word Biblical Commentary 15. Waco: Word Books, 1987.

Dockery, David S. "Typological Exegesis: Moving beyond Abuse and Neglect." Pages 161–78 in *Reclaiming the Prophetic Mantle: Preaching the Old Testament Faithfully*. Edited by George L. Klein. Nashville: Broadman, 1992.

Dozeman, Thomas B. *Commentary on Exodus*. Eerdmans Critical Commentary. Grand Rapids: Eerdmans, 2009.

———. "Innerbiblical Interpretation of Yahweh's Gracious and Compassionate Character." *JBL* 108 (1989): 207–23.

Dumbrell, William J. *Covenant and Creation: An Old Testament Covenantal Theology*. Grand Rapids: Baker, 1993.

———. *Covenant and Creation: A Theology of the Old Testament Covenants*. Nashville: Nelson, 1984.

Dunn, James D. G. "The Problem of 'Biblical Theology.'" Pages 172–83 in *Out of Egypt: Biblical Theology and Biblical Interpretation*. Edited by Craig Bartholomew, Mary Healy, Karl Möller, and Robin Parry. Scripture and Hermeneutics Series 5. Grand Rapids: Zondervan, 2004.

Dyrness, William A. *Themes in Old Testament Theology*. Downers Grove, IL: InterVarsity, 1979.

Eaton, J. H. *Kingship and the Psalms*. 2nd ed. Biblical Seminar 3. Sheffield, UK: JSOT Press, 1986.

Eichrodt, Walther. *Theologie des Alten Testaments*. 2 vols. Stuttgart: Ehrenfried Klotz, 1957.

———. *Theology of the Old Testament*. OTL. Philadelphia: Westminster, 1961.

Enns, Peter. *Exodus*. NIVAC. Grand Rapids: Zondervan, 2000.

———. *Inspiration and Incarnation: Evangelicals and the Problem of the Old Testament*. 2nd ed. Grand Rapids: Baker Academic, 2015.

Fee, Gordon D. *God's Empowering Presence: The Holy Spirit in the Letters of Paul*. Peabody, MA: Hendrickson, 1994.

Ferguson, Sinclair B. *A Heart for God*. Christian Character Library. Colorado Springs: NavPress, 1985.

Fisch, Harold. "Ruth and the Structure of Covenant History." *VT* 32 (1982): 425–37.

Fishbane, Michael A. *Biblical Interpretation in Ancient Israel*. Oxford: Clarendon, 1985.

Francis, Pope. *Laudato Si': On Care for Our Common Home; Encyclical Letter*. Huntington, IN: Our Sunday Visitor, 2015.

Freedman, David Noel. *The Unity of the Hebrew Bible*. Ann Arbor: University of Michigan Press, 1991.

Fretheim, Terence E. *Exodus*. Int. Louisville: John Knox, 1991.

Fürst, Julius. *A Hebrew and Chaldee Lexicon to the Old Testament: With an Introduction Giving a Short History of Hebrew Lexicography*. Translated by Samuel Davidson. 4th ed. Leipzig: Tauchnitz; London: Williams & Norgate, 1871.

Gentry, Peter J., and Stephen J. Wellum. *Kingdom through Covenant: A Biblical-Theological Understanding of the Covenants*. Wheaton, IL: Crossway, 2012.

Gerstenberger, Erhard S. *Theologies in the Old Testament*. Translated by J. Bowden. London: T&T Clark, 2002.

Glueck, Nelson. *Hesed in the Bible*. Cincinnati: Hebrew Union College, 1967.

Goldingay, John. *Israel's Faith*. Vol. 2 of *Old Testament Theology*. Downers Grove, IL: InterVarsity, 2006.

———. *Israel's Gospel*. Vol. 1 of *Old Testament Theology*. Downers Grove, IL: InterVarsity, 2003.

———. *Theological Diversity and the Authority of the Old Testament*. Grand Rapids: Eerdmans, 1987.

Goldsworthy, Graeme L. *According to Plan: The Unfolding Revelation of God in the Bible*. Downers Grove, IL: InterVarsity, 2002.

———. "Relationship of Old Testament and New Testament." Pages 81–89 in *New Dictionary of Biblical Theology*. Edited by T. Desmond Alexander and Brian S. Rosner. Leicester, UK: Inter-Varsity; Downers Grove, IL: InterVarsity, 2000.

———. "'Thus Says the Lord': The Dogmatic Basis for Biblical Theology." Pages 25–40 in *God Who Is Rich in Mercy*. Edited by Peter T. O'Brien and David Peterson. Homebush, Australia: Lancer Books, 1986.

Gosling, F. A. "An Unresolved Problem of Old Testament Theology." *Expository Times* 106 (1995): 234–37.

Gottwald, Norman K. *The Tribes of Yahweh: A Sociology of the Religion of Liberated Israel, 1250–1050 B.C.E.* Maryknoll, NY: Orbis Books, 1979.

Green, Joel B. *Practicing Theological Interpretation: Engaging Biblical Texts for Faith and Formation*. Theological Explorations for the Church Catholic. Grand Rapids: Baker Academic, 2011.

———. "Scripture and Theology: Uniting the Two So Long Divided." Pages 23–43 in *Between Two Horizons: Spanning New Testament Studies and Systematic Theology*. Edited by Joel B. Green and Max Turner. Grand Rapids: Eerdmans, 2000.

Green, Joel B., and Max Turner. *Between Two Horizons: Spanning New Testament Studies and Systematic Theology*. Grand Rapids: Eerdmans, 2000.

Grenz, Stanley J. *Theology for the Community of God*. Grand Rapids: Eerdmans; Vancouver: Regent College, 2000.

Gunneweg, Antonius H. J. *Biblische Theologie des Alten Testaments: Eine Religionsgeschichte Israels in Biblisch-Theologischer Sicht*. Stuttgart: Kohlhammer, 1993.

Hafemann, Scott. "Biblical Theology: Retrospect and Prospect." Pages 15–21 in *Biblical Theology: Retrospect and Prospect*. Edited by Scott Hafemann. Downers Grove, IL: InterVarsity; Leicester, UK: Apollos, 2002.

Hahn, Scott W. "Canon, Cult and Covenant." Pages 207–29 in *Canon and Biblical Interpretation*. Edited by Craig G. Bartholomew, Scott Hahn, Robin Parry, Christopher Seitz, and Al Wolters. Scripture and Hermeneutics Series 7. Grand Rapids: Zondervan, 2006.

———. "Covenant in the Old and New Testaments: Some Recent Research (1994–2004)." *CurBR* 3 (2005): 263–92.

———. *Kinship by Covenant: A Canonical Approach to the Fulfillment of God's Saving Promises*. Anchor Yale Bible Reference Library. New Haven: Yale University Press, 2009.

Hamilton, Victor P. *Exodus: An Exegetical Commentary*. Grand Rapids: Baker Academic, 2011.

Hanson, Paul D. *Dynamic Transcendence: The Correlation of Confessional Heritage and Contemporary Experience in a Biblical Model of Divine Activity*. Philadelphia: Fortress, 1978.

Harris, R. Laird. "חסד (*Ḥsd*)." Pages 305–7 in *Theological Wordbook of the Old Testament*. Edited by R. Laird Harris, Gleason Leonard Archer, and Bruce K. Waltke. Chicago: Moody, 1999.

Hasel, Gerhard F. *Old Testament Theology: Basic Issues in the Current Debate*. 4th ed. Grand Rapids: Eerdmans, 1991.

Hauerwas, Stanley, and L. Gregory Jones. *Why Narrative? Readings in Narrative Theology*. Grand Rapids: Eerdmans, 1989.

Hays, Richard B. "Reading Scripture in Light of the Resurrection." Pages 216–38 in *The Art of Reading Scripture*. Edited by Ellen F. Davis and Richard B. Hays. Grand Rapids: Eerdmans, 2003.

Heller, Roy L. *Narrative Structure and Discourse Constellations: An Analysis of Clause Function in Biblical Hebrew Prose*. HSS 55. Winona Lake, IN: Eisenbrauns, 2004.

Helmer, Christine. "Biblical Theology: Reality, Interpretation, and Interdisciplinarity." Pages 1–16 in *Biblical Interpretation: History, Context, and Reality*. Edited by Christine Helmer and Taylor G. Petrey. SBL Symposium Series 26. Atlanta: Society of Biblical Literature; Leiden: Brill, 2005.

———. "Introduction: Multivalence in Biblical Theology." Pages 1–10 in *The Multivalence of Biblical Texts and Theological Meanings*. Edited by Christine Helmer and Charlene T. Higbe. SBL Symposium Series 37. Atlanta: Society of Biblical Literature, 2006.

Hildebrandt, Wilf. *An Old Testament Theology of the Spirit of God*. Peabody, MA: Hendrickson, 1995.

Hillers, Delbert R. *Covenant: The History of a Biblical Idea*. Baltimore: Johns Hopkins University Press, 1969.

Holmgren, Fredrick C. "Faithful Abraham and the 'amanâ Covenant in Nehemiah 9,6–10,1." *ZAW* 104 (1992): 249–54.

Hood, Jason B., and Matthew Y. Emerson. "Summaries of Israel's Story: Reviewing a Compositional Category." *CurBR* 11, no. 3 (2013): 328–48.

Horowitz, Elliott S. *Reckless Rites: Purim and the Legacy of Jewish Violence. Jews, Christians, and Muslims from the Ancient to the Modern World*. Princeton: Princeton University Press, 2006.

House, Paul R. "The Character of God in the Book of the Twelve." Pages 831–49 in *Society of Biblical Literature 1998 Seminar Papers*. SBLSP 37. Orlando: Society of Biblical Literature, 1998.

———. *Old Testament Theology*. Downers Grove, IL: InterVarsity, 1998.

Howard, David M. "The Transfer of Power from Saul to David in 1 Sam 16:13–14." *JETS* 32 (1989): 473–83.

Hubbard, Robert L., Robert K. Johnston, and Robert P. Meye, eds. *Studies in Old Testament Theology*. Dallas: Word, 1992.

Hugenberger, Gordon Paul. *Marriage as a Covenant: A Study of Biblical Law and Ethics Governing Marriage, Developed from the Perspective of Malachi*. VTSup 52. Leiden: Brill, 1994.

―――. *Marriage as a Covenant: Biblical Law and Ethics as Developed from Malachi*. Biblical Studies Library. Grand Rapids: Baker, 1998.

Jackson, Wes. *Consulting the Genius of the Place: An Ecological Approach to a New Agriculture*. Berkeley: Counterpoint, 2010.

Janzen, Waldemar. *Exodus*. Believers Church Bible Commentary. Waterloo, ON: Herald, 2000.

Jenson, Philip Peter. *Graded Holiness: A Key to the Priestly Conception of the World*. JSOTSup 106. Sheffield: JSOT Press, 1992.

Joosten, Jan. "חסד, 'Benevolence,' and Ελεος, 'Pity': Reflections on Their Lexical Equivalence in the Septuagint." Pages 97–111 in *Collected Studies on the Septuagint: From Language to Interpretation and Beyond*. Edited by Jan Joosten. FAT 83. Tübingen: Mohr Siebeck, 2012.

Kaiser, Walter C. *The Uses of the Old Testament in the New*. Chicago: Moody, 1985.

Kalluveettil, Paul. *Declaration and Covenant: A Comprehensive Review of Covenant Formulae from the Old Testament and the Ancient Near East*. AnBib 88. Rome: Biblical Institute Press, 1982.

Kelly, Joseph R. "Joel, Jonah, and the YHWH Creed: Determining the Trajectory of the Literary Influence." *JBL* 132 (2013): 805–26.

Kessler, John. *Old Testament Theology: Divine Call and Human Response*. Waco: Baylor University Press, 2013.

Kinlaw, Dennis F., and John Oswalt. *Lectures in Old Testament Theology*. Wilmore, KY: Francis Asbury; Anderson, IN: Warner, 2010.

Kline, Meredith G. *Treaty of the Great King: The Covenant Structure of Deuteronomy: Studies and Commentary*. Grand Rapids: Eerdmans, 1963.

Klink, Edward W., and Darian R. Lockett. *Understanding Biblical Theology: A Comparison of Theory and Practice*. Grand Rapids: Zondervan, 2012.

Knoppers, Gary N. "Ancient Near Eastern Royal Grants and the Davidic Covenant: A Parallel?" *JAOS* 116 (1996): 670–97.

Knowles, Michael. *The Unfolding Mystery of the Divine Name: The God of Sinai in Our Midst*. Downers Grove, IL: IVP Academic, 2012.

Köhler, Ludwig. *Old Testament Theology*. Lutterworth Library 49. London: Lutterworth, 1957.

Laney, J. Carl. "God's Self-Revelation in Exodus 34:6–8." *BSac* 158 (2001): 36–51.

Lash, Nicholas. *Theology on the Way to Emmaus*. London: SCM, 1986.

Levine, Baruch A. *Leviticus*. JPS Torah Commentary. Philadelphia: Jewish Publication Society, 1989.

Lexham Analytical Lexicon to the Septuagint, The. Bellingham, WA: Lexham, 2012.

Lima, Brian. "צלם and דמות: Their Kinship Meaning in Genesis." PhD diss., McMaster Divinity College, 2015.

Lints, Richard. "Two Theologies or One? Warfield and Vos on the Nature of Theology." *WTJ* 54 (1992): 235–53.

Livingstone, Glenys. *PaGaian Cosmology: Re-inventing Earth-Based Goddess Religion*. Lincoln: iUniverse, 2008.

Martens, Elmer A. *God's Design: A Focus on Old Testament Theology*. Grand Rapids: Baker, 1981.

———. "Old Testament Theology since Walter Kaiser." *JETS* 50 (2007): 673–92.

———. "Reaching for a Biblical Theology of the Whole Bible." Pages 83–101 in *Reclaiming the Old Testament: Essays in Honour of Waldemar Janzen*. Edited by Gordon Zerbe. Winnipeg: CMBC Publications, 2001.

Mason, Steven D. *"Eternal Covenant" in the Pentateuch: The Contours of an Elusive Phrase*. LHBOTS 494. London: T&T Clark, 2008.

McCann, J. Clinton. *A Theological Introduction to the Book of Psalms: The Psalms as Torah*. Nashville: Abingdon, 1993.

McCarthy, Dennis J. *Treaty and Covenant: A Study in Form in the Ancient Oriental Documents and in the Old Testament*. AnBib 21. Rome: Pontifical Biblical Institute, 1963.

———. *Treaty and Covenant: A Study in Form in the Ancient Oriental Documents and in the Old Testament*. New ed. AnBib 21a. Rome: Pontifical Biblical Institute, 1981.

———. "What Was Israel's Historical Creed?" *Lexington Theological Quarterly* 4 (1969): 46–53.

McComiskey, Thomas Edward. *The Covenants of Promise: A Theology of the Old Testament Covenants*. Grand Rapids: Baker, 1985.

McDowell, Catherine L. *The Image of God in the Garden of Eden: The Creation of Humankind in Genesis 2:5–3:24 in Light of mīs pî pīt pî* and *wpt-r Rituals of Mesopotamia and Ancient Egypt*. Siphrut: Literature and Theology of the Hebrew Scriptures 15. Winona Lake, IN: Eisenbrauns, 2015.

McKenzie, Steven L. *Covenant*. Understanding Biblical Themes. St. Louis: Chalice, 2000.

Mendenhall, George E. *Law and Covenant in Israel and the Ancient Near East*. Pittsburgh: Presbyterian Board of Colportage of Western Pennsylvania, 1955.

Miller, Patrick D. "Theology from Below: The Theological Interpretation of Scripture." Pages 3–14 in *Reconsidering the Boundaries between Theological Disciplines: Zur Neubestimmung der Grenzen zwischen den theologischen Disziplinen*. Edited by Michael Welker and Friedrich Schweitzer. Theology: Research and Science 8. Münster: Lit Verlag, 2005.

Moberly, R. Walter L. *At the Mountain of God: Story and Theology in Exodus 32–34*. JSOTSup 22. Sheffield: JSOT, 1983.

———. *Old Testament Theology: Reading the Hebrew Bible as Christian Scripture*. Grand Rapids: Baker Academic, 2013.

Möller, Karl. "The Nature and Genre of Biblical Theology." Pages 41–64 in *Out of Egypt: Biblical Theology and Biblical Interpretation*. Edited by Craig Bartholomew, Mary Healy, Karl Möller, and Robin Parry. Scripture and Hermeneutics Series 5. Grand Rapids: Zondervan, 2004.

Montague, George T. *The Holy Spirit: Growth of a Biblical Tradition*. New York: Paulist Press, 1976.

Morgan, Donn F. *Between Text and Community: The "Writings" in Canonical Interpretation*. Minneapolis: Fortress, 1990.

Motyer, Steve. "Two Testaments, One Biblical Theology." Pages 143–64 in *Between Two Horizons: Spanning New Testament Studies and Systematic Theology*. Edited by Joel B. Green and Max Turner. Grand Rapids: Eerdmans, 2000.

Naylor, Peter. "The Language of Covenant: A Structural Analysis of the Semantic Field of Berit in Biblical Hebrew, with Particular Reference to the Book of Genesis." DPhil diss., University of Oxford, 1980.

Nelson, Richard D. *Deuteronomy: A Commentary*. OTL. Louisville: Westminster John Knox, 2002.

Nicholson, Ernest W. *God and His People: Covenant and Theology in the Old Testament*. Oxford: Clarendon, 1986.

Nihan, Christophe. "Saul among the Prophets (1 Sam 10:10–12 and 19:18–24): The Reworking of Saul's Figure in the Context of the Debate on 'Charismatic Prophecy' in the Persian Era." Pages 88–118 in *Saul in Story and Tradition*. Edited by Carl S. Ehrlich and Marsha C. White. FAT 47. Tübingen: Mohr Siebeck, 2006.

Nussbaum, Martha C. *Love's Knowledge: Essays on Philosophy and Literature*. New York: Oxford University Press, 1990.

O'Donovan, Oliver. *The Desire of the Nations: Rediscovering the Roots of Political Theology*. Cambridge: Cambridge University Press, 1996.

Ollenburger, Ben C., ed. *So Wide a Sea: Essays on Biblical and Systematic Theology*. Elkhart, IN: Institute of Mennonite Studies, 1991.

Ooi, Vincent K. H. *Scripture and Its Readers: Readings of Israel's Story in Nehemiah 9, Ezekiel 20, and Acts 7*. JTISup 10. Winona Lake, IN: Eisenbrauns, 2015.

Oswalt, John N. "Exodus." Pages 259–560 in *Genesis, Exodus*. Edited by Allen Ross, John N. Oswalt, and Philip W. Comfort. Cornerstone Biblical Commentary 1. Carol Stream, IL: Tyndale House, 2008.

Perdue, Leo G. *Reconstructing Old Testament Theology: After the Collapse of History*. OBT. Minneapolis: Fortress, 2005.

Perrin, Nicholas. "Dialogic Conceptions of Language and the Problem of Biblical Unity." Pages 212–24 in *Biblical Theology: Retrospect and Prospect*. Edited by Scott Hafemann. Downers Grove, IL: InterVarsity; Leicester, UK: Apollos, 2002.

Piper, John. *The Supremacy of God in Preaching*. Grand Rapids: Baker, 1990.

Rad, Gerhard von. *Gesammelte Studien zum Alten Testament*. Theologische Bücherei 8. Munich: Chr. Kaiser, 1958.

———. *Old Testament Theology*. New York: Harper, 1962.

———. *The Problem of the Hexateuch and Other Essays*. London: Oliver & Boyd, 1966.

———. *Theologie des Alten Testaments*. 2 vols. Einführung in die Evangelische Theologie 1. München: Kaiser, 1958.

Rendtorff, Rolf. *The Covenant Formula: An Exegetical and Theological Investigation*. Old Testament Studies. Edinburgh: T&T Clark, 1998.

Richter, Sandra L. "A Biblical Theology of Creation Care." *Asbury Journal* 62 (2007): 67–76.

Sailhamer, John. *An Introduction to Old Testament Theology: A Canonical Approach*. Grand Rapids: Zondervan, 1995.

Sakenfeld, Katharine Doob. *Faithfulness in Action: Loyalty in Biblical Perspective*. OBT 16. Philadelphia: Fortress, 1985.

————. *The Meaning of Hesed in the Hebrew Bible: A New Inquiry.* HSM 17. Missoula, MT: Published by Scholars for the Harvard Semitic Museum, 1978.

Sandys-Wunsch, John, and Laurence Eldredge. "J. P. Gabler and the Distinction between Biblical and Dogmatic Theology: Translation, Commentary, and Discussion of His Originality." *Scottish Journal of Theology* 33 (1980): 133–58.

Sarna, Nahum M. *Exodus-Shemot.* JPS Torah Commentary. Philadelphia: Jewish Publication Society, 1991.

Schaberg, Jane. *The Illegitimacy of Jesus.* New York: Crossroad, 1990.

Scharbert, Josef. "Formgeschichte und Exegese von Ex 34,6f und Seiner Parallelen." *Bib* 38 (1959): 130–50.

Schmid, Konrad. "The Emergence and Disappearance of the Separation between the Pentateuch and the Deuteronomistic History in Biblical Studies." Pages 11–24 in *Pentateuch, Hexateuch, or Enneateuch? Identifying Literary Works in Genesis through Kings.* Edited by Thomas B. Dozeman, Thomas Römer, and Konrad Schmid. AIL 8. Atlanta: Society of Biblical Literature, 2012.

Schmidt, Werner H. *The Faith of the Old Testament: A History.* Philadelphia: Westminster, 1983.

Seitz, Christopher R. *Isaiah 1–39.* Int. Louisville: John Knox, 1993.

————. *Word without End: The Old Testament as Abiding Theological Witness.* Grand Rapids: Eerdmans, 1998.

Sklar, Jay. "Sin and Atonement: Lessons from the Pentateuch." *BBR* 22 (2012): 467–91.

————. *Sin, Impurity, Sacrifice, Atonement: The Priestly Conceptions.* HBM 2. Sheffield: Sheffield Phoenix, 2005.

Smend, Rudolf. *Die Bundesformel.* Theologische Studien. Zurich: EVZ, 1963.

Snaith, Norman Henry. *The Distinctive Ideas of the Old Testament.* London: Epworth, 1947.

Sohn, Seock-Tae. "'I Will Be Your God and You Will Be My People': The Origin and Background of the Covenant Formula." Pages 355–72 in *Ki Baruch Hu: Ancient Near Eastern, Biblical, and Judaic Studies in Honor of Baruch A. Levine.* Edited by Robert Chazan, William W. Hallo, and Lawrence H. Schiffman. Winona Lake, IN: Eisenbrauns, 1999.

Sparks, Kenton L. *God's Word in Human Words: An Evangelical Appropriation of Critical Biblical Scholarship.* Grand Rapids: Baker Academic, 2008.

Sperling, S. David. "Rethinking Covenant in Late Biblical Books." *Bib* 70 (1989): 50–73.

Spieckermann, H. "God's Steadfast Love: Towards a New Conception of Old Testament Theology." *Bib* 80 (2000): 305–27.

Sponsel, Leslie E. *Spiritual Ecology: A Quiet Revolution*. Santa Barbara, CA: Praeger, 2012.

Stek, John H. "'Covenant' Overload in Reformed Theology." *Calvin Theological Journal* 29 (1994): 12–41.

Stuart, Douglas K. *Exodus*. New American Commentary. Nashville: B&H, 2006.

Suzuki, David T., and Dave R. Taylor. *The Big Picture Reflections on Science, Humanity, and a Quickly Changing Planet*. Vancouver, BC: David Suzuki Foundation/Greystone Books, 2009.

Swoboda, A. J. *Tongues and Trees: Towards a Pentecostal Ecological Theology*. Journal of Pentecostal Theology Supplement Series. Blanford Forum, Dorset: Deo Publishing, 2013.

Taylor, Bron Raymond. *Dark Green Religion: Nature Spirituality and the Planetary Future*. Berkeley: University of California Press, 2010.

Terrien, Samuel L. *The Elusive Presence: Toward a New Biblical Theology*. Religious Perspectives. San Francisco: Harper & Row, 1978.

Throntveit, Mark A. *Ezra–Nehemiah*. Int. Louisville: John Knox, 1992.

Tozer, A. W. *The Knowledge of the Holy: The Attributes of God, Their Meaning in the Christian Life*. New York: Harper, 1961.

Trible, Phyllis. "Feminist Hermeneutics and Biblical Theology." Pages 448–66 in *The Flowering of Old Testament Theology: A Reader in Twentieth-Century Old Testament Theology, 1930–1990*. Edited by Ben C. Ollenburger, Elmer A. Martens, and Gerhard F. Hasel. Sources for Biblical and Theological Study 1. Winona Lake, IN: Eisenbrauns, 1992.

———. *God and the Rhetoric of Sexuality*. OBT 2. Philadelphia: Fortress, 1978.

VanGemeren, Willem. *Interpreting the Prophetic Word*. Grand Rapids: Zondervan, 1996.

———. *The Progress of Redemption: From Creation to the New Jerusalem*. Grand Rapids: Academie/Zondervan, 1988; reprint, Grand Rapids: Baker, 1995.

Vanhoozer, Kevin J. "Exegesis and Hermeneutics." Pages 52–64 in *New Dictionary of Biblical Theology*. Edited by T. Desmond Alexander and

Brian S. Rosner. Leicester, UK: Inter-Varsity; Downers Grove, IL: Inter-Varsity, 2000.

Vaughan-Lee, Llewellyn. *Spiritual Ecology: The Cry of the Earth, a Collection of Essays*. Point Reyes, CA: Golden Sufi Center, 2013.

Vos, Geerhardus. *Biblical Theology: Old and New Testaments*. 1948. Reprint, Grand Rapids: Eerdmans, 1966.

Wall, Robert W. "Canonical Context and Canonical Conversations." Pages 165–82 in *Between Two Horizons: Spanning New Testament Studies and Systematic Theology*. Edited by Joel B. Green and Max Turner. Grand Rapids: Eerdmans, 2000.

Waltke, Bruce K. "The Book of Proverbs and Old Testament Theology." *BSac* 136 (1979): 302–17.

Waltke, Bruce K., and Cathi J. Fredricks. *Genesis: A Commentary*. Grand Rapids: Zondervan, 2001.

Waltke, Bruce K., and Charles Yu. *An Old Testament Theology: An Exegetical, Canonical, and Thematic Approach*. Grand Rapids: Zondervan, 2007.

Watts, Rikki E. "Emmanuel: Virgin Birth Proof Text or Programmatic Warning of Things to Come (Isa 7:14 in Matt 1:23)?" Pages 92–113 in *From Prophecy to Testament: The Function of the Old Testament in the New*. Edited by Craig A. Evans. Peabody, MA: Hendrickson, 2004.

———. *Isaiah's New Exodus and Mark*. WUNT 2/88. Tübingen: Mohr Siebeck, 1997.

Weinfeld, Moshe. "The Covenant of Grant in the Old Testament and in the Ancient Near East." *JAOS* 90 (1970): 184–203.

———. *Deuteronomy and the Deuteronomic School*. Oxford: Clarendon, 1972.

Weir, Jack. "Analogous Fulfillment." *Perspectives in Religious Studies* 9 (1982): 65–76.

Welker, Michael, and Friedrich Schweitzer, eds. *Reconsidering the Boundaries between Theological Disciplines; Zur Neubestimmung der Grenzen zwischen den Theologischen Disziplinen*. Theology: Research and Science 8. Münster: Lit Verlag, 2005.

Wells, M. Jay. "Figural Representation and Canonical Unity." Pages 111–25 in *Biblical Theology: Retrospect and Prospect*. Edited by Scott Hafemann. Downers Grove, IL: InterVarsity; Leicester, UK: Apollos, 2002.

Westermann, Claus. *Elements of Old Testament Theology*. Atlanta: John Knox, 1982.

Wevers, John William. *Notes on the Greek Text of Exodus*. Septuagint and Cognate Studies Series 30. Atlanta: Scholars Press, 1990.

White, Lynn. "The Historical Roots of Our Ecological Crisis." *Science* 155 (1967): 1203–7.

Williamson, Paul R. "Covenant." Pages 419–29 in *New Dictionary of Biblical Theology*. Edited by T. Desmond Alexander and Brian S. Rosner. Leicester, UK: Inter-Varsity; Downers Grove, IL: InterVarsity, 2000.

———. *Sealed with an Oath: Covenant in God's Unfolding Purpose*. NSBT. Downers Grove, IL: Apollos and InterVarsity, 2007.

Wolters, Albert M. *Creation Regained: Biblical Basics for a Reformational Worldview*. 2nd ed. Grand Rapids: Eerdmans, 2005.

Wood, Leon J. *The Holy Spirit in the Old Testament*. Grand Rapids: Zondervan, 1976.

Wright, Christopher J. H. *Knowing the Holy Spirit through the Old Testament*. Downers Grove, IL: IVP Academic, 2006.

———. "Mission as a Matrix for Hermeneutics and Biblical Theology." Pages 102–43 in *Out of Egypt: Biblical Theology and Biblical Interpretation*. Edited by Craig Bartholomew, Mary Healy, Karl Möller, and Robin Parry. Scripture and Hermeneutics Series 5. Grand Rapids: Zondervan, 2004.

———. *The Mission of God: Unlocking the Bible's Grand Narrative*. Downers Grove, IL: InterVarsity, 2006.

Wright, George Ernest. *God Who Acts: Biblical Theology as Recital*. SBT 1/8. London: SCM, 1952.

Youngblood, Ronald F. *The Heart of the Old Testament: A Survey of Key Theological Themes*. 2nd ed. Grand Rapids: Baker, 1998.

Zimmerli, Walther, and Walter Brueggemann. *I Am Yahweh*. Translated by Douglas W. Stott. Atlanta: John Knox, 1982.

Zuck, Roy B., Eugene H. Merrill, and Darrell L. Bock. *A Biblical Theology of the Old Testament*. Chicago: Moody, 1991.

Index of Modern Authors

Index of Scripture

Index of Subjects

217